PRENTICE-HALL
FOUNDATIONS OF MODERN SOCIOLOGY SERIES

PRENTICE-HALL
FOUNDATIONS OF MODERN SOCIOLOGY SERIES

Alex Inkeles, Editor

THE SCIENTIST'S ROLE IN SOCIETY
Joseph Ben-David

DEVIANCE AND CONTROL
Albert K. Cohen

MODERN ORGANIZATIONS
Amitai Etzioni

THE FAMILY
William J. Goode

SOCIETY AND POPULATION, Second Edition
David M. Heer

WHAT IS SOCIOLOGY? An Introduction to the Discipline and Profession
Alex Inkeles

THE SOCIOLOGY OF SMALL GROUPS
Theodore M. Mills

SOCIAL CHANGE, Second Edition
Wilbert E. Moore

THE SOCIOLOGY OF RELIGION
Thomas F. O'Dea

SOCIETIES: Evolutionary and Comparative Perspectives
Talcott Parsons

THE SYSTEM OF MODERN SOCIETIES
Talcott Parsons

THE AMERICAN SCHOOL: A Sociological Analysis
Patricia C. Sexton

THE SOCIOLOGY OF ECONOMIC LIFE
Neil J. Smelser

SOCIAL STRATIFICATION: The Forms and Functions of Inequality
Melvin M. Tumin

SOCIETY AND POPULATION

second edition

SOCIETY AND POPULATION

DAVID M. HEER
University of Southern California

Prentice-Hall, Inc., Englewood Cliffs, New Jersey

Library of Congress Cataloging in Publication Data

HEER, DAVID M
    Society and population.

    (Prentice-Hall foundations of modern sociology series)
    Includes bibliographical references and index.
    1. Population. 2. Demography. I. Title.
HB851.H4 1975   301.32   74-20727
ISBN   0-13-820712-7
ISBN   0-13-820704-6 pbk.

Printed in the United States of America

10   9   8   7   6   5   4

Prentice-Hall International, Inc., London

Prentice-Hall of Australia, Pty. Ltd., Sydney

Prentice-Hall of Canada, Ltd., Toronto

Prentice-Hall of India Private Limited, New Delhi

Prentice-Hall of Japan, Inc., Tokyo

In memory of Samuel A. Stouffer, who combined deep interest
In social theory with uncommon competence to test its veracity

CONTENTS

PREFACE

This book is intended both to reveal some of the ways in which an understanding of population is important to a proper study of sociology, and to help explain the causes and effects of the current "population explosion."

I have long felt that too many books (in all fields of study) fail to stimulate their readers because they overemphasize what is already known, and hardly bother with important questions which deserve to be—indeed, in some cases *must* be—answered. Only by arousing his readers' curiosity concerning *both* sides of the subject at hand—the unknown *as well as* the known—will an author get them to take that all-important first step along the path of intellectual inquiry. In this book I have tried to determine what are the important questions concerning population, and how well we can answer them so far. Anyone completing this book will realize how much room exists for further significant research.

Textbooks on population traditionally devote considerable space to describing the social composition of populations such as the distribution of populations by marital and family status, educational attainment, ethnicity, language, religion, labor-force status, occupation, industry, and income. For reasons of space, I have eliminated this rather lengthy topic and have confined the discussion of population composition to biological composition. Thus, age and sex composition are discussed rather thoroughly, and brief mention is made of genetic composition in a discussion of differential reproduction and intelligence. Furthermore, this book is focused on the populations of nation-states and of the world as a whole; no attempt is made to consider population structure and dynamics for other types of social systems. Thus we do not consider divorce, which in demographic terms represents out-migration from that social system we term "the family." In addition, we are not concerned with the population processes of strata within a society—for example, entrances to and exits from the labor force, the body of college graduates, or a particular socio-economic class. Nor do we treat the geographic distribution of social strata; hence we shall not pursue such topics as the residential segregation of whites from blacks in American cities. The social composition of the population of the United States and of other societies, the influence of population structure and dynamics on social systems other than societies, and the population structure of various social strata within societies are, of course, common topics of sudy for sociologists. Much data relating to these topics will be found in the other volumes of the Foundations of Modern Sociology Series.

I should like to express my appreciation to all those persons who have helped in the preparation of this book: to Alex Inkeles, the General Editor of the Prentice-Hall Foundations of Modern Sociology Series, who made valuable suggestions concerning the organization of this work; to the staff of Prentice-Hall, Inc.; and to Miss Linda Sayegh, Miss Dorothy Greenidge, and Mrs. Margaret Bermingham, who typed successive drafts of the manuscript.

DAVID M. HEER

SOCIETY AND POPULATION

PART ONE
THE WORLD POPULATION PICTURE

CHAPTER 1
THE GROWTH OF WORLD POPULATION

THE HISTORY OF HUMAN
POPULATION GROWTH

When one considers that even today we do not know with certainty the actual size of populations in many parts of the world, it is not surprising to discover that we have only approximate knowledge (which often means "the results of educated guesses") concerning the number of human beings living at each stage of man's existence. On the basis of careful analyses of available fact, however, we are very sure of one aspect of the expansion of man's numbers: it has been truly prodigious.

In considering the history of human population growth we must first decide what we mean by "man." *Man* obviously is the descendant of other primates, but as yet we have no clear picture of all the links between him and his prehominid ancestors. Moreover, even if all the links were apparent, we would still have the problem of defining when "man" himself appeared. For instance, do we wish to define the appearance of man as the appearance of the family *hominidae,* the genus *homo,* or the species *homo sapiens?* If we choose to trace the population history of the family *hominidae,* we may have to go back $5\frac{1}{2}$ million years; if we confine our interest to *homo sapiens,* we need go back only around 50,000 years.

Perhaps the most important stage in the evolution of man from other primates was the appearance of terrestrial, rather than tree-dwelling, creatures of fully upright posture who were able not only to use tools but also to make them. All such creatures are classed in the family *hominidae*. The first creatures to fit definitely into this category, who now bear the technical name *Australopithecines*, developed during the geological epoch before ours (the *Pleistocene*) perhaps as long as 5½ million years ago. The *Australopithecine*, an organism of completely upright posture, was free to use his flexible hands to grasp weapons for hunting other animals. Thus for the first time a mammal evolved which was dependent on tools for survival.[1]

The development of tools for hunting enabled the creatures who used them to expand their population in a slowly accelerating fashion. Deevey estimates that 1 million years ago there were only 125,000 tool-using hominid creatures, but that by 8000 B.C. the population of *homo sapiens*, by then the only hominid, was 5.3 million and growing fast.[2] According to Deevey, a population boom of sorts began around 8000 B.C. that caused about a sixteenfold increase over the next 4,000 years. Translated, this statistic means that the earth harbored a population of around 86.5 million in 4000 B.C., the approximate date of the rise of the First Egyptian Empire in the Nile Valley.

Population seems to have grown less rapidly in the following 4,000 years. Deevey estimates that at the time of Christ the population of the world was 133 million, less than a twofold increase over that of the preceding four millennia. However, there is disagreement on this point by other scholars. The United Nations, for example, reports that the population of the world at this time was between 200 million and 300 million.[3]

By 1650 A.D. the population of the world had probably risen to about 545 million. Since that date, as Table 1 shows, there has been a continually accelerating increase. According to the most recent official estimate of the United Nations, the latest recorded average annual rate of population growth (from 1963 to 1971) was 20 per thousand.[4] Some population experts believe the rate to be even higher. Accordingly, it is

1. Frederick S. Hulse, *The Human Species* (New York: Random House, 1963), pp. 164–235; Robert Reinhold, "Bone Traces Man Back 5 Million Years", *New York Times*, 19 February 1971.

2. Edward S. Deevey, Jr., "The Human Population," *Scientific American* (September, 1960), 203: 3, 195–204.

3. Population Division, United Nations, *The Determinants and Consequences of Population Trends* (New York: United Nations, 1953), p. 8.

4. Estimates of population and growth-rates from 1650 to 1900 are from A. M. Carr-Saunders, *World Population: Past Growth and Present Trends* (Oxford: Clarendon, 1936), p. 42. The growth rate from 1900 to 1950 is based on Carr-Saunders's estimate of world population for 1900 and the United Nations' estimate of world population for 1950. The source of the latter is United Nations, Department of Economic and Social Affairs, *Demographic Yearbook, 1971* (New York: United

Table 1   Estimated Population of the World since 1650

YEAR	POPULATION (IN MILLIONS)	AVERAGE ANNUAL INCREASE PER 1,000 SINCE PRECEDING DATE
1650	545	—
1750	728	3
1800	906	4
1850	1,171	5
1900	1,608	6
1950	2,486	9
1963	3,162	19
1971	3,706	20

Sources: Soo footnote 4.

very clear that in recent years the rate of population growth the world over has been unprecedented in human history.

This recent increase in population has not been *uniformly* great, however; the highest rates of increase have been found in the tropical parts of Latin America. Brazil, with about 95 million persons in 1971, was growing at a rate of 28 persons per thousand during the period 1963–71; Mexico, with about 51 million persons in 1971, was growing at a rate of 32 per thousand. Population growth substantially higher than the world average was also reported for Africa, whose growth rate for the 1963–71 period was reported as 26 per thousand per year.

Population growth rates lower than the world average during the 1963–71 period were found in Europe, the United States, Japan, and the USSR. During 1963–71 the average annual rate of population growth was 11 per thousand in the United States and 8 per thousand in Europe. During this period the lowest rates of population growth were for East Germany (− 1 per thousand) and for the United Kingdom, Hungary, and Finland (4 per thousand).[5] The population growth rate in mainland China, containing about a fifth of the world's population, is uncertain. The United Nations has recently estimated that the average annual population growth rate in mainland China from 1963 to 1971 was 18 per thousand.[6] Other experts on Chinese population,[7] however, believe the

Nations, 1972), p. 111. The estimates of world population in 1963 and 1971 are also taken from p. 111.

5. United Nations, Department of Economic and Social Affairs, *Demographic Yearbook, 1971*, pp. 111–124.

6. Ibid.

7. John S. Aird, "Population Policy and Demographic Prospects in the People's Republic of China," in Joint Economic Committee, Congress of the United States,

growth rate was substantially higher. In fact, the uncertainty concerning the growth rate in China is the main cause of the uncertainty about the world growth rate.

TWO FRAMEWORKS FOR ANALYZING THE CAUSES OF POPULATION GROWTH

Two separate frameworks of causal explanation are available for explaining world population growth. The first framework relates population to the means of subsistence. It is obvious that the population of the world can be no greater than that number which can provide itself with a minimum subsistence from the world's resources. Since for most of the period in which human beings have inhabited this planet, the majority have lived very close to a minimum level of subsistence, major population increase has only been possible when the means of subsistence could be increased proportionately.

A second framework for examining the causes of world population increase is the examination of this increase in terms of its two components, the birth rate and the death rate. On a worldwide basis, population cannot increase unless the birth rate exceeds the death rate, and the greater the difference between the two rates (in favor of births, of course), the higher will be the rate of population growth. Analysis of world population growth from the standpoint of this framework focuses on factors leading to *changes* in birth and death rates.

Population Growth and the Means of Subsistence

Societies develop because no human being can grow to maturity independently of others of his species. Human societies are in turn dependent on other animals, on plant species, and on such requisite features of the inanimate environment as water, air, and proper temperature. Human ecology is the study of the mutual relationships existing between human populations and their biological and physical environments. A key concept of human ecology is the *ecosystem*, which may be defined as "an aggregation of associated species of plants and animals together with the physical features of their habitat."[8] The past growth of world popula-

---

People's Republic of China: An Economic Assessment (Washington, D.C.: Government Printing Office, 1972).

8. Lee R. Dice, *Man's Nature and Nature's Man: The Ecology of Human Communities* (Ann Arbor, Mich.: University of Michigan Press, 1955), p. 2.

tion would not have been possible without mankind's making radical changes in his ecosystem. And these changes have not been merely quantitative; that is, modern man's relationship to his biological and physical environment is much more than an enlarged replication of the relationship of primitive man to his environment. Because of what economists call "the law of diminishing returns," the additional supply of labor occasioned by an increase in population usually results in *less* productivity than the existing labor supply. Hence, in the usual case, the means of subsistence do not automatically increase in proportion to a population increase. The mechanism by which man's means of subsistence have kept abreast of growing population is a *qualitative* change in his ecosystem—namely, a change in technology and organization serving to increase the production possible on a given amount of territory with a given quantity of labor.

A most useful way of explaining world population increase since the beginning of man's existence has been developed by Walter Goldschmidt.[9] Essentially a typology of the evolution of societies in terms of the complexity of their technology and the elaboration of their division of labor, it chronicles the improvements in technology and organization which have helped mankind to increase the total output of his necessities. According to Goldschmidt, the first type of society to evolve was one in which the predominant economic activity was nomadic hunting and food-gathering. This was followed by the development of a society in which hunting and food-gathering could take place without nomadism. The third stage of complexity consisted of societies in which the predominant economic activity was either horticulture (i.e., the cultivation of plants by means of the hoe) or the herding of animals. The fourth stage was characterized by a fully developed agriculture and the accumulation of a sufficient agricultural surplus to allow for the settlement of a portion of the population in cities. The fifth, and so far final, stage is one in which the division of labor becomes very complex, subsistence is obtained largely through the application of inanimate sources of energy (such as coal and petroleum), and much or most of the population lives in cities. Each type of society progressively allows a population of given size to procure a greater supply of goods and services from a given territory, and thus each societal type progressively allows for a higher density of population. In fact, as actual societies have progressed upward along this typology, *all* of them have experienced increased population density.

Goldschmidt's typology would seem to imply a certain discontinuity in the evolution of more efficient systems of sustenance, and hence in population growth. However, he merely intends the five-stage breakdown

9. Walter Goldschmidt, *Man's Way* (Cleveland, Ohio: World, 1959), pp. 181–218.

as a device to emphasize certain major changes without implying that the changes summarized by a given type appeared all at once.

Let us examine in somewhat more detail some of the major technological and organizational developments which have affected man's ability to support given population densities at each of the several stages. If we begin our account with the earliest representatives of the family *hominidae*, we can presume that the use of fire was unknown and that their language was extremely rudimentary. The "harnessing" of fire and the development of language undoubtedly allowed for an increase in the hominid population. So also did the improvement of tools for hunting. The spear, for example, was more efficient than the club, and the bow and arrow more efficient than the spear. Inventions such as these enabled men to evolve from small, nomadic hunting bands to more settled tribal societies. The invention of the hoe and the primitive cultivation of plants allowed for a major increase in subsistence, and thus had a profound effect on human population growth. Deevey, who as we have seen estimates that the world population increased sixteenfold in the period from 8000 B.C. to 4000 B.C., attributes this large increase to the development of horticulture and the beginnings of a more advanced agriculture.

The fourth type of society, the agricultural-state society, emerged around 4000 B.C. in the Nile delta of Egypt, the Tigris-Euphrates Valley in Iraq, the Indus Valley in Pakistan, and the Yellow and Yangtze valleys in China. The agricultural-state society is characterized above all by the presence of domesticated animals, the use of the plow, and the irrigation of agricultural land wherever possible. In addition, other technological developments, such as terracing, fertilizers, wheeled vehicles, sailboats, metallurgy, and the alphabet, date from this period, and all contributed to increased productivity. The domestication of animals allowed for a specialized herding society in certain steppe regions which were unsuitable for other types of agriculture. Such herding societies, although evolving later than horticultural societies, are of the same level of complexity, and hence have been classified by Goldschmidt as belonging in the third stage of development.

The fifth stage is the urban-industrial stage. Its beginnings in Europe may be said to coincide with Christopher Columbus's voyage to America. The voyages to the New World by Columbus and the other early discoverers were significant to technological advance for two reasons. First, the explorers brought back certain very important cultivated plants previously unknown in Europe and Asia. Among these were the potato, maize, beans, and tomatoes. Of these plants, probably the most important to Northern Europe was the potato, because the cool and rainy summers of that region are not so fitted to grain production as are warmer climates. The potato, although not native to the region, was ideally suited to it, and the produce of potatoes from one acre of land was equivalent in food value to that of two to four acres sown with grain. The potato was introduced into Ireland around 1600, and probably had its greatest impact there. By 1800 the potato was practically the sole item in the diet of the Irish common man. Meanwhile, a tremendous acceleration in population occurred: from 1754 to 1846 the population of Ireland more than doubled, increasing from 3.2 million to 8.2 million, despite heavy out-migration to the United States and other nations. The potato played an equally important role, although at a somewhat later date, in the other countries of Northern Europe—particularly in England, the Netherlands, Scandinavia, Germany, Poland, and Russia. In Russia, from 1725 to 1858 the population increased more than threefold (within the boundaries of the former year), an increase parallel in magnitude to the increase in population in Ireland.[10]

The second reason for the significance of Columbus's voyage was that it made possible a tremendous technical advance in America. First of all, the European introduction to America of the horse and other domesticated animals was a major innovation which allowed the indigenous population of America to increase greatly its means of subsistence. For example, the Indians of the Great Plains of North America, by using horses, were for the first time able to live off bison. Secondly, and more important, the Europeans had a much higher level of technology than the American Indians, particularly those Indians in what is now the United States and Canada; and by virtue of taking over territory from the Indians, the European settlers converted a very large territory from one in which the population had only a very simple technology to one whose technology was as advanced as any in the world. As a result, the population of the New World could and did grow extremely rapidly.

A major landmark of the urban-industrial stage was the invention of the steam engine by James Watt in 1769. This invention signalled the beginning of the period in which man's major supply of energy was to come from inanimate fossilized sources (coal, petroleum, and natural gas). As a result of numerous inventions, the efficient use of inanimate energy was greatly stimulated in Europe, North America, and elsewhere. We shall not go into these many inventions in detail; it will be sufficient to state two rather broad consequences of them which affected possibilities for population growth. First, a series of innovations in agriculture and manufacturing made it possible for a rapidly decreasing number of persons to produce an increasing quantity of food, clothing, shelter, and

10. William L. Langer, "Europe's Initial Population Explosion," *The American Historical Review* (October, 1963), 69:1, 1–17.

other necessities from the resources of a given area. Secondly, a revolution in the costs of transportation made it possible for different regions to specialize in those goods and services which they could produce at the lowest cost and eliminated the danger of famine caused by local failures in food production.

Although population growth was stimulated in Europe and America by the Industrial Revolution, the advance in the means of subsistence was substantially greater. Hence, for the first time in human history, certain nations experienced a rapid rise in their level of living. For example, in the United States the total output of goods and services (GNP—gross national product) per capita in constant prices increased on the average during the period from 1839 to 1959 by 1.64 percent per annum. Such an increase meant a doubling in per-capita product every forty-three years, and approximately a fivefold increase every century.[11]

As we have seen, an advancing technology and an increasing division of labor allow population to increase, and insofar as advance in technology and organization stimulate a rise in birth rate or a decline in death rate, such an advance causes population growth. However, we should also examine the other side of this relationship. Does increased population growth advance the state of technology and elaborate the division of labor? An argument by the famous French sociologist Emile Durkheim is to this effect.[12] Durkheim contends that an increase in population density is causally related to a more elaborate and productive division of labor. According to his argument, there is a natural tendency for population to expand more rapidly than the means of subsistence, and this expansion tends to sharpen the struggle for existence. Two alternatives are then possible: either men fight among themselves for the available means of subsistence, or they elaborate the division of labor to attain greater productivity. Since men have not consistently chosen the first of these two alternatives, the division of labor in human societies has become increasingly complex. Few persons would care to dispute the claim that population pressure is a contributing cause to an increasingly complex division of labor. Durkheim, however, holds that an elaboration of the division of labor can occur *only in the presence* of population pressure, and the validity of this conclusion is dubious. Durkheim's contention that population pressure is a necessary prerequisite to further development of the division of labor is, however, similar to that of certain contemporary scholars who believe that economic development will

11. Richard T. Gill, *Economic Development: Past and Present* (Englewood Cliffs, N.J.: Prentice-Hall, 1967), p. 66.

12. Emile Durkheim, *The Division of Labor in Society*, trans. George Simpson (New York: The Free Press, 1964), pp. 233–82.

not be hampered by a high rate of population growth. We shall consider their ideas in chapter 8.

Population Growth and Changes in Birth and Death Rates

The second framework for analyzing population growth concerns the factors that influence the rate of births and deaths. When compared with that of other animals, man's biological capacity to reproduce is rather limited. Unlike other animals, *homo sapiens* does not lay thousands of eggs, or typically bear offspring in litters. In the human population, women who live to the end of their reproductive period are capable of bearing only about twelve children on the average. Even so, few indeed have been (or are) the populations wherein women have ever reproduced (or still reproduce) at the level of their biological capacity. (The only such populations with which the average reader can be expected to be familiar involve the women of colonial North America who, both in French-speaking Quebec and in the English-speaking colonies of the Atlantic seaboard, reproduced at or near the level of maximum biological capacity; and the present Hutterite women, members of a small, communalistic Christian sect of the western United States and Canada, who have a similar high birth rate.)[13] Currently, the economically developed nations generaly have much lower fertility than the economically less advanced nations. Nevertheless, in all nations today fertility is substantially lower than the biological maximum.

On a worldwide level up until perhaps 300 years ago, the birth rate and the death rate were both very high, and each averaged to a level almost exactly equal to the other. Thus, if the death rate averaged around 50 per thousand, the birth rate would also average that amount. Of course, in any given year birth rates and death rates would not be exactly equal; death rates in particular tended to vary considerably from year to year.

In years with an adequate food supply, population growth, at least

13.   For a discussion of Hutterite fertility and its relation to biologically maximum fertility, see J. W. Eaton and A. J. Mayer, "The Social Biology of Very High Fertility among the Hutterites," *Human Biology* (1953), 25, pp. 206–63; Christopher Tietze, "Reproductive Span and Rate of Reproduction among Hutterite Women," *Fertility and Sterility* (1957), 8:1, 89–97; and Mindel C. Sheps, "An Analysis of Reproductive Patterns in an American Isolate," *Population Studies*, 19:1 (July, 1965), pp. 65–80. For a discussion of fertility in the colonial United States, see Wilson H. Grabill et al., *The Fertility of American Women* (New York: John Wiley, 1958), pp. 5–24. Fertility in French-Canada during the early eighteenth century is discussed in Jacques Henripin, *La Population Canadienne au début du XVIIIe siècle: nuptialité, fécondité, mortalité infantile* (Paris: Presses Universitaires de France, 1954).

in agricultural societies, was about 5 or 10 per thousand.[14] Years of food scarcity tended to have very high death rates. Not only did food shortage sometimes cause actual starvation; more importantly, it caused malnutrition and undernourishment, and under these conditions the death rate from various infectious diseases rose markedly. One of the most famous epidemics in human history was the Black Death, which occurred in Europe during the years 1347–52. An epidemic of bubonic plague began in Constantinople in 1347 and spread throughout the Mediterranean region and the European Atlantic coast during the following year. It then moved inland and continued until it struck Russia in 1352. The Black Death killed approximately one-quarter of the population of Europe, and the continent was not able to regain its former population for many years.[15]

The birth rate in pre-industrial societies was more stable than the death rate. However, at least in pre-industrial Europe the level of the birth rate was indirectly affected by the death rate because of a direct influence of the death rate on the age at marriage. In much of Europe, marriage was linked to inheritance. Since a marriage could not be contracted until the couple acquired land, they often had to wait for the death of the bridegroom's father. Following a period with an abnormally high death rate, a greater proportion of men would find themselves inheritors of land, and the average age of inheritance would be low. More men marrying and a decline in the age at marriage would result in a relatively high level of fertility. On the other hand, during periods when the death rate was low, fewer men would inherit land, and those inheriting would do so only at a later age. As a result, marriage would be less frequent and at a later age, and fertility would decline.[16]

Since the advent of the urban-industrial era, sharp rises in the death rate have accompanied each major war. However, the scientific-industrial revolution has markedly reduced peacetime mortality throughout the world. It is believed that mortality in Europe began to decline very slowly in the eighteenth century, quite possibly as a result of the more ample diet occasioned by the introduction and diffusion of the potato. It was not until the late nineteenth century that mortality in Europe and the area of European settlement began to decline rapidly, and the speed of *that* decline probably was caused by a combination of

14.   Carlo M. Cipolla, *The Economic History of World Population* (Baltimore, Md.: Penguin, 1902), p. 78.

15.   William Petersen, *Population*, 2d ed. (New York: Macmillan, 1969), pp. 388–91.

16.   Goran Ohlin, "Mortality, Marriage, and Growth in Pre-Industrial Societies," *Population Studies* (March, 1961), 14:3, 190–97.

factors which had to await a variety of other human developments before they came into being: (1) a rise in the level of nutrition; (2) greatly improved sanitation, especially in cities, because of improvements in sewage and water supply systems; (3) medical advance in the prevention of infectious disease through inoculation; and (4) medical advance in the cure of infectious disease, particularly through the use of antibiotics. Outside of the economically developed nations, death rates remained high until the end of World War II. After World War II, a very pronounced reduction of mortality in these nations—a reduction much more rapid than had ever occurred in Europe or the United States—became the chief cause of the large recent acceleration in the world growth rate. Nevertheless, the level of mortality in these nations still remains, with some notable exceptions, distinctly higher than that of the economically developed nations.[17]

The very rapid decline of mortality in the underdeveloped nations after World War II resulted in large measure from inoculation for infectious disease, reduction of malaria through DDT spraying, and the cure of infectious disease through antibiotics. However, a large proportion of persons in these nations were and continue to be malnourished and living in unsanitary conditions.

The nations experiencing economic advance from the scientific industrial revolution were characterized not only by declining mortality but also by a fall in fertility. The *theory of the demographic transition* has been advanced as a comprehensive explanation of the effects of economic development both on mortality and on fertility decline. The classic theory is as follows. The initial stage is one of elevated birth and death rates; and because the birth rate is only approximately equal to the death rate, the natural increase in population is just about nil. In the second stage, there is a high rate of population growth caused by a decline in the death rate which proceeds at a much faster pace than the decline in the birth rate. In the third stage, the rate of population growth is positive but of lesser magnitude than in the second stage; in this third stage, the birth rate is declining more rapidly than the death rate. In the final stage, population growth is small or negative, since a low birth rate now approximates in magnitude a low death rate.[18]

17. On the decline of mortality in Europe, see David V. Glass and D. E. C. Eversley, eds., *Population in History* (Chicago, Ill.: Aldine, 1965), and for a general discussion of trends in mortality in different areas of the world see Population Division, United Nations, *The Determinants and Consequences of Population Trends* (New York: United Nations, 1953), pp. 47–70.

18. See Warren S. Thompson, *Population and Peace in the Pacific* (Chicago, Ill.: University of Chicago Press, 1946), pp. 22–35; C. P. Blacker, "Stages in Population Growth," *Eugenics Review* (October, 1947), 39:3, 88–102; Kingsley Davis, *Human*

The writers who popularized the idea of the demographic transition emphasized the simultaneous occurrence of economic development, industrialization, and urbanization as causes of the initial decline in mortality and the secondary decline in fertility. The fall in mortality was very plausibly explained: economic development led to a rise in the standard of living, including a higher level of nutrition, better sanitary facilities, and improved medical care. The supposed impact of industrialization, urbanization, and economic development on fertility, however, was spelled out less clearly. Until rather recently, most demographers accepted these three factors as necessary and sufficient for fertility reduction but paid relatively little attention to the *exact* ways in which changes in these three factors would affect fertility.

The theory of the demographic transition, popularized just after the end of World War II, was congruent with all of the facts then known about mortality and fertility. In this immediate postwar period the known facts referred to the world demographic situation just before World War II, because the vital events occurring during and just after the war were heavily influenced by the war itself and were therefore considered abnormal. During the period just before World War II, the industrialized nations of Europe, North America, and Oceania all had such low fertility and mortality that their intrinsic natural increase was nil. All of these nations were therefore considered to be in the fourth and final stage of demographic transition. Moreover, the demographic history of all these industrialized nations appeared to confirm the theory of demographic transition. All of them had experienced major *secular* (very long-term) declines, both in mortality and in fertility, with the decline in mortality generally preceding the decline in fertility. Furthermore, if one looked at the nations of the world in cross-sectional perspective, all of the developed nations with low fertility and mortality were in great contrast with the underdeveloped nations, all experiencing high fertility and, most of them, high mortality.

In the years following World War II, however, events cast increasing doubt on the classic statement of the demographic transition with respect to fertility. Demographers with faith in the theory of the demographic transition could not at first believe that fertility in the United States was actually rising to a level higher than that which had existed before World War II. At first the observed postwar jump in the birth rate was explained by the birth of babies temporarily postponed because of World War II. When this factor was found inadequate to explain the postwar increase

Society (New York: Macmillan, 1949), pp. 603–8; and Frank W. Notestein, "The Economics of Population and Food Supplies," in *Proceedings of the Eighth International Conference of Agricultural Economists* (London: Oxford University Press, 1953), pp. 15–31.

in fertility, much attention was paid to the effect of changes in age at marriage and at child-bearing on annual measures of fertility. P. K. Whelpton showed that a decline in age at marriage and in the maternal age at which children were born could result in a temporary inflation of the annual fertility measures even though there was no change in the average number of children per woman completing the reproductive period.[19] Since after World War II, the United States did experience a pronounced decline in the age at marriage and in the intervals between marriage and the birth of each child, it could plausibly be argued that the size of completed families in the United States was not rising. Only by the late 1950s had sufficient data accumulated to prove conclusively that the size of completed families in the United States among recent marriage cohorts was significantly above the level attained by those women who were married in the decade before World War II.[20]

Demographers were then faced with the embarrassing situation that fertility in the United States had increased despite the supposed fact that fertility would not rise once the final stage of demographic transition had been reached. Moreover, fertility had risen in a period which saw increased industrialization, increased urbanization, and a dramatic rise in the level of economic development.

During the last few years, corroborating evidence has been produced from various historical periods in other societies of direct rather than inverse associations between economic development and the trend in fertility. For example, several historical demographers have recently produced evidence indicating that English fertility may well have increased during that nation's period of industrial development in the early nineteenth century,[21] and similar increases may have occurred in the Netherlands during its periods of commercial and industrial development.[22]

A summation of this evidence suggests that a more adequate theory of fertility transition must distinguish between direct and indirect effects of economic development. The direct effect of economic development

19. Pascal K. Whelpton, *Cohort Fertility: Native White Women in the United States* (Princeton, N.J.: Princeton University Press, 1954).

20. U.S. Bureau of the Census, "Fertility of the Population: March 1957," in *Current Population Reports*, Series P-20, No. 84 (8 August 1958).

21. J. T. Krause, "Some Implications of Recent Work in Historical Demography," *Comparative Studies in Society and History* (January, 1957), 1:2, 164–88; H. J. Habakkuk, "English Population in the Eighteenth Century," *Economic History Review* (December, 1953), 6:2, 117–33.

22. William Petersen, "The Demographic Transition in the Netherlands" *American Sociological Review* (June, 1960), 25:3, 334–47.

and the consequent increase in economic well-being is probably an increase in fertility. The observed long-range historical fact that increased economic development usually has resulted in a reduction in fertility must then be caused by indirect effects of economic development conducive to fertility reduction which outweigh the facilitating effect of economic development. Some of the most important of these indirect effects of economic development conducive to fertility decline may be a decline in infant and childhood mortality, an increase in demand for an educated labor force, the introduction of social-security systems, and an increase in population density. The reasons why these and other changes accompanying economic development foster fertility decline will be discussed in chapter 5.

CHAPTER 2
FUTURE HUMAN SOCIETIES AND THEIR ENVIRONMENTAL CONSTRAINTS

THE FUTURE GROWTH OF WORLD POPULATION

Although we do not know enough about world population to be able to predict its future growth, we can (and it will be instructive for our present purposes) *project* it, assuming a continuation of the probable growth rate during very recent years. A population projection is simply the arithmetic spelling out of certain assumptions concerning the way in which populations grow. In this projection we shall assume that the rate of population growth will remain constant at 20 per thousand to the year 2400. The fantastic results are presented in table 2.

A population growing at a constant rate such as the one we have imagined doubles itself in a fixed time-period. When the rate of increase is 20 per thousand, this doubling occurs every thirty-five years. At this rate of increase, every century the population increases approximately sevenfold.

From table 2 one may also examine the population densities which would occur in connection with our assumed rate. In 1971 the population per square mile of terrestrial area in the world (excluding polar regions but including inland waters) was 70.7.[1] By the year 2400 it would be 376,218.

1. Calculated from the data provided in United Nations, Department of Economic and Social Affairs, *Demographic Yearbook, 1971* (New York: United Nations, 1972), p. 111.

Table 2   Projection of World Population Assuming an Annual Increase of 20 per thousand

YEAR	POPULATION (IN BILLIONS)	PER SQUARE MILE
1971	3.71	70.7
1975	4.01	76.5
2000	6.62	126.2
2025	10.91	208.0
2050	17.99	343.0
2075	29.66	565.5
2100	48.91	932.6
2200	361.39	6,890.7
2300	2,670.32	50,915.6
2400	19,731.13	376,218.0

This last figure may be compared with certain current population densities. In 1970 Manhattan Island (New York County) had a density of 66,923 persons per square mile, the highest for any political unit in the United States. For the city of New York the population density then was 26,343, and for New York City and its surrounding suburbs (the New York urbanized area) it was 6,683. By comparison, the population density in the well-populated state of Massachusetts in 1970 was only 727 per square mile, and in the United States as a whole, a low 57.5.[2]

BALANCE BETWEEN FUTURE POPULATION GROWTH AND FUTURE INCREASES IN THE MEANS OF SUBSISTENCE

I have presented this population projection not because many students of population seriously believe that it will come to pass, but rather to show the inevitability of a decline in population growth sometime in the future. When it will come is a matter of opinion, but all experts appear to agree that the world will never have anywhere near the population that has been projected here for the year 2400. A decline in the growth rate may come about because human beings will voluntarily restrict their fertility. On the other hand, if the world birth rate is not reduced, the growth of world population may outstrip the growth in means of subsistence. If this happens, mankind's death rate must inevitably rise.

The question of whether mankind could avoid an increase in its

2. U.S. Bureau of the Census, *United States Census of Population: 1970*, Final Report PC(1)-A1, pp. 52, 81, and 152 and Final Report PC(1)-A34, p. 21.

death rate as a consequence of population growing faster than the means of subsistence was initially raised by Thomas Robert Malthus in 1798 in his famous first essay on population.[3] In this initial study, Malthus concluded that avoiding a mortality rise would not be possible. The means of subsistence, he claimed, grew only at an *arithmetic* rate, whereas populations tended to grow at a *geometric* rate. When the imbalance between growth in the means of subsistence and in population became too great, factors such as hunger, epidemic disease, and war—which Malthus termed *"positive checks"*—would operate to raise the death rate and reduce the population to a level compatible with the means of subsistence. In his later writings, Malthus abandoned his pessimistic dogmatism and expressed the hope that man could avoid an application of positive checks through certain *preventive checks*—that is, checks on the birth rate. Malthus proposed late marriage as the best means to reduce the birth rate, since he believed any limitation of births within marriage was immoral.[4]

In the period since the death of Malthus, mankind's situation has been much more fortunate than Malthus envisioned. The positive checks to population growth have not increased their force. On the contrary, death rates today are much lower throughout the world than they were in Malthus's time. Malthus did not foresee the great rise in the means of subsistence which occurred throughout the world after his death, nor did he envision that in many nations birth control within marriage would become an important means of population control.

Nevertheless, the question Malthus raised is no less important today than during his lifetime. The human species in the not-too-distant future *will* experience a rise in its death rate unless the means of subsistence can be increased at the same rate as the population. A rise in mortality can be avoided only through a sizable reduction in the birth rate, a substantial increase in the means of subsistence, or some combination of these two. But none of these more pleasant possibilities is certain to occur.

Harrison Brown, an eminent geochemist, has estimated that with improvements in practice and the development of new technology, world food production can be eventually increased so that it will be sufficient to support 50 billion persons.[5] However, even if we accept the argument

3. Thomas Robert Malthus, *Population: The First Essay* (Ann Arbor: Ann Arbor Paperbacks, 1959).

4. Thomas Malthus, "A Summary View of the Principle of Population," in Thomas Malthus et al., *Three Essays on Population* (New York: Mentor Books, 1960), pp. 13–59.

5. Harrison Brown, *The Challenge of Man's Future* (New York: Viking, 1954), pp. 145–48. For a more pessimistic view of this matter see Donella H. Meadows et al., *The Limits to Growth* (New York: Universe Books, 1972).

that eventually the world can support 50 billion persons, we cannot assume that future death rates will not rise. The crucial question is not
how many persons can eventually be supported on this planet, but how
fast the means of subsistence can be increased. For example, suppose
it would take 300 years to increase the means of subsistence sufficiently
to support 50 billion persons on earth at the present level of living. Suppose also that population growth continued at its present rate, doubling
the population every thirty-five years. Then we would witness the impossible situation of a world population of 50 billion only some 125
years hence, long before the means of subsistence had risen correspondingly. Clearly, if it should take 300 years to increase the means of subsistence sufficient to support 50 billion individuals, then the world rate
of population growth cannot continue at its present level but must
be reduced in the meantime either by lower fertility or by higher
mortality.

In the next two sections of this chapter we will review some of the
possibilities of increasing the supply of various resources necessary for
human subsistence. It should be emphasized at the outset that this discussion will be in large part speculative, since experts are not always in
agreement concerning the feasibility of many of the proposed measures
for increasing the supply of these necessities.

Food

Because our knowledge concerning the important question of how
rapidly the world's food production can be increased is rather limited,
there is great disagreement on the matter among agricultural experts.
Statements of opinion tend to shed more heat than light. Arguments
over future food availability notwithstanding, much of the world's population is *now* malnourished: millions do not even get enough to eat to
prevent gnawing hunger from being an almost constant companion, and
many more millions eat a qualitatively inadequate diet in which the
principal lack is insufficient protein. In principle, given the proper conditions, the earth's food production could be greatly expanded; but in
practice, speaking from an economic and technological point of view,
such an expansion could only be undertaken at the cost of massive
amounts of money, materials, and energy (all of which those most in
need have the least), and even then not to a much greater degree until
further advances in technology have been made. In principle, food production can be increased through an *expansion of agriculture acreage*,
by means of a *greater yield per acre*, or through *greater exploitation of
the oceans*. We shall now discuss each of these three possibilities.

The great increase in world population in the last few centuries was accompanied by a great increase in cropland. In part this was made possible by the continual settlement of many areas, including much of North and South America, Australia, New Zealand, and Siberia, in which agriculture had not previously existed. The increase in cropland also occurred at the expense of forest and pasture land in long-settled agricultural areas. Finally, an increased use of irrigation made agriculture feasible in many arid regions where it had not previously been possible. Can a similar increase in cropland occur in the near future? Several noted experts believe not.[6] Factors that impede the further large-scale expansion of cropland are that much of the present cropland of the world is becoming either severely eroded or waterlogged and is no longer suitable for cultivation and that cropland is also being continuously reduced by urbanization. Moreover, these experts believe that with present technology no new large areas of the world can be opened to agriculture at a feasible cost.

Those agricultural specialists who believe that a large increase in cropland is possible believe that new cropland can be created from the vast tropical rain forests of northern South America, Africa, and Indonesia.[7] These tropic areas, now virtually uninhabited, may contain four-fifths as much potential cropland as the 3.5 billion acres presently cultivated.[8] It should be emphasized, however, that these areas are now unpeopled for the very good reason that with present technology no one can make a living there. These tropic rain-forest areas have the advantages of large amounts of water and sunlight. They have the disadvantages of such poor soil and of being so infested with insects and fungi that all previous attempts at agriculture have failed. Thus, opening these large areas to agriculture, if ever feasible, will first require an intense amount of research to obviate the present obstacles.

The second means of increasing food production that we cited previously is increasing the yield per acre of already cultivated lands. The term *Green Revolution* has been used in reference to certain quite spectacular increases in yield per acre of wheat and rice recently obtained in some of the less developed nations. Before the Green Revolution, yields per acre in these nations were considerably lower than elsewhere.

6. See Lester R. Brown, *Man, Land, and Food* (Washington, D.C.: U.S. Dept. of Agriculture, Economic Research Service, Foreign Regional Analysis Div., 1963); and statement of John J. Haggerty in House Committee on Agriculture, *World War on Hunger*, 89th Congress, 2nd sess., 1966 (Washington, D.C.: Govt. Printing Office, 1966), pp. 68–79.

7. Harrison Brown, *The Challenge of Man's Future* (New York: The Viking Press, 1954), pp. 133–35.

8. Statement of John J. Haggerty, *World War on Hunger*, p. 74.

For example, the rice yields per acre in India were less than one-third as high as those in Japan.[9] Much of the difference in rice yield between India and Japan was caused by special high-yielding strains developed by the Japanese and their use of very large amounts of fertilizer. But an additional factor is that Japan's temperate climate is more favorable to high yields than India's tropical climate, and even with the most advanced farming practices and the best strains, it is not likely that rice yields in India could equal those in Japan.

The essence of the Green Revolution has been the introduction of new strains of wheat and rice suitable for tropical areas which, given an adequate amount of water, ample fertilizer, and, if necessary, insecticides, produce much more heavily than the original strains. For example, the "miracle rice," IR-8, is capable of doubling the yield of most local rices in tropical Asia. The Mexican dwarf wheat developed by Nobel Prize winner Norman Borlaug has had even more remarkable results in those areas to which it is suited; for example, in Mexico wheat yields almost tripled between 1950 and 1965. It must be emphasized however, that very large parts of the Third World have not and cannot profit from the new seeds. In some areas fertilizer may be too expensive, or if applied may simply wash away because the land is too hilly. Furthermore, the Mexican wheats have an advantage over other strains only when they are grown under irrigated or high-rainfall conditions, and the new strains of rice cannot be grown under conditions of natural flooding where they may become submerged.[10]

Insufficient water is therefore a major roadblock to higher yields per crop. Ample water, if made available, would also serve another need. In warm climates a year-round supply of water permits several crops a year rather than the one crop whenever the year is sharply divided into rainy and dry seasons.

In many parts of the world groundwater is pumped from wells and applied to crops either throughout the growing season or for that part of the growing season when rainfall is inadequate. An increasing use of groundwater has been an extremely important component of the increased yields of wheat recently obtained in India and Pakistan.[11] However, groundwater is a capital resource which is not automatically replenished. In many areas the amount of groundwater is steadily declining. For example, in Arizona the groundwater level has receded more than

9. *The State of Food and Agriculture· 1966* (Rome, Italy: Food and Agricultural Organization of the U.N., 1966), p. 140.

10. Lester R. Brown, *Seeds of Change* (New York: Praeger, 1970), pp. 3–43.

11. Ibid., p. 25.

100 feet from its earlier level.[12] Larger pumps may secure greater quantities of water for the near future, but they hasten the time when all groundwater will be exhausted. In areas adjacent to rivers, water for crops may also be made available through construction of reservoirs. But storage of water in reservoirs means that land inundated for the reservoir can no longer be used for production; moreover, a part of the water stored in reservoirs is lost through evaporation. Providing crops with ample water in many arid regions will henceforth require very lengthy transport of water, which will be quite expensive. For example, the Feather River project, which will divert water from northern to southern California, is estimated to cost $2 billion, and its construction to take thirty years.[13]

Desalinization of water is being undertaken in several parts of the world; however, its cost is now so great that it is used only for drinking water and not for agriculture. Even if the price of desalinated water should become much lower, its agricultural use would probably have to be restricted to areas immediately adjacent to a coast, since the cost of transporting it long distances would be very high. The use of water for agriculture must also compete with its use by industry. For example, more than 2,500 tons of water are necessary to manufacture one ton of synthetic rubber.[14] If pollutants can be removed, much of the water used for industrial purposes can be reused for some other purpose. In view of the increased expense in obtaining water, however, we must learn to reuse water much more often than we have in the past.

To some extent, yields per acre can be improved simply through the application of more labor without increasing the supply of other inputs such as water or commercial fertilizer. At least in Indonesian rice paddies, it would appear that total production can be almost indefinitely increased through additions to the number of cultivators.[15]

Finally, yields of food per acre can be improved considerably if men can learn to live without protein from animal sources. From five to eight calories of food from plants are needed to produce each calorie of foodstuff obtained by humans from animals.[16] Thus, food from animal sources is extremely wasteful of plant calories, and this is a chief reason

12. Georg Borgstrom, *The Hungry Planet* (New York: Macmillan, 1965), p. 417.

13. Ibid., p. 425.

14. Ibid., p. 423.

15. Clifford Geertz, *Agricultural Involution* (Berkeley, Calif.: University of California Press, 1963), p. 32.

16. Borgstrom, *The Hungry Planet*, p. 28.

why in many Asian nations very little food comes from such sources. At present a very large proportion of mankind suffers from a protein deficiency. If men could get the right kind of protein exclusively from plants, they could obtain more calories for themselves because of feeding fewer animals, and they might also obtain more much-needed protein for themselves. Recently a packaged combination of different vegetable products, including an oil-seed meal and a cereal which together create a balanced protein product, has been developed and marketed under the name of *Incaparina*.[17] Wider distribution of this product holds great promise. Another means of obtaining inexpensive protein may be the development of yeast factories. Yeast, a source of high protein, can be grown with great efficiency from sugar cane.[18] Algae may be yet another future source of high-quality protein, but the intensive cultivation of algae would demand the expenditure of very large amounts of capital, and the cost of maintaining production might be either high or low.[19]

Man may also be able to increase the amount of food gathered from the sea. In fact, since the end of World War II the production of food from marine sources has increased more rapidly than that from terrestrial sources.[20] Much of this increase in fisheries production came about from stepped-up fishing activity in the Southern Hemisphere, particularly off the coast of Peru. It is believed that we are currently fully exploiting or even overexploiting the fish from the North Atlantic Ocean, but that further increases in catch can be obtained from oceans in the Southern Hemisphere, particularly the Indian Ocean.[21] Incidentally, a promising new product from the new fishing grounds off the coast of Peru is fish protein concentrate. This fish flour, obtained from grinding whole fish, is now largely used as feed for poultry and livestock but can be used to provide valuable and inexpensive protein to human beings as well.

The problem of increasing world food production is made much more difficult because the greatest need for increased production is in the rapidly growing economically backward nations where the obstacles to securing a sufficient food production increase appear to be greatest.

17.　Nevin S. Scrimshaw, "Adapting Food Supplies and Processing Methods to Fit Nutritional Needs," in *World Population and Food Supplies, 1980*, ASA Special Publication No. 6 (Madison, Wis.: American Society of Agronomy, 1965), pp. 31–41.

18.　Ibid., p. 39.

19.　Ibid.

20.　*The State of Food and Agriculture: 1971* (Rome, Italy: Food and Agricultural Organization of the U.N., 1971), p.1.

21.　S. J. Holt, "The Food Resources of hte Ocean," *Scientific American* (September 1969), 221:3, pp. 178–94.

We cannot be sure that the less developed nations will be able to increase their food production sufficiently to keep up with their increase in population. If they do not, and if the United States and others of the food-surplus nations can no longer meet the food deficits of these nations, death rates in the latter will surely rise. It is clear, however, that by providing extensive technical and scientific assistance, the developed countries can greatly help the less developed nations increase their food supplies.

Energy and Minerals

The future demand for energy and minerals will be increased not only by population growth but also by economic development. The world's population is now doubling approximately every thirty-five years. But the world consumption of energy has been growing at a rate which ensures a doubling of consumption approximately every twelve years, and production of iron ore at a rate which ensures doubling approximately every eleven years.[22] In the early 1960s over 92 percent of the world's energy consumption was derived from fossil fuel resources (i.e., from coal, petroleum, and natural gas), and less than 8 percent from the generation of hydroelectric power, atomic energy, or other means.[23] Nevertheless, in the face of a very rapid increase in energy consumption, mankind will soon be confronted with the exhaustion of its supply of energy from fossil fuels.

The United States is extremely favored in its reserves of fossil fuels. Yet in 1954 Harrison Brown estimated that the fossil fuel resources in the United States might last no longer than 75 years, or at most no longer than 250 years.[24] Estimates of when the world's fossil fuels will be exhausted are of course subject to considerable error, since we do not have accurate knowledge of what or where all reserves actually exist, especially with regard to petroleum and natural gas, nor can we predict how fast the demand for fossil fuels will grow in the near future. Nevertheless, it is clear that the era of fossil fuel consumption will be but a very short time period in the total span of human history. Recent events

22. Approximate doubling times were computed from data in United Nations, *Statistical Yearbook, 1965* (New York: United Nations, 1966), pp. 347 and 186.

23. Sir Harold Hartley, "World Energy Prospects," in *The World in 1984*, Vol. I, ed. Nigel Calder (Baltimore: Penguin Books, 1965), p. 71.

24. Harrison Brown, *The Challenge of Man's Future* (New York: Viking Press, 1954), p. 164. For another similar estimate, see Richard L. Meier, *Science and Economic Development: New Patterns of Living* (Cambridge, Mass.: The MIT Press, 1966), p. 29.

make it apparent that unless energy can be produced from other sources as cheaply as from fossil fuels, the world will have to get along with less energy or pay more for what it gets.

Further development of water power will provide some small relief when fossil fuels have been exhausted. However, we must expect that in the future the major sources of energy will come from atomic power and perhaps from the direct tapping of solar energy. If nuclear fission becomes the major source of the world's energy, the supply of high-grade uranium and thorium ores will eventually be exhausted. However, if all the uranium and thorium within one ton of ordinary rock could be utilized for energy release, energy equivalent to that within fifty tons of coal could be obtained.[25] Thus, in principle man could use ordinary rock for his fuel-energy needs.

Because future technological developments cannot be predicted in advance, we cannot forecast in detail the future cost of energy. In some areas and for certain purposes, atomic energy is now the least expensive energy source; operating costs at nuclear power plants are now relatively low. The major reason why atomic energy is not now usually competitive with fossil fuels is the high cost of the interest payments on the enormous uranium or thorium inventory which is currently necessary for nuclear energy production. A major reduction in the cost of atomic power will result when and if a safe and environmentally harmless breeder reactor is developed. Current nuclear reactors are capable of utilizing only uranium-235, which makes up only 1.5 percent of the fission energy contained in uranium, and cannot utilize the very much more common uranium-238. The breeder reactors will allow fission of uranium-238 and will produce perhaps fifty times as much energy from a given amount of uranium as is obtainable by current methods. The United States government has announced a national policy of hastening the development of the breeder reactor. Conversely, unless a safe and effective breeder reactor can be developed quickly, an acute shortage of uranium ores is likely to develop before the end of the century which would cause the cost of atomic power to rise substantially.[26]

The future cost of metals will also be greatly affected by the future costs of energy. All nations are exhausting their supplies of high-grade iron ore and the other high-grade metallic ores necessary for modern industry. For example, the United States is increasingly mining taconite,

25. Drown, *The Challenge of Man's Future*, p. 174.

26. See "Energy" in Roger Revelle et al., eds., *The Survival Equation* (Boston, Mass.: Houghton Mifflin, 1971), pp. 208–17; Chauncey Starr, "Energy and Power," *Scientific American* (September 1971), 225:3, pp. 37–49; and M. King Hubbert, "The Energy Resources of the Earth," *Scientific American* (September 1971), 225:3, pp. 61–70.

a relatively low-grade iron ore. Obtaining metal from low-grade rather than high-grade ores requires a much greater expenditure of energy. Thus, the cost of metals will be much affected in the future by the costs of energy production.

LIFE IN A MORE CROWDED WORLD

Although demographers may disagree on how fast the world's population will grow and when the human population will reach its peak, almost all of them would agree that the world's population will probably be considerably more dense in coming years than it has been in the past. Assuming that present standards of living throughout the world will at least be maintained and that death rates will not rise, what will be some of the other consequences of life in a more crowded world?

Perhaps one of the most important consequences will be the emergence of tighter social controls on certain activities. For example, a very large increase in the amount of vehicular traffic will necessitate more complex traffic rules. Traffic may become so dense that human beings may have to abdicate the management of their automobiles to computers. Controls over water and air pollution will also have to become more strict. As populations increase, the efficiency with which water is used and reused will have to increase greatly. Industrial plants which place large quantities of pollutants into water will have to be zoned into areas so that they are the last users of water. As the number of large cities grow, air pollution will tend to become much more intense. Each city will find that more and more of its air has been polluted from emissions rising over other cities. Hence, national and even international controls over air pollution will become necessary. Since a constantly expanding population may seem undesirable, many nations may attempt to reduce the fertility of their populations through such measures as monetary rewards for bearing fewer children or for having oneself sterilized.

A direct result of crowding will be that the amount of space per capita will decrease. This will have immediate consequences even in the United States, where general living space is still ample, although even now the country suffers from overcrowding in its places of prime scenic and historic interest. In recent years the number of persons visiting areas of scenic or historic interest in our national park system has been more than 200 million a year, approximately twenty times the annual number of visitors in the 1930s.[27] If our population continues to increase,

27. U.S. Bureau of the Census, *Statistical Abstract of the United States, 1965* (Washington, D.C.: Government Printing Office, 1965), p. 201 and U.S. Bureau of the Census, *Statistical Abstract of the United States, 1972* (Washington, D.C.: Government Printing Office, 1972), p. 201.

we may have to prohibit visits to such places except on the basis of reservations made long in advance.

Environmental mastery in a more crowded world will depend on man's ability to make changes continually in his relation to his environment. Many well-intentioned changes actually prove to be harmful: because ecological chains are so complicated, each environmental change is subject to the possibility of unintended consequences. A familiar recent example of unintended consequences resulting from attempts at environmental change is the reduction of many bird populations following the attempt to kill harmful insects with DDT, dieldrin, and other powerful insecticides. Systems research, using high-speed computers, may help to prevent reoccurrences of such ecological errors, but it is doubtful that we will ever be able to avoid completely all the possible harmful consequences of environmental change.

CHAPTER 3
THE GEOGRAPHIC
DISTRIBUTION
OF POPULATION

THE GENERAL DISTRIBUTION
OF THE WORLD'S POPULATION

In spite of man's flexibility in adapting to a large number of different environments, human beings have found certain environments much more congenial than others. As a result, vast areas of land have either a scanty population or none at all. Antarctica is perhaps the most conspicuous example of a large land area which has no permanent human inhabitants. As figure 1 shows, other sparsely populated areas of the world are found in the arctic zones of North America and Asia, the vast desert region extending from Northern Africa through central Asia, the arid interior of Australia, the mountainous areas in North and South America and Africa, and elsewhere. The world distribution of population is so uneven that nearly half of the world's population lives on 5 percent of this planet's total land area.[1]

The distribution of the world's population can best be explained through two frames of reference, or "frameworks," one environmental and the other historical. If one were interested in an ideal distribution of population, one would have to pay attention only to environmental factors, but the human population on earth is not ideally located (no matter how the ideals might be defined), and the actual distribution of population on earth is as much affected by historical as by environmental factors.

1. United Nations, *Determinants and Consequences of Population Trends* (New York: United Nations, 1953), p. 163.

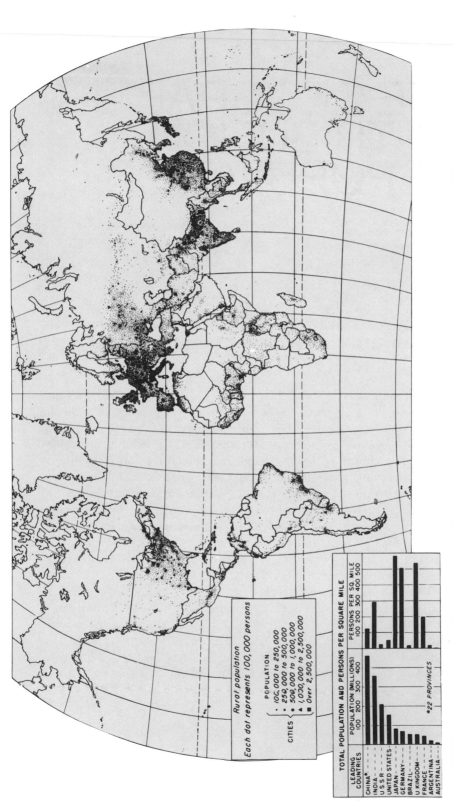

FIGURE 1 Distribution of World Population. Source: John W. Alexander, *Economic Geography* (Englewood Cliffs, N.J.: Prentice-Hall, Inc., 1963).

The environmental factors affecting population distribution at a given point in time are: (1) *climate,* (2) *location of water, soil, energy, and mineral resources,* and (3) *transport relationships.*

Climate bears some rather obvious relationships to population distribution. Large parts of the world attract either no people at all or at best only a few hardy or adventurous ones because of the temperature. Man can, of course, live in almost any environment having an unfavorable temperature, but he finds other environments less costly, both monetarily and energy-wise. Very cold climates present extreme obstacles to human habitation: they are very unfavorable for food production, and clothing and shelter must be more elaborate. At present the very cold climates are inhabited only where they contain valuable minerals or where the area is strategic for military or scientific reasons. The hot tropic areas of the world are much more densely populated than the polar areas. However, the tropics also present some difficulties for human habitation: tropic environment causes a higher incidence of infectious disease, mainly because there is no seasonal check on (that is, no cold-weather hiatus for) the insect, bacterial, and fungus populations; and a combination of high heat and humidity, unless artificially altered through air conditioning, reduces human work efficiency.

Large groups of people need very large quantities of water at cheap cost, since an ample supply of water is necessary not only for direct use as drinking water and for cleanliness, but also for agriculture and manufacturing. Human population is dense mostly in areas where the rainfall is adequate. If rainfall is deficient, a dense population can be maintained only if there is abundant groundwater, a large nearby river, facilities for transporting water inexpensively by pipeline or aqueduct, or processing plants for the inexpensive desalinization of seawater.

The quality of soil under cultivated use is also an important determinant of population distribution. The three best soils are (1) alluvial deposits in river valleys, (2) volcanic soils, and (3) the chernozem (black earth) soils of certain temperate grasslands. Soils such as these are capable of producing large quantities of food per acre and hence can support quite dense populations. The soils of poorest quality are the latosols (leached red and yellow), covering much of tropic Africa and Latin America, and the podzolic (organic/mineral—ashy) soils of the arctic and subarctic regions. In their areas, population is usually very slight. The absence of soil, as in mountainous regions of rock surface, is an even more severe inhibitor of high population density.

A mineral or energy resource may also attract population. If such resources are to be exploited, the population must be at least large enough to provide the labor force necessary for mining or extraction. If the resource is very bulky, additional population may locate near it because it is often more profitable to use the resource where it is taken from the earth than elsewhere. Iron and steel industries thus, often tend to locate near coal mines because a large amount of coal is used in manufacturing iron and steel. In turn, an area with a large iron and steel industry tends to attract so many manufacturers of fabricated metal products that a coal-mining area often becomes a major center of heavy industry.

The third environmental determinant of population distribution is transport relationships. Since almost all of the resources for human subsistence can be used at some site other than that in which they are found naturally, certain areas may become important centers of population if their costs of transport from resource areas to market areas are low. With present technology, cost of water transport is usually much cheaper than transportation by land. Hence, coastal areas and islands are apt to be areas which can cheaply assemble raw materials from elsewhere, process them, and ship the finished product to other markets. England exemplifies an area with very favorable transport relationships. The density of population in other nations is hampered by poor transport relationships. Countries with a rugged terrain, such as Mexico and Colombia, have poor transport relationships because the costs of highway and railroad construction are so high. Similarly, transport relationships are poor in land-locked nations situated at great distances from markets or resource areas.

If the population of the world were able to be redistributed to maximize human comforts, environmental factors would be the sole basis for redistribution. However, since this population apparently has not been distributed with its own comfort in mind, the explanation for the existing population distribution must then depend on various historical factors, such as *past demographic trends, environmental advantages,* and *social policies.*

Demographic trends undoubtedly have had a crucial influence on the present distribution of the earth's population. The United States, for example, possesses a very large share of the total natural resources of the world, but only a small share of its population. Before the sixteenth century, the area which is now the United States was populated by tribes with such a low level of technology that their population density was very slight; since that century, despite a very rapid growth in population, the United States has not had time to develop a very dense population. Hence the amount of natural resources per capita of total population in the United States remains extremely high relative to that of almost all of the remainder of the world. By contrast, China, India, Pakistan, Indonesia, and many other nations have had a positive growth rate for such a long period of time that resources per capita have become extremely limited.

Actually, once it has had the effect of drawing enough people to its locus, an environmental advantage is never exhausted—not even if drastic changes are made in the original surroundings. It is never exhausted because it helps to determine the density of all future populations: once an area becomes densely populated, it achieves and stands a good chance to retain a transport advantage over more thinly populated competitive regions in marketing its produce, and this factor alone will continue to attract people. Proof of the thesis that environmental advantage is never exhausted may be seen in the present concentration of population on the northeast coast of the United States (which, however, might not prove to be the most popular distribution area if the United States were suddenly depopulated and could be populated again). The existing high density of population in this section of the nation is at least partly because it was the closest to Europe, and it gained a transportation advantage by attracting both the bulk of the first European settlers and the lion's share of the early market-produce business.

New York may be America's largest city as a result of its past environmental advantages. New York's port does not now have any noticeable intrinsic advantage over those in Norfolk, Baltimore, or Philadelphia; all of these are closer to America's heartland. What gave New York its greatest advantage over its competitors was the building of the Erie Canal, completed in 1825. Upon the canal's opening, the freight rate from Buffalo to New York declined from $100 to $10 a ton, and travel time from fifteen to six days.[2] As a result, the population of New York City soon outstripped that of its principal rivals (Baltimore, Philadelphia, and Boston) which, without canals, did not have cheap access to the interior. Today railroads and highways are New York's chief links to the hinterlands, and New York no longer has a transport advantage in obtaining goods from inland America. Because of the great lead in population which she attained as a result of the Erie Canal, however, New York has been able to maintain its position as the largest city in the United States.

The third historical factor influencing population distribution is social policy. Because dense populations tend to maintain themselves, past social policies that helped to determine these densities are important in explaining current population densities. For example, although Brazilia has recently been made the capital of Brazil, Rio de Janeiro the previous seat of government, had in 1970 a population of 4.3 million, in contrast to less than 3 hundred thousand in Brazilia, mainly because it was Brazil's capital for so many years. Beside the choice of the capital city, other social policies which can also determine population distribu-

2. *Encyclopaedia Britannica*, 1965, s.v. "Erie Canal."

tion within a nation may be found in current and past legislation concerning tariffs, agricultural subsidies, migration, and area development. The current population distribution among nations is also influenced by such past and present social policies as warfare and restrictions on international migration.

Changes in population distribution result from several factors. In the very long run, they may be due to environmental changes, but environmental changes usually occur very slowly and hence are quite unimportant to short-run changes in population distribution. Changes in technology, in population growth rates, and in social policy are probably the most important determinants of short-term shifts in population distribution.

URBANIZATION

In many nations one of the most striking characteristics of the last 200 years has been the tremendous change in the proportion of population living in cities—a change termed *urbanization*. Kingsley Davis has estimated that the proportion of the total world population living in urban areas of 100,000 population or more increased from around 2 percent in 1800 to about 18 percent in 1960.[3] Urbanization has been closely associated with economic development. In the history of the now developed nations, each increase in material well-being was associated with a greater proportion of the total population living in urban areas. For example, in the United States the proportion of all population classified as urban residents increased from 5.1 percent in 1790 to 73.5 percent in 1970.[4] Currently, the most economically developed nations are also for the most part the most urbanized, and the least developed the least urbanized. For example, in the United States, the world's most wealthy nation, 55.5 percent of the population lived in urbanized areas of more than 100,000 population in 1970,[5] while in India, one of the world's poorest nations, only 8 percent of the population lived in urban areas of this size class in 1964.[6]

The urbanization of the world during the last 200 years has had

3. Kingsley Davis, "The Urbanization of the Human Population," *Scientific American* (September, 1965), 233:3, 44.

4. U.S. Bureau of the Census, *United States Census of Population: 1970*, Final Report PC(1)-A1, p. 42.

5. Ibid., p. 43.

6. United Nations, *Demographic Yearbook, 1964* (New York: United Nations, 1965), pp. 178–79.

two fundamental causes. First, as a nation becomes more wealthy, its inhabitants desire to spend less of their income on food and more on other goods and services. Consumer goods other than food are almost invariably produced more cheaply in cities than in the countryside, because cities are centers of transportation and thus can assemble raw materials and ship out a finished product at a relatively low cost, and also because cities can provide a labor force sufficient to produce commodities by mass production—a method which in most cases results in cheaper costs all around. Cities are also the best locations for many specialized services. If, for example, a medical specialist were to locate in the middle of the countryside, he would have a hard time making a living because he would see so few patients; if, however, he located in a city, he would have patients not only from that city but also from many outlying areas to which the city is linked by its transportation network. Thus such specialized services as wholesale trade, higher education, hospital services, banking, and insurance are almost invariably located in urban areas. Because cities can provide many services which rural areas cannot, they often attract people who might have equal or better economic opportunity elsewhere. In such cases, the urban economic opportunity stimulates urbanization, and urbanization in turn stimulates the economic opportunity available in cities.

The second major reason for urbanization has been the changing character of food production. Before the scientific-industrial revolution the number of input goods necessary to achieve the production of agricultural products was very few, and the input goods used were usually produced by the farmer himself. Today, at least in the developed nations, the situation is very different. To create their produce, farmers increasingly rely on artificial fertilizers, insecticides, machinery, and inanimate sources of energy. These many inputs to agricultural production cannot be produced directly on the farm but instead are usually produced in urban centers. As a result, a large part of "farm" work is now done not on the farm but in cities. Furthermore, for the many persons in the developed nations who do not themselves live on farms, food which remains on the farm is of no direct use. To be useful to urbanites, farm produce must be transported from the farm, processed, and then distributed, and these additional activities are commonly carried out by persons who themselves dwell in cities. Hence for any typical food product, the farmer receives only a very small share of the total price. For example, in the United States in 1966 a quart of milk cost the consumer 28¢, while the farmer received only 2.8¢ for it.[7]

Concomitant with increasing urbanization in the developed nations

7. Robert E. Dallos, "Milk: Case History of a Rising Price," *New York Times*, 7 August 1966.

has been a phenomenon which I shall call *suburbanization*. "Suburbanization" can mean several things, though perhaps its most common meaning would be "an increase in the proportion of the total population in a metropolis which lives outside the official limits of the central city of that metropolis." In the United States and other developed nations there has certainly been a much more rapid growth in the political areas of the metropolis outside the central city than within its bounds. However, the suburbanization to which I wish to refer can occur *both* in the central city *and* in surrounding adjacent cities and towns. What I wish to discuss is a tendency for the parts of the metropolis nearest the central business district to decline in population while those most removed from the central business district increase dramatically.

Suburbanization has been perhaps most pronounced in the United States, but the phenomenon exists in all developed nations. The process of suburbanization can be well illustrated by the example of the New York urbanized area during the period from 1950 to 1970. During those years the total population of the New York-northeastern New Jersey urbanized area increased from 12.3 million to 16.2 million persons. The urbanized land area however, increased even more than the population per square mile so that the population per square mile for the whole urbanized land area declined from 9,810 to 6,683. In Manhattan, the center of the urbanized area, the population declined from 89,000 persons per square mile to 69,000. Consider now the pattern of population density to the east of Manhattan. Brooklyn and the Bronx, densely settled boroughs immediately adjacent to Manhattan on the southeast and northeast respectively, experienced little change in population density. In Brooklyn the decline in population was from 36,000 persons per square mile to 34,000; in the Bronx, density remained constant at 34,000 persons per square mile. Queens Borough, somewhat farther east from Manhattan than Brooklyn or the Bronx, had a slight gain in population from 14,000 to 17,000 persons per square mile, whereas Nassau County, on Long Island immediately east of Queens Borough and outside the limits of New York City, more than doubled its population from 2,200 persons per square mile to 4,700. Simultaneously, Suffolk County, located to the east of Nassau County, experienced a phenomenal rise in density from 300 persons per square mile to 1,200.[8]

Suburbanization has several causes. One is that residential use of land must compete with other land uses. Increasingly, land adjacent to the central business district is taken over for expressways, parking lots, and commercial use, and as a result, residential density declines.

---

8.   U.S. Bureau of the Census, *United States Census of Population, 1960*, Vol. 1, Part 1, p. 45; and Vol. 1, Part 34, p. 13; and U.S. Bureau of the Census, *U.S. Census of Population: 1970*, Final Report PC(1)-A34, p. 21.

A second cause involves changes in the demand for residential space brought about by changes in income, the number of leisure hours, and the cost of travel. Larger incomes have allowed larger proportions of more salaries to be spent on travel to and from work, and shorter work-days have given the commuter more time for such travel. In addition, the automobile has greatly reduced the cost and time of commuting be-tween the central city and suburban areas, some remote enough not to be linked to the central city by public transport. Further, families have moved out of the areas adjacent to the central business districts to escape high land costs, soaring rents, and a general lack of elbowroom.

Thirdly, with an increasing volume of goods shipped by truck rather than by railroad, and with a rising proportion of workers commuting by automobile rather than by public transportation, it has also been possible for a larger proportion of factories to locate away from the cen-tral business area. An increasing dispersion of jobs also reinforces a dis-persion of residence.

A fourth cause for suburbanization relates to the quality of existing city housing and the phenomenon of rising per-capita income. In the areas adjacent to the central business district, housing is generally rather crowded. As the average income of the population of the inner-city area increases, the residents wish to spend more money on housing. The usual pattern is one of demanding more space per capita. Hence, dwelling units are remodeled, and a house which originally was built for two families is converted to a single-family house. In Boston, which lost about 20 percent of its population from 1950 to 1970 the proportion of housing units with more than one person per room declined from 12.7 percent to 7.6 percent.[9] Similar declines in crowding within housing units have occurred in Manhattan and in the East Side of London, two areas which have also declined in total population.[10]

SOCIAL EFFECTS OF HIGH
AND LOW POPULATION DENSITY

Before we study the effects of differences in population density, we must define the term. The most common definition of *population density,*

9. U.S. Bureau of the Census, *United States Census of Population, 1950*, Vol. 3, Chapter 6, p. 86; and U.S. Bureau of the Census, *U.S. Census of Population and Housing: 1970*, Final Report PHC(1)-29, p. P-3 and p. H-3.

10. U.S. Bureau of the Census, *United States Census of Housing, 1950*, Vol. 1, Part 4, P. 32–29; U.S. Bureau of the Census, *U.S. Census of Housing: 1970*, Final Report HC(1)-A34, p. 44; and Peter Hall, *The World Cities* (New York: McGraw-Hill, 1966), pp. 38–44.

as it applies to a given place, is "the number of persons per unit of area in that place." A difficulty with the population per areal unit is that the density we compute is only for the place itself and does not take into account the density of contiguous areas.

A second definition of population density for a given place might be "the number of persons per unit of housing space in that place." Such a definition is very different from the first. Thus in impoverished rural areas the amount of living space per capita may be very small, but the distance between dwellings very large. Moreover, an area containing high-rise luxury apartments would have a low density according to this definition, whereas according to the first definition its density would be very high. Furthermore, the social effects also appear to vary depending on the definition. For example, a recent study of local areas within Chicago revealed that the number of persons per housing unit *was* associated with various pathologies, whereas persons per unit of area was not.[11]

A third definition of population density has been termed *population potential*. Although the concept of population potential is somewhat harder to comprehend than the two preceding definitions of population density, it is for many purposes the most useful of the possible definitions. *Therefore, in future references to population density, we shall take it to refer to population potential.* Population potential measures not only the population per area at a particular location, but also the number of persons who are contiguous to that location. Making use of population-distance ratios, it is computed for a given reference point by dividing the total population at each separate point in the nation (or other unit) by the distance of that point from the reference point, and then summing these population-distance ratios over all points in the nation (or other areal unit). Stated in mathematical notation, the definition of population potential is as follows:

$$\text{Population potential at reference point} = \sum_{i=1}^{k} \frac{\text{Population at point } i}{\text{Distance of point } i \text{ from the reference point}}$$

In the United States the point of highest population potential is New York City; the central districts of all other large urban areas also have high population potential. In rural parts of the United States a belt of relatively high population potential covers the whole area from

11. Omer R. Galle, Walter R. Gove, and J. M. McPherson, "Population Density and Pathology: What are the Relationships for Man?" *Science* (7 April 1972), 176, 23–30.

Boston to Norfolk on the East and from St. Louis to Milwaukee on the West.[12]

Assuming that population potential is the most satisfactory way to define population density, we will still have difficulty in ascertaining its social effects, since there are many problems in separating the effects of population density from the effects of the many other variables that are commonly associated with it. For example, if we wish to examine the differential effects of the high population potential characteristic of central cities in the United States from the lower population potential of their suburbs, we should have to separate the effects of such facts as these: (1) central cities tend to have older, more crowded housing than their suburbs; (2) central cities tend to contain higher proportions of lower socio-economic groups and of blacks, the foreign-born, and persons not living in family units; (3) central cities may or may not contain a higher proportion of new arrivals than their suburbs.

As a result of these difficulties in disentangling the effect of other variables, our empirical knowledge of the social effects of population density is still rather slight. It may therefore help our understanding of the effects of differences in population density if we consider two sets of deductive arguments in connection with the empirical knowledge that is available. First of all, when population density is high, an individual is in close physical contact with many more persons than when it is low. It is then likely that both the total number of persons with whom he will have social contact and the range in types of persons will vary directly with the population density. Secondly, human beings are biologically limited both in the number of persons with whom they can be acquainted and in the number they can know well. Therefore, a higher proportion of all social contacts in the area of high population density might be expected to be superficial or secondary relationships which are functionally specific and affectively neutral, whereas a high proportion of all contacts where population density is low would be primary relationships, functionally more diffuse and expressive of stronger emotions.

From these considerations it is plausible to argue that very low or very high population densities are inimical to human welfare. A very low population density, though sought and appreciated by a few, for the vast majority leads to loneliness occasioned not only by the absolute paucity of other human contacts but by the fact that the types of persons who may be most congenial to a given individual may be altogether lacking in the restricted circle of possible acquaintances. It may also lead to the inability to procure many necessary services, except at prohibitive

---

12. For a further discussion of population potential, see Otis Dudley Duncan et al., *Statistical Geography* (Glencoe, Ill.: The Free Press, 1961), pp. 52–55.

costs of transportation and may restrict the flow of new and useful ideas. High population density, on the other hand, will at least allow the individual an opportunity to form congenial associations with the like-minded. It will also allow him to procure many specialized services and will foster the spread of new and useful ideas. However, the sheer number of social contacts which high population density forces on one may cause mental stress to develop, of a type and intensity which may be clearly exemplified by the strain one encounters in driving in the midst of a rush-hour traffic jam.

Some interesting experiments by John B. Calhoun on populations of laboratory rats illustrate the pathology which can be created by the mental stress occasioned by extreme population densities.[13] In Calhoun's experiments, all of the rat populations were supplied with an abundance of food and were free from the attacks of predators. However, under conditions of high population density, mother rats failed to build nests or to nurse their young adequately. As a result, infant mortality among the high-density rats was very high. Maternal mortality also rose with increased population density. Many male rats developed various disorders, including homosexuality, extreme aggression, cannibalism of infant rats, and a very obvious desire for isolation.

The mental stress and even loneliness of life for humans living in areas of high population density has been stressed by Louis Wirth.[14] Wirth argued that the excessive number of superficial contacts made necessary in a situation of high population density reduces the possibility of primary relationships and contended that life in the big city is essentially lonely. However, more recent data suggest that Wirth's view of the loneliness of big-city life exaggerates the extent to which primary contacts are lacking in areas of high population density. William Foote Whyte's *Street Corner Society* showed the existence of very strong primary ties among the young men living in the North End of Boston, an Italian working-class district of high population density.[15] Similarly, Young and Willmott's *Family and Kinship in East London* reported extensive primary relationships in that dense working-class area.[16] In fact, Young and

13. John B. Calhoun, "Population Density and Social Pathology," *Scientific American* (February, 1962), 206:2, 139–48.

14. Louis Wirth, "Urbanism as a Way of Life," *American Journal of Sociology* (July, 1938), 44:1, 1–24.

15. William Foote Whyte, *Street Corner Society* (Chicago, Ill.: University of Chicago Press, 1943).

16. Michael Young and Peter Willmott, *Family and Kinship in East London* (London; Routledge & Kegan Paul, 1957).

Willmott found primary relationships to be considerably stronger in Bethnal Green, their study area in London's East End, than in Greenleigh, their suburban study area, a "new town" situated some twenty miles away from downtown London.

It should be noted that the high-density areas studied by Whyte and by Young and Willmott were both areas of stable and homogeneous population. It is likely that high population density has relatively little harmful effect in such conditions, whereas it may become distinctly harmful if it occurs in conjunction with a heterogeneous population containing many recent arrivals. The murder of Catherine Genovese which occurred in 1964 in Queens Borough, New York, may illustrate the type of social pathology occasioned by high population density in conjunction with these other conditions. Miss Genovese was stabbed in three separate attacks and finally killed by her assailant, while none of the thirty-eight neighbors who witnessed the attack attempted to discourage her assailant or *even to notify the police.* The incident fostered great anxiety among opinion leaders in the United States concerning the adequacy of primary social controls in densely populated urban areas.[17]

We shall discuss more thoroughly, in the chapter on migration, the consequences to an already populous area of a high proportion of recent arrivals. In concluding this discussion of the social effects of differences in population density, it would be well to repeat that this topic, although as yet inadequately studied, is one of great significance.

17. *The New York Times*, 27 March 1964, p. 1; 28 March 1964 (editorial), pp. 18 and 28; and 3 May 1964, Sec. 6, p. 24.

PART TWO
POPULATION
PROCESSES

CHAPTER 4
MORTALITY

The *crude death-rate* is perhaps the most commonly used measure of mortality. It may be defined as "the ratio of the number of deaths which occur within a given population during a specified year to the size of that population at midyear." Frequently, however, the crude death-rate does not provide a very accurate indicator of mortality conditions, since it is very much affected by age structure. A young population will always have a lower crude death-rate than an older population, even though the death rates at each age in the two populations are identical. Furthermore, differences between two populations in their sex ratio will also affect the crude death-rate, since at each age, death rates for females are usually somewhat lower than for males.

An exact comparison of mortality in two different populations can be made by a separate presentation of the death rates in each age-sex group of each population. This method is illustrated in Table 3, which presents male age-specific death rates for the United States and for Peru in 1961. Table 3 shows clearly that at each age, mortality is distinctly higher for males in Peru than for males in the United States. The table also demonstrates the very great differences in mortality by age within each of these two populations. For both nations the death rates by age form roughly a U-shaped distribution. Death rates are relatively high in the first year of life, rapidly decline in early childhood, reach their minimum around ages 10 to 14, and then rise gradually but steadily until they reach their maximum at old age.

Table 3   Male Age-Specific Death Rates for the United States and for Peru, 1961 (per 1,000 population)

AGE	U.S.	PERU
0	29.2	176.3
1–4	1.1	17.0
5–9	0.5	7.0
10–14	0.5	2.5
15–19	1.2	4.5
20–24	1.7	6.3
25–29	1.7	7.0
30–34	2.0	7.4
35–39	2.8	8.4
40–44	4.5	10.4
45–49	7.3	13.6
50–54	12.4	18.4
55–59	17.9	25.2
60–64	27.9	35.8
65–69	41.4	53.0
70–74	57.4	76.3
75–79	83.4	114.9
80–84	128.3	190.6
85 and over	219.6	278.7

Source: U.S. Dept. of Health, Education, and Welfare, "Life Tables," in *Vital Statistics of the United States, 1961*, Vol. 2, Sec. 2, p. 7; and Eduardo E. Arriaga, "New Abridged Life Tables for Peru: 1940, 1950–51, and 1961," *Demography* (1966), 3:1, 226.

Life tables provide the most complete picture of mortality in a given population. Two types of table can be constructed, the most common of which, termed a *period* life table, summarizes the age-sex-specific mortality conditions pertaining in a given year or other short time-period. The second type of life table, called a *cohort* or *generation* life table, summarizes the age-sex-specific mortality experience of a given birth cohort (a group of persons born at the same time) for its lifetime, and thus extends over many calendar years.

Both types of life table assume a cohort of fixed size at birth—usually 100,000—and provide the following data for each year of age: (1) the probability of death during the year for those persons entering an exact age x (q_x); (2) the number of deaths occurring between exact age x and exact age $x + 1$ (d_x); (3) the number of survivors to exact age x (l_x); (4) the number of years of life lived by the cohort between exact age x and age $x + 1$ (L_x); (5) the total years of life lived by the cohort from age x to the end of the human lifespan (T_x); and (6) the mean number of years of life remaining from age x to the end of the lifespan (e^o_x).

A variant of the complete life table, which provides mortality data for each single year of age, is the abridged life table, which provides data for persons in age-groups, usually of five-year intervals. An abridged life table for United States males in 1969 is presented in Table 4. In this table the prefix n refers to the number of years in the age interval. Thus $_nL_x$ denotes the number of years of life lived between age x and age $x + n$.

Perhaps the most commonly used datum from the life table is the *average* or *mean expectation of life at birth* $(e°_0)$. A principal advantage of the mean expectation of life at birth as a summary measure of mortality is that, unlike the crude death-rate, it does not depend on the age structure of the population.

Two additional summary measures of mortality are also free of distortion due to differences in age composition. One of these is termed an *age-standardized* or *age-adjusted death rate*. This is obtained by computing for each age-sex group the product of its specific death-rate and a fraction equal to the proportion belonging to that particular age-sex group in a "standard" population and then summing these products over every age-group and each sex. Mortality in various populations may be easily compared when the same standard population is used to "weight" the age-sex-specific mortality rates in each population. Another summary measure of mortality in frequent use is the *standard mortality ratio,* which equals 100 times the ratio of the actual crude death-rate in a population to the rate which would have been expected if for each age-sex group in the actual population the death rate were identical to that in some "standard" population. Mortality in various populations can again be easily compared when standard mortality ratios are computed for several populations, in every case using the same set of rates as the standard in constructing the "expected" death rate.

Mortality Differentials

In the previous section we discussed how mortality rates vary by age and sex, and what methods are available for comparing mortality after making allowances for differences between populations in their age-sex composition. We are now in a position to discuss some other types of mortality differentials. Some of the mortality differences of prime interest to sociologists are those discriminating between: (1) times of peace and war, (2) different social classes within a nation, (3) developed and less-developed nations, and (4) current national levels compared to previous levels in those nations. Let us discuss each of these four differentials in turn.

Wars may or may not have a major effect on a nation's mortality.

Table 4 Abridged Life Table for the Male Population: United States, 1969

AGE INTERVAL	PROPORTION DYING	OF 100,000 BORN ALIVE		STATIONARY POPULATION		AVERAGE REMAINING LIFETIME
Period of life between two exact ages stated in years x to $x+n$	Proportion of persons alive at beginning of age interval dying during interval $_nq_x$	Number living at beginning of age interval l_x	Number dying during age interval $_nd_x$	In the age interval $_nL_x$	In this and all subsequent age intervals T_x	Average number of years of life, remaining at beginning of age interval $\overset{o}{e}_x$
0–1	0.0237	100,000	2,372	97,868	6,683,185	66.8
1–5	.0037	97,628	359	389,637	6,585,317	67.5
5–10	.0025	97,269	244	485,693	6,185,660	63.7
10–15	.0026	97,025	251	484,575	5,709,967	58.9
15–20	.0082	96,774	795	482,066	5,225,392	54.0
20–25	.0112	95,979	1,079	477,232	4,743,326	49.4
25–30	.0102	94,900	969	472,072	4,266,094	45.0
30–35	.0114	93,931	1,074	467,079	3,794,022	40.4
35–40	.0160	92,857	1,498	460,815	3,326,943	35.8
40–45	.0243	91,369	2,223	451,699	2,966,128	31.4
45–50	.0372	89,146	3,319	438,068	2,414,429	27.1
50–55	.0580	85,828	4,974	417,452	1,976,361	23.0
55–60	.0894	80,854	7,232	387,127	1,558,909	19.3
60–65	.1336	73,622	9,335	344,544	1,171,782	15.9
65–70	.1885	63,787	12,023	289,624	827,238	13.0
70–75	.2718	51,764	14,069	224,037	537,614	10.4
75–80	.3509	37,695	13,229	155,322	313,577	8.3
80–85	.4556	24,466	11,148	93,387	158,255	6.5
85 and over	1.0000	13,320	13,320	64,868	64,868	4.9

Source: U.S. Public Health Service, "Life Tables" in *Vital Statistics of the United States*, 1969, Vol. 2, Sec. 5, p. 7.

To the present, the United States has been singularly lucky in this respect. The total number of deaths of American citizens due to the wars in Korea and Vietnam has been negligible. Even in World War II the number of battle deaths among armed forces personnel was less than 300,000,[1] which was only a small fraction of the almost 6 million deaths occurring normally to civilians during the less-than-four-year period in which the United States was at war.[2] Various other nations have not shared our luck—Russia is a prime example. The French demographer Jean-Noel Biraben has estimated that in the Soviet Union during World War II the crude death rate reached a peak of 53 per thousand in 1942, compared with a rate of 18 per thousand just before the war in 1940.[3] Of course, in certain parts of the Soviet Union the death rate was considerably greater than in the nation as a whole. It has been estimated that in the winter of 1941–42, when Leningrad was besieged by the German Army, approximately one-third of that city's three million inhabitants died of cold and hunger.[4]

A future war might well result in a level of mortality substantially above that previously experienced. In 1963, United States Secretary of Defense Robert McNamara testified that in the event of nuclear war, fatalities in the United States might approach 100 million persons, or somewhat more than half our total population.[5]

Nations usually exhibit important differences in mortality according to social class. For the United States, data on this topic are not plentiful since many of the usual indicators of social class are not available from death certificates. Nevertheless, standard mortality ratios by educational attainment and by family income for the adult population of the United States have been computed by means of matching death certificates for the months of May through August 1960 with the April 1960 Census schedules. Although these ratios may not be of the highest validity (since only 77 percent of the death certificates could be matched to the Census schedules), their pattern is striking. To illustrate, among white males 25

1. U.S. Bureau of the Census, *Statistical Abstract of the United States, 1966* (Washington, D.C.: Government Printing Office, 1966), p. 260.

2. U.S. Public Health Service, *Vital Statistics of the United States, 1964*, Vol. 2, Part A (Washington, D.C.: Government Printing Office, 1966), p. 2.

3. Jean-Noel Biraben, "Essai sur l'evolution demographique de l'U.R.S.S.," *Population*, 18, No. 2a (June, 1958), pp. 41–44.

4. Leon Gouré, *The Siege of Leningrad* (Stanford, Calif.: Stanford University Press, 1962), p. 218.

5. Testimony before the House Armed Services Committee, February, 1963, quoted in speech by Senator George McGovern (D., S.D.), *Congressional Record*, 2 August 1963.

to 64 years of age, those with less than five years of schooling had a standard mortality ratio of 115 whereas those who were college graduates had a ratio of 70; among white females of this age group, the corresponding ratios were 160 and 78.[6]

Data on infant deaths by social-class indicators have also been made available for the United States. A mail questionnaire was sent to a probability sample of parents of legitimate live births in 1964–66 and a second probability sample of parents of infants dying before age one during these same years. From the data collected, death rates by family income, father's education and mother's education were computed. For both whites and blacks of each sex striking differences by social-class indicators were shown. For example, for white female infants, the number of deaths per 1,000 live births was 22.4 when family income was less than $3,000 as compared to 17.4 when family income was $10,000 or more; and 29.2 when mother's education was eight years or less as compared to 16.0 when mother's education was sixteen years or more.[7]

For the United States the differential mortality of whites and non-whites is of interest. This differential is at least in part a reflection of social class, since a very large proportion of all nonwhites are of lower social class. Currently, nonwhites have a considerably higher mortality rate than whites. The mean expectation of life at birth for white men and women in the United States in 1969 was 71.3 years, whereas that for nonwhite men and women was only 64.3 years. Furthermore in 1969 the death rates for nonwhites from 20 to 49 years of age were approximately double those of whites.[8] Nevertheless, the mortality differential between whites and nonwhites is now less than it used to be. In 1969 the mean expectation of life at birth of nonwhites was only 10 percent less than among whites, whereas in 1900 it had been 31 percent lower.[9]

Mortality differences among nations are still substantial although the range in mortality level among nations is considerably less now than it was before World War II. Although expectation of life in the less developed nations cannot usually be known precisely since so many of them lack a complete registration of deaths, it can be reasonably estimated that the people of several nations in Africa currently have an expecta-

6.   Evelyn Kitagawa, "Social and Economic Differentials in Mortality in the United States, 1960" in International Union for the Scientific Study of Population, *International Population Conference*, London, 1969 (Liege, Belgium, 1971), pp. 980–95.

7.   Brian MacMahon et al, "Infant Mortality Rates: Socioeconomic Factor," *Vital and Health Statistics*, Series 22, No. 14, p. 12.

8.   U.S. Public Health Service, "Life Tables" in *Vital Statistics of the United States, 1969*, Vol. 2, Sec. 5, p. 8.

9.   Helen C. Chase, "White-Nonwhite Mortality Differentials in the United States," *Health, Education, and Welfare Indicators* (June 1965) pp. 27–38.

tion of life at birth of only thirty-five years or less. In Burma, the Khmer Republic (Cambodia), India, Indonesia, Pakistan, and Vietnam the expectation of life at birth is estimated to be no more than about fifty years. On the other hand, in the United States, Canada, Australia, New Zealand, Japan, the Soviet Union, and most of the European nations, the mean expectation of life at birth for both sexes is about seventy years or more. The lowest mortality in the world is found in Norway, the Netherlands, and Sweden, where the expectation of life at birth for males (at least seventy-one years) is about four years greater than in the United States, and that for females (around seventy-six years) is about two years greater than in the United States.[10]

In at least some parts of Europe mortality decline has been reliably reported since the latter half of the eighteenth century. This decline, however, was quite gradual until the latter part of the nineteenth century. Within the past century the reduction in mortality in Europe and the other now-developed nations has been an event of truly phenomenal magnitude. To illustrate: in 1900 the average expectation of life at birth in the United States was only 47.3 years, compared to 70.4 years in 1969. In the United States and other nations with reduced mortality, the declines in infancy and childhood, and among young adults, have been much greater than for older persons. For example, the death rate for white infants under one year of age in the United States declined from 159 per thousand in 1900 to 19 per thousand in 1969 or by 88 percent. Similar percentage declines were attained for all ages below thirty-five. On the other hand, the death rate for white persons eighty-five years old and over declined by only 19 percent.[11]

The trend in mortality in the less developed nations cannot be plotted as precisely as in the developed nations. However, it is clear that a major reduction in mortality occurred in many nations in a very short time-period following World War II. For example, in Chile, where death registration is quite complete, the crude death-rate declined from 19.3 per thousand in 1945 to 15.0 in 1950, and was further reduced to 12.3 by 1960. Deaths of infants under one year of age per 1,000 live births declined from around 150 in 1945 to slightly over 100 in 1950 and later years, and even sharper declines were obtained in the mortality of children and young adults.[12] In India the crude death-rate probably declined from about 27 per 1,000 in 1941–50 to about 19 per thousand in

10. *United Nations Demographic Yearbook, 1971* (New York: United Nations, 1972, pp. 746–65.

11. Chase, "White-Nonwhite Mortality Differentials," pp. 27–38; U.S. Public Health Service, "Life Tables", p. 8.

12. *Recent Mortality Trends in Chile*, National Center for Health Statistics, Series 3, No. 2 (Washington, D.C.: U.S. Public Health Service, 1964).

1958–59.[13] But perhaps the most dramatic decline in mortality occurred in Ceylon, where the crude death-rate declined from around 20 per 1,000 in 1940–44 to less than 10 per 1,000 in 1958.[14]

In the more recent past, mortality rates have apparently stabilized in many countries. In the United States the expectation of life at birth has remained essentially constant since 1954.[15] Even in Chile, where mortality is still quite high compared to that in the developed nations, there has been little decline in age-specific mortality rates since 1953.[16] The reasons for this recent stabilization will be discussed in the next section.

DETERMINANTS OF MORTALITY

Mortality is a consequence both of *morbidity* (sickness) and of the *case-fatality* rate—that is, of the proportion of sick persons who die. Whereas *curative medicine* is aimed specifically at reducing case-fatality rates, *preventive medicine* (the most important components of which are adequate nutrition, environmental control, immunization, and health education) may help to reduce either morbidity *or* case-fatality. Let us first discuss the contributions of each of the various types of preventive medicine, and then the role of curative medicine.

Although famine, a common cause of death in former times, has in recent years been largely eliminated by the speedy transport of food to areas temporarily bereft of their own supply, *level of nutrition* is still an important determinant of mortality. Recent studies have provided conclusive proof that a very important cause of high mortality levels among children under five is an inadequate diet, especially with respect to protein. For example, in a Mayan area of Guatemala, Gordon, Behar, and Scrimshaw (a team of public-health physicians and nutritionists) conducted an experiment in which over a four-year period the children of one village were given a daily high-protein dietary supplement consisting of milk, a banana, and *Incaparina* (a product described in chapter 2).[17]

13. *Population Bulletin of the United Nations, No. 6—1962* (New York: United Nations, 1963), pp. 37–38.

14. Ibid., p. 38.

15. U.S. Public Health Service, "Life Tables," p. 12.

16. *Recent Mortality Trends in Chile*, National Center for Health Statistics, Series 3, No. 2 (Washington, D.C.: U.S. Public Health Service, 1964), p. 1.

17. Nevin S. Scrimshaw, "The Effect of the Interaction of Nutrition and Infection on the Pre-School Child" in *Pre-School Child Malnutrition: Primary Deterrent to*

The mortality rates of children under three years of age in this village were then compared to those of children in a nearby control village and to the mortality rates existing in the test village before the experiment. Although little reduction was secured in the death rate of babies less than one month old, among infants one to eleven months old the death rate was only 19 per thousand, compared to 106 per thousand in the control village, and 113 per thousand in the test village prior to the experiment. For children six to eighteen months old the death rate in the experimental village was 30, compared with 97 in the control village, and at nineteen to thirty-six months of age the death rates were 10 and 25 respectively. The improved diet of the test village resulted not only in a lower incidence of such diseases as diarrhea and measles, but also in a lessening of their severity, so that both morbidity *and* case-fatality rates were reduced. If such inexpensive sources of protein as Incaparina can be widely used, clearly they will have a great effect on the mortality of infants and young children in the less developed nations. Achieving widespread acceptance of Incaparina or a similar substance will, however, demand a widespread program of health education.

Various measures of *environmental control* are also of great aid in preventing disease. The quarantine of persons affected by infectious disease, one of the earliest public-health actions ever to be enforced by governmental action, is an example of effective environmental control. Two other major measures of environmental control are adequate disposal of sewage, and a pure water supply. In the opinion of one expert, these two have done more for the health of human beings than any other hygienic measures.[18]

The English barrister Edwin Chadwick was the person most responsible for the idea that proper sanitation should be the responsibility of governments. In *The Sanitary Conditions of the Working Population of Great Britain*, published in 1842, Chadwick persuasively argued the causal connection between sanitary care and disease, and urged that each local unit of government appoint a physician as a salaried health officer. The Public Health Act of 1848, passed largely at Chadwick's urging, provided for the first time a statutory authority for such health officers.[19] An additional impetus for improving water supplies was obtained when John Snow, a London physician, proved that the incidence of cholera

---

Human Progress (Washington, D.C.: National Academy of Sciences—National Research Council, 1966), pp. 63–73.

18. C. Fraser Brockington, *Public Health in the Nineteenth Century* (Edinburgh: E. & S. Livingstone, 1965), p. v.

19. Ibid., pp. 136–63.

during the epidemic of 1848 was especially high in those areas of the city where the drinking water was of lowest quality.[20] A similar discovery with respect to typhoid fever was soon made by another English physician, William Budd.[21]

More recently, a major advance in environmental control has been obtained through the use of insecticides such as DDT to kill the mosquitoes which carry malaria. Mass sprayings of DDT in tropical nations soon after World War II were responsible for large-scale reductions in mortality from this cause within a very short time.

Immunization against specific infectious diseases began with Edward Jenner's discovery in 1771 that smallpox could be prevented by injection of material obtained from persons infected with the milder disease of cowpox. In the latter half of the nineteenth century the bacteriological and viral theory of disease was developed by Louis Pasteur, Robert Koch, and others. Pasteur, who also invented the process we call "pasteurization," dramatically proved (particularly to his less knowledgeable and imaginative critics) that immunization against certain diseases could be accomplished by inoculation with a live but attenuated organism, when he developed first his famous vaccine which saved thousands of European sheep and cattle from the scourge of anthrax, and then the celebrated vaccine which prevents rabies from developing in human beings. Since the late nineteenth century, vaccines have been developed for many if not all of the important infectious diseases.[22] All told, mass immunization has played a major role in making death from infectious disease exceedingly uncommon in the developed nations, and in causing a substantial decline in mortality from such diseases in the less developed nations.

Mortality levels may also be influenced by programs of *health education*. Instruction concerning proper nutrition and personal hygiene has without a doubt played an important role in the mortality decline during the past century. Future declines in mortality from such diseases as lung cancer and heart disease may depend on further education concerning smoking, diet, and exercise.

The technology of curative medicine has also made great advances since the middle of the nineteenth century. One of the most important, made around 1865, was Joseph Lister's development of antisepsis (antiseptic methods), which greatly reduced the possibility of infection during

20. Charles Wilcocks, *Medical Advance, Public Health and Social Evolution* (Oxford: Pergamon Press, 1965), p. 105.

21. Ibid., p. 106.

22. Ibid., pp. 118–34.

and after surgery.[23] Another major advance, begun in 1928, was the development of antibiotics, which was initiated by Alexander Fleming's discovery that the mold *penicillium notatum* could kill staphylococci.[24] Then, too, widespread use of antibiotics during and after World War II led to very substantial reductions in deaths from wounds and from many diseases such as tuberculosis, bubonic plague, typhoid, and typhus.

At present, mortality from infectious disease is quite rare in the developed nations and has been very greatly reduced in the poorer nations. (In the developed countries, most deaths now occur from degenerative disease.) Because little progress has been made in further reducing mortality from these diseases, there has been little change in mortality levels in the developed nations since about 1955. In the less developed nations, perhaps the chief drawback to a reduction in mortality is malnutrition. A second impediment to mortality reduction in the poorer nations is the great scarcity of physicians, auxiliary health personnel, and hospitals and clinics, particularly in the rural areas where most of the populace lives. Better health facilities and more adequate nutrition will both depend on the degree of economic advance which these nations can make, although perhaps, if eating habits can be changed and if products such as Incaparina can find mass acceptance, better nutrition can be obtained at little additional monetary cost.

THE SOCIAL EFFECTS OF SOCIETAL DIFFERENCES IN MORTALITY

It is possible that the dramatic decline in mortality since the end of the nineteenth century has evoked more changes in social structure than any other single development of the period. However, there has been so little research that any discussion must be speculative.

Contemporary citizens of developed nations rarely encounter death, except among the aged. This situation contrasts greatly to that which prevailed in these nations formerly. To illustrate how different the situation was in our own country during the past, let us note some of the bereavements suffered by three presidents of the United States and their families. George Washington's father died when George was only eleven. Upon her marriage to George, Martha Washington was a twenty-six-year-old widow. She had already borne four children, two of whom had died in infancy; and of her two surviving children, one died at age

23. Ibid., pp. 115–17.

24. Ibid., pp. 201–9.

seventeen and the other in early adulthood. Thomas Jefferson lost his father when Tom was only fourteen. His wife Martha had also been previously widowed when she married Jefferson at the age of twenty-three, and died herself only eleven years later. Of the six children that Martha bore to Tom, only two lived to maturity. Abraham Lincoln's mother died when she was thirty-five and he was nine. Prior to her death she had three children; Abraham's brother died in infancy, and his sister in her early twenties. Abraham Lincoln's first love, Anne Rutledge, died at age nineteen. Of the four sons born to Abraham and Mary Todd Lincoln, only one survived to maturity.[25] Clearly, a life with so many bereavements was very different from most of our lives today.

A seemingly direct consequence of the reduction in the frequency of bereavement is a decline in the institutions of mourning. In his book *Death, Grief, and Mourning*, the English anthropologist Geoffrey Gorer points out that at the beginning of the twentieth century there were strict rules of etiquette that the bereaved must observe toward others and that others should show toward him. At present, however, neither the bereaved nor the circle of his acquaintances knows quite how to act toward the other, and in fact a common reaction is to try to deny the very existence of the bereavement. In Gorer's opinion, the lack of bereavement ritual and the frequent attempt to act as if the death had not occurred combine to retard healing and prolong the period of the bereaved's emotional upset.[26]

Another apparent consequence of the decline in mortality is a change in the character of religion. In their book *Popular Religion*, a content analysis of trends in popular inspirational literature in the United States since 1875, Schneider and Dornbusch point out a sharp decline in the emphasis placed on how religion will benefit one in the next world, and a marked increase in the emphasis on how religion will aid one in this world.[27] Evidently, the intensity of popular feeling concerning an afterlife has waned. Probably a very important reason for wanting an afterlife is to reunite oneself with friends and relations who have already died. In a high-mortality society, persons of all ages have many close friends and relatives who have recently died; in a low-mortality society, only the elderly find themselves in this position. Thus mortality decline should reduce the general concern with immortality.

25. *The 1973 World Almanac* (New York: Newspaper Enterprise Association, 1073), pp. 771–77.

26. Geoffrey Gorer, *Death, Grief, and Mourning* (Garden City, N.Y.: Doubleday, 1965).

27. Louis Schneider and Sanford M. Dornbusch, *Popular Religion: Inspirational Books in America* (Chicago, Ill.: University of Chicago Press, 1958).

It is also possible, however, that extremely negative attitudes toward traditional religion may also abate with the reduction of mortality. This seemingly self-contradictory action might be based thus: supposing that the experience of prematurely losing one's parent, spouse, or child would provoke in certain individuals severe doubt that there can be a deity who is both benevolent and omnipotent, the smaller the number of persons who have such an experience, the fewer will be the number who will develop or tend to cling to extremely negative attitudes toward such a belief.

A third possible consequence of mortality decline may be a change in family structure. When there is a large probability of early widowhood and orphanhood, it is hazardous for a nuclear family—i.e., a married couple and its children—to isolate itself too far from its kin group. This is because the death of either the father or the mother would make it very difficult for the orphaned children to receive proper rearing and support. Thus, in high-mortality societies we commonly see the nuclear family strongly dependent on some larger kin-group. By contrast, in the low-mortality, developed nations of today, the nuclear family often lives at a considerable distance from other kin, and its ties with relatives, although present, are considerably weaker than they would be in a society with high mortality. In turn, the possibility of a large number of relatively isolated nuclear families has important implications for the process of economic development. A high economic level is not possible without an elaborate division of labor, and much geographical mobility is necessary if very specialized occupational positions are to be filled by the best possible people. Hence, a high level of mortality, by impeding the possibility of a relatively isolated and independent nuclear family, also hinders the process of economic development.

A fourth possible consequence of high mortality may be a reduced intensity of certain interpersonal ties. In a society wherein many children will die before reaching the age of five, parents may frequently steel themselves for the possibility of their child's early death by forbidding themselves to develop a strong emotional attachment. The same may also apply to marriage. Arranged marriages are common in high-mortality societies, whereas in societies with low mortality, marriage is commonly contracted by free choice to a person for whom one has a strong emotional commitment. In a society in which a strong love relationship might soon be disrupted by death, there should be less dissatisfaction with a system of arranged marriages than in societies where mortality is low. Conversely, one may speculate that the pressure for easy divorce may increase as mortality declines, since the number of years one must expect to live jointly with one's spouse becomes so much longer.

A fifth possible consequence of societal differences in mortality is a difference in orientation to time. It may be hypothesized that when mortality is high, individuals tend to have a weaker orientation toward the future and a stronger orientation toward the present than when mortality is low.[28] If so, this may have further effects on the degree of achievement motivation in the society, since achievement always involves a sacrifice of present values for future goals. Furthermore, where mortality is high, parents may be loath to make sacrifices for the future success of their children, since the probability of the child's living to maturity is by no means certain.

Finally, the level of mortality in a society appears to influence its fertility directly. We shall examine in detail some of the reasons for this effect in the following chapter.

28. For a similar view see Stephen Enke, *Economics for Development* (Englewood Cliffs, N.J.: Prentice-Hall, 1963), p. 405.

CHAPTER 5
FERTILITY

FERTILITY MEASUREMENT

We noted in the last chapter that because death rates vary considerably by age, an accurate comparison of mortality among different populations demands a control for differences in age composition. The crude birth-rate (again, births per 1,000 of the total population) does not adequately provide this control.

For females, the period of fecundity (i.e., the biological capacity to conceive and bear children) may extend from about age fourteen to almost age fifty. It is impossible to be more precise, since there is considerable individual variation in the reproductive span, factors such as diet may be important in explaining variations in the span among different populations, and—last but hardly least—a full study of the topic has never been made. We do know, however, that the fecundity of women is distinctly higher in the middle years of the reproductive period than at other times, and that adolescents and women past the age of forty have relatively low fecundity.[1] But even less is known about the reproductive span of men than of women. One can state rather imprecisely that the production of spermatozoa begins at puberty and gradually increases until full maturity is reached, and that after the age of forty there is a decline in the amount of active sperm-

1. Moni Nag, *Factors Affecting Human Fertility in Nonindustrial Societies: A Cross-Cultural Study* (New Haven, Conn.: Department of Anthropology, Yale University, 1962), pp. 104–20.

atozoa. Of course, some men never achieve a high rate of sperm production, others experience an early decline in production, and still others possess abundant spermatozoa even in extreme old age.[2]

The implication of these biological facts for fertility measurement is that the proportion of the total female or male population capable of reproduction is often no more than about half. Furthermore, within the group of reproductive age, differences in age composition must be taken into account.

Although it is possible to compute fertility rates for both males and females, presentation of female fertility rates is much more common than that of male rates. This is largely a matter of convention and the availability of data. Both male *and* female fertility rates *should* be computed for those populations which, because of war losses or other reasons, have a very abnormal sex ratio. This is appropriate because whenever there is an excess of females, male fertility rates are apt to be much higher than those for females, whereas when men are in surplus, female rates may exceed those for males. Moreover, one must always be aware that fertility differentials which exist for females may not exist in the same manner for males.

The most exact comparison of fertility in two different populations is obtained by presenting *age-sex specific birth-rates*—i.e., the ratio of the births to individuals of a given age and sex to the total number of same-sexed individuals at that age, for each age-sex group for which reproduction is biologically possible. It is often more convenient, however, to compare two populations according to one summary measure of fertility, and several such summary measures are available. The *general fertility rate* for females is defined as "the number of births per 1,000 women 15 to 44 years of age." This measure provides considerable but not perfect control for differences in age composition. A general fertility rate can also be computed for males; the most commonly used base is men 15 to 54 years old. The *total fertility rate,* which can be computed for either women or men, is simply the summation of age-sex specific birth-rates over each age in which reproduction is possible. For females the formula for the total fertility rate is

$$\sum_{x=15}^{49} b_x$$

where b_x is the number of children borne per woman of age x. A variant of the total fertility rate is the *gross reproduction rate,* which can also be

2. A. S. Parkes, ed., *Marshall's Physiology of Reproduction*, Vol. 1, Part 2 (Boston, Mass.: Little, Brown, 1966), p. 81; and Moni Nag, *Factors Affecting Human Fertility*, p. 105.

computed either for women or for men. For females the gross reproduction rate is

$$\sum_{x=15}^{49} b^f_x$$

where b^f_x is the number of female children borne per woman of age x.

The gross reproduction rate for males is, similarly, the summation, over each age in the male reproductive period, of the ratio of births of male children fathered by men of a given age to the total number of men of that age. The gross reproduction rate for each sex is therefore approximately half the value of the total fertility rate for that sex. The total fertility rate and the gross reproduction rate both offer an exact control for differences in age composition, since in the computation of either of these measures each age-group is always given the same "weight" as any other age-group.

In discussing mortality we mentioned that two types of measures were possible: period measures and cohort measures. The same distinctions can be made for fertility measures. For example, the *period total fertility rate* for females in 1970 would consist of a summation of age-specific birth-rates for women of each age in 1970, whereas the total fertility rate for the birth cohort of 1919 20 would consist of a summation of the birth rate for 10-year-old girls in 1930, 11 year-olds in 1931, and so on, up to and including 49-year-old women in 1969. It is an empirical observation that the fluctuation over time in period fertility measures is considerably greater than the fluctuation in measures for birth cohorts. This is because period fertility rates are greatly affected by changes in the timing of births. A decline in the mean age at childbearing temporarily inflates the period total fertility rates (or their variants, the *period gross reproduction rates*) even though there is no change in the total fertility or gross reproduction of any birth cohort. On the other hand, a rise in the average age of childbearing temporarily deflates the period rates even though there is no change for any birth cohort. It is now widely recognized that the decline in the age at childbearing in the United States in the 1950s produced period fertility rates that were somewhat higher than the rates which can be expected for any birth cohort.

Even when the registration of births is imperfect, as in many of the less developed nations, and the direct measurement of fertility lacks validity, much useful fertility data can be obtained from census data. The proportion of the total population under age 15 is a very good general indicator of the level of fertility in a population; equally suitable is the ratio of children under five to women 15 to 49 years of age. In many censuses, women are questioned concerning the number of children they have ever borne. The number of children ever born to women 45 to 49 years of age as determined from the census bears a very close relation to the total fertility rate for the birth cohort born 45 to 49 years before the census.

We have covered in some detail the simpler and more frequently used measures of fertility. Before moving to another topic, it would be appropriate to point out that there are other fertility measures in quite common use. These include fertility rates for married and unmarried persons, for married persons by duration of marriage, and rates by parity (i.e., the number of live births a woman has already had) and by duration of parity (the number of years since a woman has had her last child).

DIFFERENTIAL FERTILITY

There is a very extensive body of data describing differences in fertility among nations at a given time; within a single nation over time among geographic areas within a single nation, such as its rural and urban areas; and among such social categories as individuals with varying amounts of educational attainment, or income, or of different occupation, religion, or ethnic group. However, much of the existing data are difficult to interpret because it is not certain that the difference in question is caused by a difference in the classifying variable or in some variable associated with it. For example, the fertility of Jews in the United States is lower than that of any other major religious group, but controversy has developed as to whether the cause of this lower fertility is associated with the Jewish culture itself or whether it is merely a result of the fact that Jews differ substantially from other Americans in their residence, occupation, or some other factor.[3]

Although the interpretation of fertility differences must be done with caution, a knowledge of some of the actual variations in fertility among different populations and strata is valuable, if only to give an idea of the possible range in human fertility which may be observed. Currently, the Hutterites—the aforementioned communalistic religious group now residing in South Dakota, North Dakota, Montana, and the prairie provinces of Canada—apparently hold the world's record for high fertility. An analysis of the fertility of a Hutterite community conducted by Eaton and Mayer showed that, among married women 45 to 54 years of age, the mean number of children ever born was 10.6. This high number was

3.   See Ronald Freedman et al., "Socio-Economic Factors in Religious Differentials in Fertility," *American Sociological Review* (1961), 26:4, 608–14; and Calvin Goldscheider, "Fertility of the Jews," *Population Index* (1966), 32:3, 330.

achieved despite the fact that these women first married at an average age of more than twenty years. If allowance were made for the reproductive time lost by marriage delay, one would estimate that the average woman of this group has the biological capacity to bear at least twelve children. The period gross reproduction rate of all Hutterite women (married and unmarried) in 1946–50 was 4.00.[4] Although a few populations, such as those of the eighteenth-century British[5] and French colonies[6] of North America have approximated the Hutterite figure, fertility in most nations, including the less developed nations, currently falls considerably short of the record set by the Hutterites. The other end of the fertility range is exemplified by Sweden, wherein the female gross reproduction rate in 1970 was 0.94.[7] For females in the United States in 1972 the gross reproduction rate was almost as low, about 0.99.[8]

Let us now look at some of the commonly described types of fertility differentials. We shall successively discuss fertility differences (1) between the developed and less developed nations at the current time, (2) in the now developed nations over time, (3) between urban and rural areas, (4) according to social class, and (5) according to religious or ethnic group.

In general, the nations with the lowest per-capita income have the highest fertility, and vice-versa. For example, India has a female gross reproduction rate of about 2.70, whereas in the developed nations the female gross reproduction rate usually ranges from about 1 to 2.[9] However, the relationship between national levels of income and of fertility is not invariant. Certain nations with a relatively high income, such as Venezuela, have very high fertility, and other nations with a relatively low income, such as Greece and Japan, have very low fertility. Moreover, the relation between national fertility level and per-capita income is not so pronounced as the relation between fertility and infant mortality, or

4. Joseph Eaton and Albert J. Mayer, "The Social Biology of Very High Fertility among the Hutterites: The Demography of a Unique Population," *Human Biology* (1953), 25:3, 206–64.

5. Wilson H. Grabill et al., *The Fertility of American Women* (New York: John Wiley, 1958), pp. 5–13.

6. Jacques Henripin, *La Population Canadienne au debut du XVIII Siecle* (Paris: Institut National D'Etudes Demographiques, 1954).

7. *Population Index* (April-June 1972), 38:2, 235–44.

8. Estimated from data contained in U.S. Bureau of the Census, *Current Population Reports*, Series P-25, No. 499 (May 1973), p. 2.

9. *United Nations Demographic Yearbook, 1965* (New York: United Nations, 1966), pp. 605–17); *United Nations Demographic Yearbook, 1969* (New York: United Nations, 1970), pp. 474–77.

even between fertility and per-capita newspaper circulation (an accurate and widely available index of average educational level). Furthermore, when the relation of income to fertility is considered in a simultaneous statistical analysis holding constant the effects of four other variables, per-capita income is found to have a positive rather than a negative relation with the national fertility level.[10]

In all of the economically developed nations the level of fertility is now substantially less than what it was a hundred or more years ago. However, the decline in fertility has not been an altogether regular process. The fertility decline for the white population of the United States from 1800 to 1972, shown in figure 2, illustrates this irregularity very well. Fertility decline was quite regular from 1800 to 1935; thereafter we observe the pronounced "baby boom" of the 1940s and 1950s, followed by the very sharp drop in fertility in the 1960s and early 1970s. Analysis of the long-term trend in fertility in several of the developed nations has demonstrated that variation in the business cycle has a marked effect on fertility. Other things being equal, fertility tends to rise above the long-term trend when times are exceptionally prosperous, especially for the young adults just entering into parenthood, and to fall when the economy is depressed.[11]

In most nations fertility, particularly when measured for females, is substantially higher in rural areas than in urban. For example, in the United States in 1970 the average number of children ever born to all women 35 to 44 years old was 2.8 in urbanized areas (cities of 50,000 population or more and their suburbs), and 3.5 among farm residents.[12] Part of this difference resulted because a smaller proportion of women had ever married in urbanized areas than on farms. However, the difference between urbanized areas and farms in the United States was almost as pronounced among married women as among all women, and among married women the difference was present regardless of the size of the husband's income.[13] Substantial urban-rural fertility differences,

10. David M. Heer, "Economic Development and Fertility," *Demography* (1966), 3:2, 423–44.

11. Virginia Galbraith and Dorothy S. Thomas, "Birth Rates and the Interwar Business Cycles," *Journal of the American Statistical Association* (December, 1941), 36, 465–76; Dudley Kirk, "The Relation of Employment Levels to Births in Germany," *Milbank Memorial Fund Quarterly* (April, 1942), 40:2, 126–38; and Richard Easterlin, *The American Baby Boom in Historical Perspective* (New York: National Bureau of Economic Research, 1962).

12. U.S. Bureau of the Census, *1970 Census of Population*, Final Report PC(1)-D1, pp. 675–76.

13. Ibid., pp. 181–86.

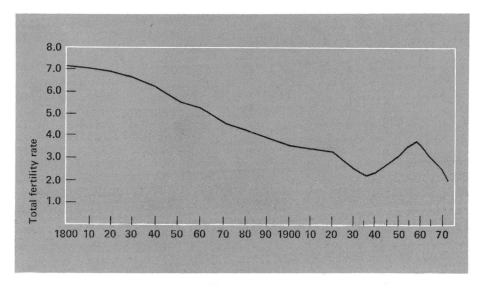

Figure 2 Total Fertility Rate for the White Population of the United States, 1800–1972. Source: Ansley J. Coale and Melvin Zelnik, *New Estimates of Fertility and Population in the United States* (Princeton, N.J.: Princeton University Press, 1963), p. 36; U.S. Public Health Service, *Vital Statistics of the United States*, Vol. I, Section 1, p. 7; and estimates by the author derived from U.S. National Center for Health Statistics, *Monthly Vital Statistics Reports*, 19, No. 12 (1971) and 21, No. 12 (1973).

at least for females, are also found in all of the European nations and in Latin America.[14] In parts of Africa and Asia, however, there appears to be much less urban-rural difference in fertility.[15] The reason for this has not been fully clarified. The lack of a strong urban-rural fertility difference here may be due in part to the fact that, unlike the situation in Western nations, the cities attract many single men rather than single women. Another factor may be a higher level of infant and childhood mortality in the cities, which tends to increase the number of children born, if not the number of children surviving.

Many studies have noted that fertility in the developed nations tends to be highest among persons of the lower social classes, and lowest

14. *Population Bulletin of the United Nations, No. 7—1963* (New York: United Nations, 1965), pp. 122–34.

15. Ibid., and Warren C. Robinson, "Urbanization and Fertility: The Non-Western Experience," *Milbank Memorial Fund Quarterly* (1963), 41:3, 291–308.

among persons of the middle and upper classes. Recent evidence indicates that this inverse relationship was much more pronounced in the early years of the twentieth century than it is at present. However, the data available to study social-class differences in fertility are not entirely adequate. Almost all of the data refer only to female fertility, and very little is known about social-class fertility differences for males. Moreover, much of the female data is for those currently married, which may differ somewhat from data applicable to the total female population. Fertility data by social class are further confounded by several other factors (most notably by differences in residence) which must be controlled if the intrinsic relation between social class and fertility is to be ascertained. In the United States the poorest and least educated persons are more often found in rural than in urban areas, and within the urban population a larger proportion of the working class than of the middle class has a farm background. Although for the United States as a whole in 1960 there was a generally inverse relation between the educational attainment of all women and the number of children they had ever borne by ages 35 to 44, this relationship was less pronounced in the urbanized areas than in the nation as a whole.[16] Furthermore, in the United States in 1962, among married women 35 to 44 years old residing in urban areas and with no farm background, the difference in fertility according to level of educational attainment, although slight, was somewhat U-shaped rather than inverse.[17]

In the years following World War II the previously existing inverse relationship between husband's income and fertility began to change toward a direct relationship. This change can best be illustrated for white married women living in urbanized areas. In 1960 among such women fifty years old and over, those with husband's income of $10,000 or more had fewer children ever born than the women in any other income class. In contrast, among the women 30 to 39 years old in 1960, those with husband's income of $10,000 or more had a higher number of children ever born than the women with husbands in any other income class.[18] On the other hand, following 1960 there was a reversal in this trend toward a direct relationship between husband's income and fertility. For the United States as a whole among all married women 35 to 44 years of age, women whose husband's 1969 income was $15,000 or more had an average of 3.0 children whereas women whose husband's 1969

16. U.S. Bureau of the Census, *1970 Census of Population*, pp. 100–101.

17. Otis Dudley Duncan, "Farm Background and Differential Fertility," *Demography* (1965), 2, 240–49.

18. U.S. Bureau of the Census, *United States Census of Population*, 1960, Vol. 2, Part 3A, p. 182.

income was less than $2,000 had an average of 3.3 children ever born. Among that subset of these women living in urbanized areas, there was almost no relation between husband's income and fertility; the average number of children ever born was 3.0 for those women with husband's 1969 income of $2,000 or less and also 3.0 for those with husband's 1969 income of $15,000 or more. The relationship in 1970 between children ever born and husband's 1969 income for white women varied somewhat by state. In most of the highly urbanized states in the Northeast, there was essentially no relationship between husband's 1969 income and the number of children ever born. Conversely in other states, particularly in the South and Southwest, there was a substantial inverse relationship.[19]

Many studies show that within a nation there are often substantial fertility differences among its different religious or ethnic groups. In many cases we do not have enough data to test whether the difference is caused by some feature of the group's culture, or whether it is merely an accidental result of the group's residence, level of mortality, literacy, income, or some other accidental factor. However, a detailed study of the Protestant-Catholic fertility differential in the United States in 1955 indicated that this difference was accentuated when Protestants and Catholics are equated on such factors as urban-rural residence, income, and educational attainment.[20] On the other hand, many almost wholly Catholic nations in Europe have quite low fertility. In explanation of this aparent contradiction, Lincoln Day has hypothesized that Catholic fertility is elevated only in nations where Catholics feel they are subject to political persecution by non-Catholic groups.[21] In such nations, the laity follow more closely the doctrine of the Church with regard to birth control; moreover, the Catholic clergy are also more likely to promote the large-family ideal.

A good example of the effect of other confounding factors on the fertility of an ethnic group is obtained by examining the relative fertility of American blacks. For the United States as a whole in 1960 the average number of children ever born to women 35 to 44 years old was 2.4 for whites and 2.8 for blacks. In New York State, on the other hand, the respective figures were 2.1 and 1.8.[22]

19.   U.S. Bureau of the Census, *Census of Population: 1970*, Final Report PC(2)-3A, pp. 246–247 and Final Reports PC(1)-D2 through PC(1)-D52, Table 162.

20.   Freedman et al., "Socio-Economic Factors in Religious Differentials in Fertility."

21.   Lincoln H. Day, "Natality and Ethnocentrism: Some Relationships Suggested by an Analysis of Catholic-Protestant Differentials," *Population Studies* (March 1968), 22, 27–50.

22.   U.S. Bureau of the Census, *United States Census of Population, 1960*, Vol. 2, Part 3A, pp. 1, 20–21, and 296.

MECHANISMS DIRECTLY
AFFECTING FERTILITY

A causal analysis of fertility differentials may involve a great number of factors and complicated chain reactions. It is therefore appropriate to make a systematic classification of the mechanisms which directly affect fertility and through which all other factors must operate. An excellent categorization of these mechanisms has been devised by Kingsley Davis and Judith Blake.[23] Their most basic concept is that the birth of a child is not possible unless: (1) sexual intercourse has occurred, (2) intercourse has resulted in pregnancy, and (3) pregnancy has been brought to successful term. Building on this concept, they have devised a list of eleven variables which directly affect fertility. They term these "intermediate variables" since any other variables which may affect fertility must ultimately act through one of these. We shall list these now under their own section heading and then, since societies differ very greatly in their values on at least some of these variables, we shall consider all eleven in some detail.

Intermediate Variables
Affecting Fertility

I.   Factors affecting exposure to intercourse
   A.   Those governing the formation and dissolution of unions in the reproductive period
      1.   Age of entry into sexual unions
      2.   Permanent celibacy; proportion of women never entering sexual unions
      3.   Amount of reproductive period spent after or between unions
         a.   When unions are broken by divorce, separation, or desertion
         b.   When unions are broken by death of husband
   B.   Those governing the exposure to intercourse within unions
      4.   Voluntary abstinence
      5.   Involuntary abstinence (from impotence, illness, and unavoidable but temporary separations)
      6.   Coital frequency (excluding periods of abstinence)
II. Factors affecting exposure to conception
      7.   Fecundity or infecundity, as affected by involuntary causes

23. Kingsley Davis and Judith Blake, "Social Structure and Fertility: An Analytic Framework," *Economic Development. and Cultural Change* (1956), 4, 211–35.

8. Use or non-use of contraception
    a. By mechanical and chemical means
    b. By other means
9. Fecundity or infecundity, as affected by voluntary causes (sterilization, subincision, medical treatment, etc.)

III. Factors affecting gestation and successful parturition
    10. Foetal mortality from involuntary causes
    11. Foetal mortality from voluntary causes

1. *Age of entry into sexual unions.* In the nations of European culture a couple is not supposed to marry until the husband is able to support a wife and family. In preindustrial Europe the age of marriage was relatively low, but beginning at least as early as the eighteenth century the age at marriage began to rise. This rise was so substantial that actual fertility levels were reduced far below their biological potential. During the twentieth century, age at marriage in Europe has been declining concomitant with the increased acceptance of birth control within marriage.[24] Ohlin has suggested that the earlier rise in the European age at marriage could plausibly be explained by the decline in mortality, since the average man now had to wait longer before inheriting land or advancing from his apprenticeship.[25]

In many Asian nations, on the other hand, the age at first marriage has always been very early, since marriages are arranged and the husband is not expected to support his family entirely by his own efforts.

In recent years Ireland has presented the extreme in late age at marriage. In 1961, 45 percent of all females 25 to 29 years old had never married, and 67 percent of males. The other extreme is India, where in the same year and in the same age-group the proportion of women who had never married was only 2 percent and the proportion of males a mere 17 percent.[26]

2. *Permanent celibacy.* A rather high proportion of permanent celibates is frequent in nations which have a late average age at marriage. Ireland again represents the extreme of high proportions celibate. In Ireland in 1961, in the 45 to 49-year age-group, 22 percent of all women and 31 percent of all men had never married.[27]

3. *Amount of reproductive period spent after or between unions.* To some extent in all societies, actual fertility is reduced below the biologically

24. J. Hajnal, "European Marriage Patterns in Perspective," in David V. Glass and D. E. C. Eversley, eds., *Population in History* (Chicago, Ill.: Aldine Publishing Co., 1965), pp. 101–43; and Ansley J. Coale, "Factors Associated with the Development of Low Fertility: An Historic Summary," Paper #WPC/WP/194, delivered at the United Nations World Population Conference, Belgrade, Yugoslavia, 1965.

25. G. Ohlin, "Mortality, Marriage, and Growth in Pre-industrial Populations," *Population Studies* (March, 1961),14:3, 190–97.

26. Data for both Ireland and India are from *United Nations Demographic Yearbook, 1963* (New York: United Nations, 1964), pp. 726–27 and 730–31.

27. Ibid., pp. 730–31.

maximum level because part of the reproductive period is spent after or between sexual unions. Where monogamy is institutionalized, it is almost inevitable that a certain proportion of widows never remarry, since there are almost always considerably more widows than widowers, and many widowers prefer to remarry never-married women. Periods of separation between marital unions are also important in some societies in reducing fertility. Perhaps the best-known locus of this practice is Jamaica.[28] There, few sexual unions are undergirded with legal marriages, and many of the consensual unions break up. The breakup may be caused by marital (legal or otherwise) incompatibility, or in many cases may occur simply because the woman does not want to incur the chance of an additional pregnancy.

4. *Voluntary abstinence.* Certain primitive societies enjoin periods of voluntary abstinence on special ceremonial occasions. Almost all societies enjoin a period of abstinence during late pregnancy and also during the early postpartum period. The former has no detrimental effect on fertility and the latter has little since almost all women have very low biological fecundity during this time. Of the various forms of voluntary abstinence, the "rhythm method" probably has the greatest effect on fertility. This method of birth control demands abstinence in the days before and around the time of ovulation, which generally occurs around the midpoint of the menstrual cycle. When properly practiced, it will reduce conception rates by a rather large amount.

5. *Involuntary abstinence.* In a few societies a large proportion of men must absent themselves from their wives periodically to obtain gainful labor. For example, this is often the case in highland Peru, where many of the men migrate to the coast during the season when sugar cane is harvested.[29]

6. *Frequency of intercourse.* Much theoretical evidence suggests that this variable may be rather important in determining differences in fertility between individuals. Whether or not it affects the fertility of different populations is another matter. It is possible, however, that factors such as diet, temperature, humidity, and the prevalence of certain enervating diseases may have effects on the average frequency of sexual intercourse in different populations. This is clearly a field where we need much more information than we now have.

7. *Fecundity or infecundity as affected by involuntary causes.* Several factors may affect the probability of conception, given the fact that intercourse occurs at a specified frequency. On a worldwide basis, perhaps the chief of these is the incidence of venereal disease, particularly gonorrhea. Venereal disease affects the fecundity of both men and women. Empirical studies have shown that it is a very frequent cause of childlessness in parts of tropical Africa, and in the recent past it has also apparently been a very important cause of childlessness among American blacks.[30] A survey

28. See Judith Blake, *Family Structure in Jamaica: The Social Context of Reproduction* (New York: The Free Press, 1961).

29. David M. Heer, "Fertility Differences between Indian and Spanish-speaking Parts of Andean Countries," *Population Studies* (July, 1964), 18:1, 71–84.

30. Reynolds Farley, "Recent Changes in Negro Fertility," *Demography* (1966), 3:1, 188, 203.

of the Belgian Congo (now Zaire) conducted in the latter part of the 1950s showed that in certain areas up to 35 percent of all women 45 years old and over had never borne a child, and that the incidence of childlessness was very strongly correlated with the incidence of venereal disease in the area.[31]

A second factor which may involuntarily affect fertility is altitude. It is quite likely that high altitude, for example, depresses to some extent the fecundity of the inhabitants of the Indian-speaking areas of Bolivia, Peru, and Ecuador.[32]

Finally, extreme hunger has been found to cause amenorrhea (and hence temporary sterility) in women, and a reduced sperm-count in men.[33]

Modern medical science has made considerable progress in reducing the proportion of persons who are involuntarily childless. The use of antibiotics to cure venereal disease has been very important in this respect. Another advance has been the use of artificial insemination to impregnate women whose husbands are sterile. New drugs have recently been developed which stimulate ovulation and allow certain women to conceive who otherwise would probably never be able to do so.

8. *Use or non-use of contraception.* According to popular belief, contraception is the most important of all of the intermediate variables affecting fertility. Actually, although there is no doubt that contraception is very influential in reducing levels of fertility, it is definitely not so overwhelming a contribution that the other variables can be ignored.

Contraceptive techniques date back to antiquity.[34] The simplest technique, coitus interruptus (i.e., withdrawal of the penis from the vagina just before ejaculation) is mentioned in the Old Testament. At least among those who choose to use it, coitus interruptus is highly effective, and it is still a very important means of contraception in Europe. A condom made of linen was invented in the sixteenth century: the first manufacture of rubber condoms took place in the late nineteenth century; and in the 1930s appeared the latex condom, cheaper and better than its rubber predecessor. The condom is now one of the most popular and effective forms of contraception in the world. The diaphragm, invented in the 1880s, has also become a popular and highly effective method of contraception.

In the early years of the 1960s a revolution in contraceptive technology occurred with the widespread acceptance of two new methods—the oral contraceptive and the IUD (intrauterine device)—whose use could be separated from the act of intercourse. The oral contraceptive is coitus-independent and is also the first contraceptive that is almost completely effective when used according to instructions. By 1965 it had

31. A. Romaniuk, "Fecondite et sterilite des femmes Congolaises," in *International Population Conference, New York, 1961* (London: International Union for the Scientific Study of Population, 1963), 2, 109–17.

32. W. James, "The Effect of Altitude on Fertility in Andean Countries," *Population Studies* (July, 1966), 20:1, 97–101.

33. Ancel Keys et al., *The Biology of Human Starvation* I (Minneapolis: University of Minnesota Press, 1950), 749–63.

34. For a very complete account of the history of contraceptive practices, see Norman Himes, *Medical History of Contraception* (New York: Gamut Press, 1963).

become the most widely used contraceptive in the United States: in that year, among married white women eighteen to thirty-nine years old, 24 percent had used the pill as their most recent method of contraception.[35] The intrauterine device has the great advantage that once it is inserted, the wearer has no need to make any further contraceptive efforts. It is not perfectly reliable, but is probably at least as effective as the condom or diaphragm when these are used during each act of intercourse. The IUD has been the principal contraceptive employed in the family planning programs of many of the Asian nations.

9. *Fecundity or infecundity as affected by voluntary causes.* The surgical operations of tubal ligation in the female and vasectomy in the male provide an individual permanent freedom from further parenthood without destroying sexual pleasure or creating any alternations in personality. Of the two operations, vasectomy is the simplest and least costly. At one time vasectomy was much less popular than tubal ligation, but its prevalence increased dramatically during the decade of the 1960s so that by 1970 the number of sterilized husbands was actually greater than the number of wives who had experienced a tubal ligation. By 1970, among couples where the wife was 35 to 39 years of age, the proportion of couples in which either husband or wife had had a sterilizing operation for contraceptive purposes was 18 percent, as compared with only 11 percent in 1965.[36] Currently, medical researchers are attempting to perfect a method of vasectomy which will allow an effective reversing operation. Under present methods the chance of reversing the effect of a vasectomy is only around 50 percent. If a surely reversible method of vasectomy can be obtained, it may become one of the most widely used methods of birth control among couples who have completed their desired family size.

On a worldwide basis, prolonged breast-feeding is one of the most important means by which a woman may temporarily reduce her fecundity. Women are sterile during their period of postpartum amenorrhea and a short period of anovulatory cycles following the resumption of their menses. Prolonged lactation has a pronounced effect on the length of the period of postpartum sterility. Potter estimates that the period of postpartum sterility averages thirteen months in a population which engages in prolonged lactation, and only four months in a population with no lactation.[37]

10. *Fetal mortality from involuntary causes.* On the average, about 20 percent of all known pregnancies are spontaneously aborted.[38] There is much individual variation in the proportion of pregnancies which mis-

35. Charles F. Westoff and Norman Ryder, "United States: Methods of Fertility Control, 1955, 1960 and 1965," in *Studies in Family Planning*, No. 17 (February, 1967).

36. Larry L. Bumpass and Harriet B. Presser, "Contraceptive Sterilization in the U.S.: 1965 and 1970," *Demography* (November 1972), 9:4, 531–48.

37. Robert G. Potter, Jr., "Birth Intervals: Structure and Change," *Population Studies* (November, 1963), 17:2, 155–66; and Robert G. Potter et al., "A Case Study of Birth Interval Dynamics," *Population Studies* (July, 1965), 19:1, 81–96.

38. Potter, "Birth Intervals: Structure and Change."

carry, but little is known how populations may vary in this respect. 11. *Fetal mortality from voluntary causes.* Induced abortion is one of the most important means of birth control. Primitive and hazardous methods of abortion have been practiced throughout human history. Modern surgical methods make induced abortion a very safe operation when conducted properly.[39] However, in those nations where abortion is still illegal, the operation is frequently hazardous to health, and even to life.

Abortion can now be performed with a very minimum amount of legal restriction in the United States, Japan, Denmark, the United Kingdom, the USSR, the People's Republic of China, Poland, Czechoslovakia, the German Democratic Republic, Hungary, and Yugoslavia. In many of these nations the frequency of induced abortion is very high. In Hungary, for example, the number of abortions officially reported is considerably higher than the number of live births.[40] The recently-invented suction-pump method of abortion, which reduces by half the proportion of cases with postoperative complications, has now been widely adopted in the United States, mainland China, and the East European nations, replacing the method of dilatation and curettage.[41]

It is very difficult to obtain exact statistics on the incidence of abortion in nations where it is illegal except for stringent medical indications. For the United States during the 1950s when abortion was still almost entirely illegal, a group of leading experts estimated that the number of illegal abortions was between 200,000 and 1,200,000 per year.[42] A study recently conducted in Chile concluded that approximately one in every three or four pregnancies in that nation was interrupted by abortion.[43] And authoritative claims have been made that the number of illegal abortions in France and Italy approximates the number of live births, but the evidence on which these claims are based is quite fragmentary.

39. Christopher Tietze, "The International Medical Experience," in *Abortion Experience in the United States*, ed. H. J. Osofsky and J. D. Osofsky (New York: Harper and Row, 1973); "Mortality, Morbidity in Legal Abortions Drop as Women Learn Early Procedures Safer," *Family Planning Digest*, 2, No. 3 (May 1973), pp. 8–9.

40. A. Klinger, "Abortion Programs," in *Family Planning and Population Programs*, ed. Bernard Berelson et al. (Chicago, Ill.: University of Chicago Press, 1966), pp. 465–76.

41. Christopher Tietze, "Two Years' Experience with a Liberal Abortion Law: Its Impact on Fertility Trends in New York City," *Family Planning Perspectives* (Winter 1973) 5:1, pp. 36–41; Anibal Faundes and Tapani Luukainen, "Health and Family Planning Services in the Chinese People's Republic," *Studies in Family Planning* (July 1972), 3:7 Supplement, pp. 165–76; K. H. Mehlan, "The Socialist Countries of Europe," in *Family Planning and Population Programs*, ed. Bernard Berelson et al. (Chicago, Ill.: University of Chicago Press, 1966), pp. 208–9.

42. Mary G. Calderone, ed., *Abortion in America* (New York: Hoeber-Harper, 1958), pp. 178–80.

43. Mariano Requena, "Social and Economic Correlates of Induced Abortion in Santiago, Chile," *Demography* (1965), 2, 33–49.

FACTORS AFFECTING THE DECISION
TO HAVE CHILDREN

The eleven intermediate variables we have cited are concerned with the means by which change in the fertility of a population can be affected. An understanding of these variables gives one a good idea of the *involuntary* biological factors which constrain fertility. However, the level of fertility itself can be explained only when we also consider *voluntary* decisions concerning childbearing. Biological factors place a natural upper limit on the fertility of the individual, but the individual can reduce his own fertility to whatever degree he chooses. Even in primitive societies excess fertility can always be avoided, though the price for doing so may be very great. To consider two extreme examples: (1) couples may decide to refrain from sexual intercourse to avoid a further pregnancy; and (2) the pregnant woman can always decide to abort the fetus even at the risk of her life.

An excellent conceptual scheme for the analysis of the factors affecting the decision to have children has been devised by the economist Joseph Spengler.[44] He considers the decision to have an additional child a function of three variables: (1) the preference system, (2) the price system, and (3) income. Provided we define these terms in a broader sense than they usually receive in the economic literature, these three concepts provide for a complete classification of all factors that affect this decision. The *preference system* simply describes the value a married couple places on an additional child relative to the value of all other goals they might achieve without having that child. The *price system* delineates the cost of an additional child relative to the cost of attaining all other goals that might be achieved if the decision were made not to have another child. Costs must be very broadly defined and must include not only monetary costs but expenditures of time and effort as well. *Income* must also be broadly defined to include not only monetary income but the total amount of time and energy that a couple has for pursuit of all of its possible goals in life. (Because the term *resources* fits the definition more closely than the term *income*, I shall henceforth use the term *resources*.) Given these definitions of the three variables affecting the decision to have an additional child, we can presume that the probability of deciding in favor of another child will vary directly with the relative value anticipated from that child, inversely with the predicted relative cost, and directly with the amount of resources foreseen as available for all goals.

44. Joseph J. Spengler, "Values and Fertility Analysis," *Demography* (1966), 3:1, 109–30.

Spengler's scheme is very useful in analyzing the long-term changes in fertility which have occurred over the last century in the now-developed nations, the fertility differences which now exist between the developed and less-developed nations, and fertility differentials within a nation.[45] Although all of these might be discussed, I shall like to concentrate attention on how this scheme helps to clarify the long-term trends in fertility within the now-developed nations.

The now-developed nations have a long history of increasing per-capita monetary income. They also have a long history of decreasing hours devoted to gainful employment and increasing amounts of leisure time. If there had been no change in either price or preference system, one might then have expected that the long-term trend in fertility would have been upward. Clearly, since over the long run fertility has tended downward, changes in the preference and price system must have discouraged rather than encouraged fertility to an extent that counterbalanced the elevating effects of increased money and leisure time. On the other hand, for a long period during the 1940s and 1950s in all of the developed nations which did not suffer severely from World War II (the United States, Canada, Australia, and New Zealand), we observe a substantial fertility rise. At least for the United States it has been well documented that this period of rising fertility was also one of very rapid rise in monetary income for young adults.[46] It is therefore plausible to presume that during this period the elevating effect of rising income more than counterbalanced any depressing effects of changes in the preference or price system.

In the last hundred years or so, there have undoubtedly been several changes in the preference system in the now-developed nations which have tended to reduce desired family size. One of the most important changes is probably the decline in mortality. As emphasized earlier, the secular (long-term) decline in mortality has had greater relative effect in infancy and childhood than among adults. Therefore, if fertility had not declined, the reduction in mortality would have tended to increase somewhat the number of living children per living parent. This may be illustrated by presenting ratios of children to adults of parental age for typical stable populations differing only in mortality.[47]

45. Of course a complete explanation of fertility differentials must also take into account changes in such nonvolitional biological factors as the incidence of venereal disease, and nutritional status.

46. Richard Easterlin, *The American Baby Boom in Historical Perspective* (New York: National Bureau of Economic Research, 1962).

47. A stable population is one with a calculable and unchanging rate of growth and a calculable and unchanging age composition. Stable populations are more fully described in chapter 7.

For example, the United Nations estimates that for a stable population with a gross reproduction rate of 2.5 and a life expectation at birth of 20 years, the ratio of population under 15 years to that 15 to 59 years is 0.56; whereas when the expectation of life at birth is increased to 70 years with no change in the gross reproduction rate, this ratio is increased to 0.83.[48] Thus, as the level of mortality declined, one would expect the value of an additional birth to wane.

A second possible effect of mortality reduction on the preference system relates to a possible connection between the level of mortality and the amount of emotional energy that parents invest in each of their children. It may be supposed that the pain of bereavement at a child's death is directly proportional to the amount of emotional energy that the parents have invested in that child. Therefore, where mortality levels are high, one might expect parents, in the interests of self-protection, to place relatively little emotional involvement in any one child. Since parents have limited amounts of emotional energy, a reduction in mortality, by encouraging parents to place more libido in the existing children, should reduce their desire to have an additional child.[49]

A third reason why mortality reduction should lead to a lower preference for additional children is obtained if one assumes that parents want to be reasonably certain of having a specified minimum number of children survive to maturity. Where mortality is high, one cannot be sure that any of one's existing children will survive to maturity. When mortality is as low as it is in the now-developed nations, parents can be highly certain that their child will survive from birth to maturity. Thus, a decline in mortality reduces the value of an additional child as insurance for the possibility that one or more of the existing children may die. The effect of mortality reduction in this respect can even be quantitatively measured. If one assumes (1) that each couple is capable of bearing twelve children, (2) that a perfect means of birth control is available and utilized, and (3) that all couples want to be 95 percent certain of having at least one son who will survive to the father's sixty-fifth birthday, the gross reproduction rate (a computer simulation study shows) will fall from 5.2 when the expectation of life at birth is 20 years, to 0.95 when the expectation of life rises to 74 years.[50]

48. United Nations, Department of Economic and Social Affairs, *The Aging of Populations and its Economic and Social Implications* (New York: United Nations, 1956), pp. 26–27.

49. This idea was first advanced in an oral communication by Dr. Laila Sh. El Hamamsy, Director of the Social Research Center, American University in Cairo, Egypt.

50. David M. Heer and Dean O. Smith, "Mortality Level, Desired Family Size, and Population Increase," *Demography* (1968), 5:1, pp. 104–21.

A second long-term change in the preference system relates to the value which parents can achieve from the productive labor of their children. In the agrarian society of the United States in the eighteenth century, with the supply of land practically unlimited, children could be a very productive asset to their parents at a very early age. When the amount of land per capita declined, as it did in the United States during the nineteenth century, the value to the farmer of the labor of an additional child probably declined correspondingly. Moreover, in all of the now-developed nations, industrialization resulted in a further substantial reduction in the value of child labor. Although such labor was quite common in many of the early factories, the situation of the child in the factory was much less satisfactory than if he were working under the direction of his father on the family farm. As a result, much moral sentiment developed against child labor, and in all of the developed nations legislation emerged restricting it. The productive value of child labor was still further reduced by compulsory education laws which, becoming increasingly severe, lowered still further the productive value of an additional child to its parents.

A third long-term change in the preference system relates to the change in the institutions which provide support for the elderly. In the preindustrial period and in the early stages of the Industrial Revolution, the elderly could expect to receive financial support only from their own kin—mainly from their own sons. Gradually, business corporations and governments developed social-security schemes for the aged and for widows. With the full development of these schemes, it was no longer necessary for parents to bear enough children so that they would have one or more sons to support them in their old age. Thus the value to parents of bearing additional children was further diminished.

A fourth change in the preference system was a decline in the rewards which could be expected from society at large for bearing a large number of children. When mortality was high, a high rate of fertility was a positive necessity if the population was not to decline. Governmental and religious authorities who did not wish to see the nation's population decline encouraged a high level of fertility. As mortality declined, the necessity for a high level of fertility merely to maintain the existing level of population subsided. As a result, many governments and religions have changed their attitudes from one favoring large families to one opposing them.

A fifth possible change in the preference system may have resulted because economic development tends to promote a shift from allocation of social status by ascription to allocation by achievement. Where status is ascribed at birth, one need spend little effort in advertising one's status; whereas when status is achieved, its level tends to be transitory, and individuals may develop an intense need for conspicuous consumption (i.e., a compulsion to show off possessions that are not necessarily needed or wanted, but are regarded as status symbols) to demonstrate their rank. If the preference for conspicuous consumption increases, then the preference for children, who do little to publicize one's status, must decline.[51]

Over the past century the development of new and improved methods of birth control has not only reduced the relative preference for children but has also increased their price relative to that of other goals. When available methods of birth control are crude and undeveloped, or when knowledge of better methods is lacking, the decision not to have an additional child involves a high expenditure of resources as well as substantial inconvenience, interference with sexual pleasure, and even the hazard to life and health incurred by resort to a primitive means of abortion. During the 1960s, for example, the increasing use of the highly effective oral contraceptive in the United States and other nations may have been one of the major reasons for their sharp fertility decline.

Economic development has produced other changes in the price system affecting desired family size. One of the most important concomitants of economic development has been urbanization. By raising population densities, urbanization usually causes an increase in the relative price of living space. Since rearing children demands considerable amounts of living space, the relative cost of children rises with each increase in its relative price. Although we may presume that over the past hundred years or so the relative cost of living space has in general been increasing, it is possible that the rise has not been invariant. One may speculate that in the United States in the 1940s and 1950s, increasingly widespread use of the automobile, together with governmental policies which subsidized home ownership, made possible the acquisition of suburban homes at a relative cost probably substantially lower than that during previous decades. Part of the American Baby Boom of the 1940s and 1950s may be explained by this short-term change in the relative cost of living space. Conversely, during the late 1960s and early 1970s the very high interest rate for home mortgages increased the effective cost of living space for young married couples and may have been an important factor in the sharp decline in fertility during those years.

Another factor affecting desired family size is that the labor cost of child care tends to rise in relation to the labor cost of producing material goods. While economic development makes possible a much

---

51. For an argument of this type with respect to the middle class of England during the late Victorian period see J. A. Banks, *Prosperity and Parenthood* (London: Routledge & Kegan Paul, 1954).

larger production of factory goods per man-hour of labor, the number of man- and woman-hours necessary to supervise and socialize a child has certainly not declined, and in fact most probably has risen. Therefore, when a married couple is deciding whether or not to have another child, they can assume that an additional child will burden the wife with the responsibilities of child care for about three more years, or more precisely by the number of years intervening between this birth and the last one. Moreover, with another child to supervise, she will have to work harder during the period when the older children are still under her care. This increased effort must be set against the possible remuneration from a job. Since the amount of material goods which can be bought with each hour of labor outside the home has steadily increased with each advance in national economic level, there has been a substantial secular increase in the price of child-care services relative to the price of material goods.

A final long-term change in the price system which affects the decision to have children concerns the quality of education which parents demand for their children and which is socially imposed. A society increasingly oriented to a complex technology requires that children be given an increasingly lengthy education, and parents recognize more and more that their own child will be at a substantial disadvantage unless his education meets society's new norm. Even where the direct cost of education is met by the state, longer education increases the cost to the parent in terms of more years of child dependency. Hence the secular increase in the standard of education has also helped to depress family size.

DIFFERENTIAL REPRODUCTION
AND THE LEVEL OF INTELLIGENCE

Population genetics studies the "gene pool" of a population and the factors that cause it to change. One of the most important problems in human population genetics is to measure the changes, if any, which may be taking place in the *genetic* component of human intelligence. The term "genetic" is emphasized because it has already been clearly demonstrated that intelligence-test scores are influenced not only by the character of one's genes but also by one's environment.

The eugenics (eugenic = well-born) movement has been concerned not only with investigating changes in the human gene pool, especially as they might affect intelligence, but also with advocating programs which would encourage the reproduction of presumably genetically superior elements of the population and discourage the reproduction of the supposedly inferior. One of the principal founders of the eugenics movement was the English scientist Francis Galton, who published his first ideas advocating a eugenic program in 1865. In the late nineteenth and early twentieth centuries many eugenicists became convinced that the average level of innate human intelligence was declining, at least within the developed nations. They further predicted that this decline, if unchecked, would have disastrous consequences for society.[52]

In support of their belief that the mean level of innate intelligence was declining, the eugenicists argued that intelligence was at least in part genetically determined (i.e., determined by the character of one's genes at conception). Furthermore, they believed that genetic intelligence was inheritable—that is, that the genetic intelligence of the child would tend to vary directly with that of his parent. On these two points the eugenicists were in concurrence with the views of most scientists. In addition, the eugenicists believed that the growth rate of the more intelligent segment of the population was lower than that of the less intelligent portion. This belief was principally derived from the following three pieces of indirect "evidence."

First of all, numerous studies in all developed nations showed an inverse relation between the socio-economic status of the husband and the fertility of his wife. Secondly, numerous studies demonstrated an inverse relation between a woman's educational attainment and the number of children she had borne. The third source of evidence came from studies relating the intelligence of children, as measured by psychological tests, to the number of their siblings. These studies all showed an inverse relation between intelligence and sibling number.[53]

To make inferences from any of these data to the growth rates of population segments differing in intelligence obviously demands many additional assumptions. For example, from the first set of data one must assume that unmarried people can be ignored and that socio-economic status and intelligence are so highly correlated that they can be regarded as identical; to make inferences from the second set one must assume that education and intelligence are extremely closely associated, and furthermore that the population growth-rates for women in each intelligence grouping are the same as those for men. To make inferences from the third set of data, one has to assume that the intelligence of parents is very closely associated with that of their children, that couples who have

52. For the history of the eugenics movement see C. P. Blacker, *Eugenics: Galton and After* (London: Gerald Duckworth, 1952), and Mark H. Haller, *Eugenics: Hereditarian Attitudes in American Thought* (New Brunswick, N.J.: Rutgers University Press, 1963).

53. For a review of these studies see Anne Anastasi, "Intelligence and Family Size," *Psychological Bulletin* (May, 1956), 53:2, 187–209.

no children can be ignored, and that there are no environmental factors operating among children in large families to reduce their measured intelligence.

Although the evidence for declining intelligence was only inferential, many noted demographers, psychologists, and geneticists made quantitative estimates of how rapidly the level of intelligence was declining. For example, in 1934 Lorimer and Osborn estimated that the average IQ in the United States was declining one point per generation.[54] Other writers estimated that the drop per generation was as much as four points.[55]

Opportunities soon arose to determine whether or not intelligence-test scores were actually declining. Much to the surprise of many experts, all of the large studies designed to investigate generational trends in intelligence found that the intelligence level was increasing. The largest of these studies was conducted in Scotland, where the entire group of eleven-year-old children was first tested in 1932 and then again in 1947. The average IQ in the later test was found to average about two points higher than in the earlier one.[56]

A rise in measured intelligence is not necessarily contradictory with a decline in the genetic component of intelligence. It is plausible that an increase in favorable environmental factors, such as a high level of education among parents, and hence more intellectuality in the home, had counterbalanced the adverse factor of declining genetic inheritance. Moreover, there was no doubt that the level of education among parents was continually rising, and if this increased education among parents did indeed increase the measured intelligence of their children, it could cause the IQ of the later generation to be considerably higher than that of the earlier.

Clearly, the question of declining innate intelligence could not be settled without further data. The next step was to measure the intelligence of a group of children and then find out how many offspring they had had by the end of their reproductive years. For example, if one begins with a group, or cohort, all tested at age ten, one should first subdivide it according to intelligence-test score. For each subgroup of like scores, one should then find out the average number of children borne or fathered who survived to age ten. One would then have the growth

54. Frank Lorimer and Frederick Osborn, *Dynamics of Population* (New York: Macmillan, 1934), chapter 8.

55. Anastasi, "Intelligence and Family Size," p. 97.

56. Scottish Mental Survey Committee, *The Trend of Scottish Intelligence* (London: University of London Press, 1949).

rate of each intelligence grouping over the span of a generation. However, this would not yet tell us whether or not the annual growth-rate of subgroups of differing intelligence varied, since the length of generation may vary by level of intelligence. We may define the *mean length of generation* as "the average age of parents at the birth of their children." If more intelligent people receive more education and marry later than the less intelligent, their average generation length will be longer. Therefore, in order to obtain the annual growth-rate for each intelligence grouping, one must divide the generational growth-rate by the mean length of generation.

In 1963, Bajema completed the first study, which closely conformed to the previously mentioned ideal "research design."[57] Bajema began with a group of 1,144 native white individuals born in 1916 and 1917 who had been tested for intelligence in the sixth grade of the Kalamazoo public school system. He was able to obtain life-history data for 979 of these 1,144, and was able to determine for each individual the number of his or her children who survived to age one.

One of the most original aspects of Bajema's study is his investigation of subsequent mortality dependent upon sixth-grade IQ. Bajema found that the higher the IQ, the higher the proportion who survived to age 45. For example, among individuals with an IQ of 120 or higher, 96 percent survived, whereas among those with an IQ of less than 80, only 87 percent survived. Among survivors to age 45, Bajema found that the group with an IQ of 120 or more had the highest number of children (2.62), whereas the group of lowest intelligence (IQ less than 80) had the smallest, only 1.65. An important reason why the lowest-IQ group had so few children on the average was that substantial proportions had never married and/or had never had children.

Although the survivors to age 45 with an IQ of 120 or more had the highest average number of offspring, they were closely followed by the survivors with an IQ of 80 to 94. Thus, survivors of highest intelligence, and those of less-than-average intelligence, each had higher fertility than survivors of near-average intelligence, while those with distinctly subnormal intelligence had the lowest fertility of all. For all persons, including those who did not survive, there was a slight tendency for IQ to be positively associated with number of offspring.

Bajema also found the average length of generation to be slightly longer in the high-IQ group than in the other groups. Computing the annual growth-rate of each IQ grouping by dividing its average number

57. Carl Jay Bajema, "Estimation of the Direction and Intensity of Natural Selection in Relation to Human Intelligence by means of the Intrinsic Rate of Natural Increase," *Eugenics Quarterly* (December, 1963), 10:4, 175–87.

of offspring by its mean generation length, he found that the group with an IQ of 120 or more had the highest annual growth-rate. The group with an IQ of 80 to 94 had the second highest growth-rate, and the group with an IQ of less than 80 had a negative growth-rate which was distinctly lower than that of the other groups. Incidentally, Bajema found, in common with other studies, a negative correlation between the individual's IQ and the number of his siblings, and also a slight negative correlation between the fertility of his females and their subsequent educational attainment.

Two other studies, with a somewhat less adequate research design, have findings congruent with those of Bajema. One was a large study of siblings and parents of persons committed to the Minnesota State School and Hospital for the mentally retarded;[58] the second was a relatively small study conducted in Cambridge, England.[59] Both studies showed clearly that feeble-minded persons who marry tend to have large families, but that since a high proportion of them never marry, the average number of offspring of the total group of feeble-minded is not large. Both studies also confirmed the relatively high reproduction of the top IQ groups.

The question of whether or not the IQ of the population is declining is still not settled. All of the better studies to date are confined to rather small localized areas and to the experience of birth cohorts who have recently completed their reproductive span. It is possible, for instance, that the average level of intelligence in many nations declined for a considerable period of time but is no longer declining. It is possible again that if we limit attention, as studies so far have done, to persons born in urban areas, there will be a positive relation between IQ and subsequent offspring, but that if attention is expanded to rural areas as well, a negative relation might result. Obviously, many more studies are necessary before we have a clear idea of the differential reproduction of groups varying in measured intelligence. Furthermore, no one has as yet succeeded in isolating the genetic component of intelligence from the important environmental influences which affect IQ tests. Until this feat has been accomplished, we must be cautious both in coming to, and in making deductions from conclusions.

Moreover, we need further research not only on *trends* in innate intelligence but also on the *consequences* of changes thereof. Is a declin-

58. J. V. Higgins et al., "Intelligence and Family Size: A Paradox Resolved," *Eugenics Quarterly* (June, 1962), 9:2, 84–90.

59. John Gibson and Michael Young, "Social Mobility and Fertility," in *Biological Aspects of Social Problems*, J. E. Meade and A. S. Parkes, eds. (Edinburgh: Oliver & Boyd, 1965), pp. 69–80.

ing average intelligence really so harmful, as the eugenicists have blithely assumed? One might perhaps argue that in a future world in which all menial work is performed by computer-controlled machines, only the small minority of persons retained as managers and professionals would need a high level of intelligence. The rest of the population, whose sole role would be that of consumer, might do very well with but a modicum of intelligence.

Furthermore, we should pay attention not only to changes in the *mean value* of intelligence but also to the *distribution* of intelligence. At present most persons are of average intelligence; relatively few are of extremely high or extremely low mental competence. It is possible, however, that we are evolving a population wherein relatively few persons will be of average intelligence—most will be either distinctly bright or distinctly subnormal. This could occur if individuals marry others of similar intelligence, and if persons of average intelligence reproduce at a level below that of the rest of the population, as found in Bajema's sample. Would such a development be good or bad? Given the present state of knowledge, we cannot even attempt an answer.

SIBLING NUMBER
AND CHILD DEVELOPMENT

The advocates of planned parenthood have vigorously proclaimed the advantages of small families for the development of the child. Pronatalists have asserted just as loudly that children develop best in the atmosphere of a large family. The relation between sibling number and subsequent personality is a question of great importance, but unfortunately to date we know relatively little about it.

In the preceding section we noted that there was a small but negative correlation between the measured intelligence of children and the number of their siblings. Although this negative correlation may be entirely caused by the lower intelligence of the parents of very large families, other interpretations are possible. An alternative explanation is that a large number of siblings reduces contact with adults and hence impedes the development of linguistic abilities and leads to a lowering of measured intelligence. Support for the view that lack of adult contact lowers measured intelligence is provided by data which demonstrate that the average IQ of twins is about five points lower than that of singletons, even within groups homogeneous for family size and socio-economic level.[60] As yet, however, there has been no study which has gathered data

60.   Anastasi, "Intelligence and Family Size."

on the IQ of both parents and children together with data on the number of children in the family. Without such a study it is impossible to determine the degree of influence which sibling number exerts on the development of intellectual ability.

A few existing studies are concerned with the effect of number of siblings on the child's personality and on his adjustment to his parents. One of the best of these studies concludes that within each social class the fewer the number of their siblings, the better was the adjustment of adolescents to their parents. Among the "only child" children, 38 percent had a superior adjustment to parents, but among those with five or more siblings only 16 percent had it.[61] According to two other studies, a large number of siblings seemed to have a slightly adverse effect on the child's general social adjustment.[62] One of these studies showed that the negative effect of a large sibling number was greater among working-class children than among middle-class children.[63] This may be related to social-class differences in the frequency of unwanted conceptions.

Unwanted conception must definitely be taken into account in considering the impact of sibling number on child development.[64] In the United States, as recently as 1960 to 1965, 17 percent of all births were unwanted by either spouse at time of conception. Births of higher order were more likely to be unwanted than births of lower order, and unwanted conceptions were more common the lower the socio-economic status of the parents.[65] Although in the succeeding five years, the rate of unwanted births in the United States declined by some 36 percent,[66] unwanted births in the United States still constitute a sizeable fraction of the total. It is quite possible that a large number of siblings has *no* effect on a child's development if *all* of the children have been wanted.

61. Ivan Nye, "Adolescent-Parent Adjustment: Age, Sex, Sibling Number, Broken Homes, and Employed Mothers as Variables," *Marriage and Family Living* (November, 1952), 14:4, 327–32.

62. Glenn R. Hawkes et al., "Size of Family and Adjustment of Children," *Marriage and Family Living*, 20:1, 65–68; and Murray J. Strauss and Diane J. Libby, "Sibling Group Size and Adolescent Personality," *Population Review* (July, 1965), 9:1 and 2, 55–64.

63. Strauss and Libby, "Sibling Group Size and Adolescent Personality."

64. Edward Pohlman, "Results of Unwanted Conceptions: Some Hypotheses up for Adoption," *Eugenics Quarterly* (March, 1965), 12:1, 11–17.

65. Larry Bumpass and Charles F. Westoff, "The 'Perfect Contraceptive' Population," *Science*, (September 18, 1970), 169, pp. 1177–82.

66. Charles F. Westoff, "Changes in Contraceptive Practices among Married Couples," in Charles F. Westoff, ed., *Toward the End of Growth: Population in America* (Englewood Cliffs, N.J.: Prentice-Hall, 1973), pp. 19–31.

On the other hand, even when parents desire a large family, the burden of caring for many offspring may compel them to give less individual attention to each, and hence serve to impede development. Again, further research is necessary.

We may also ask what effect sibling number has on one's opportunity for adult success. A study by Blau and Duncan provides a very good answer.[67] Basing their findings on a probability sample of 20,000 American men between 20 and 64 years of age, they found that the number of siblings was negatively related both to educational attainment and to current occupational level. Although their data revealed sibling number to have less effect on future success than father's education or occupation, they were also able to show that the number of siblings had an effect on adult achievement even after holding constant the effect of father's occupation. Specifically, after controlling for the effect of father's occupation, they demonstrated that men who had been only children had the best chance for high educational attainment and occupational success, that men with one to three siblings had better than average prospects, but that men with four or more siblings were clearly disadvantaged. Their data revealed that almost the sole reason for the greater occupational success of those with fewer siblings was their higher educational attainment. No doubt a major reason for the higher educational level of those men with fewer siblings is simply economic. Parents of small families can better afford to educate their sons than parents of large families. However, if a large number of siblings does exert an adverse influence on IQ or on social adjustment, then these factors may also contribute to the negative relation between sibling number and educational attainment.

67.   Peter M. Blau and Otis Dudley Duncan, *The American Occupational Structure* (New York: John Wiley, 1967), pp. 295–313.

CHAPTER 6
MIGRATION

CONCEPTS AND MEASUREMENT

Measuring migration is somewhat more complicated than gauging fertility or mortality. To measure shifts in usual place of residence from one area to another, several considerations must be taken into account. First of all, the "usual place of residence" must be defined. Although this is no problem for most individuals, an explicit definition must be provided persons with more than one "usual residence," such as college students, members of the armed forces, and inmates of institutions.

Secondly, a careful definition of "place of origin" and "place of destination" is necessary. Because these places can be anything from a particular housing unit to a nation or even a continent, the number of migrants will depend on the terms of the definition. In the United States, for example, the number of persons who change households is much greater every year than the number who move to a new county; and that number, in turn, is larger than the number who move to a different state. The U.S. Bureau of the Census makes a distinction between migrants and movers: *migrants* are persons who move to a new *county*; movers are those who move to a new *household*, whether or not they cross a county line. Another common distinction is made between persons who move between nations, *international migrants*, and those who move within a nation, *internal migrants*.

A third consideration is whether to measure the total number of moves during a given time-period or merely the change in place of residence, if any, from the beginning to the end of the period. Most migration analysts are content with the latter measurement, even though with its use the number of residence changes in a relatively long period, such as five years, will be smaller than the sum of the number of changes of residence recorded each year during that period.

Although a student of migration might be happy with a simple description of the number of persons within an area who have moved into a different subarea (e.g., the number of persons in the United States moving into a new state), he would probably want to know where these migrants were going and whence they had come. For the fifty States and the District of Columbia (making fifty-one units) there are a total of 2,550 possible migration "streams," each characterized by a different state of origin and of destination. This is because for any given state there are fifty different streams of out-migrants and fifty streams of in-migrants. The *gross interchange* between place *A* and place *B* is the sum of the number of in-migrants from *B* to *A* and the number of out-migrants from *A* to *B*. The *net migration* for place *A* from place *B* is the difference between the number of in-migrants from *B* to *A* and the number of out-migrants from *A* to *B*. The *effectiveness of migration* between *A* and *B* is the absolute value of the ratio of the net migration to the gross interchange. Theoretically, this ratio can vary from a value of 1, when all migration is unidirectional. to a value of 0, when the migration streams in each direction are of equal magnitude. Commonly, this ratio is nearer to 0 than to 1.

To measure the *crude rate of migration* to different subareas within a given total area, the number of migrants during the year is divided by the midyear population of the total area. The *rate of out-migration* from a given place of origin during a given year is commonly computed by dividing the number of out-migrants from that place by the midyear population of the place of origin, and the *rate of in-migration* to a given place of destination is computed by dividing the number of in-migrants by the midyear population of the place of destination. The *net migration rate* is perhaps the most commonly computed migration rate. For any given place it is simply the ratio of the net number of migrants to or from the place, divided by its population at midyear. Migration rates standardized for age and sex may also be computed. If the requisite data are available, age-specific migration rates for different years may be combined to produce migration rates for cohorts.

Ideally, migration data should be secured by a registration of all geographical movements. International migration can usually be measured in this way. Several nations, of which Sweden is one, have a compulsory registration of all internal movements. However, to measure internal mobility in the United States, we must make use of census and survey data which ask persons where they lived at some earlier date. Mobility data gathered from this source slightly underestimate the total amount of movement because they ignore persons who move and then die before the time of the survey. For nations with low mortality, such as the United States, this cannot cause any serious bias in the data except for the oldest age-groups.

TRENDS, DIFFERENTIALS, AND MAJOR STREAMS

It is much easier to discuss general trends in mortality and fertility than in migration. One reason is that for migration the relevant data are often not available. A second reason is that trends in migration vary from nation to nation, and there has been no generalized change such as has occurred in mortality and fertility. At any rate, for the sake of brevity we shall confine our discussion to trends in the United States.

For this country, annual data on internal migration are available only since the "year" 1947–48, and since then there has been little variation in the rate of geographical mobility. Approximately 19 percent of the total population has moved every year, about 6 percent have changed their county of residence, and about 3 percent have moved to a new state.[1] Fragmentary data suggest that rates of internal migration prior to 1947–48 were essentially of the same magnitude as they have been since that date.[2]

Statistics on immigration into the United States from abroad are available since 1820. The absolute number of persons moving into the nation reached a peak in 1907, when about 1,300,000 immigrant aliens entered the country. However, there have been several major peaks in the rate of immigration into the United States. The apex of the first peak occurred in 1854, when 428,000 immigrants entered the United States; in that year the rate of immigration was 16.1 per thousand of U.S. population. The apex of the last peak, in 1907, coincided with the acme of the absolute number of immigrants; in that year the immigration rate was 14.8 per thousand. The first of the peak periods corresponds to the "old migration" predominantly composed of Irish leaving their native land because of the potato famine, and Germans, often leaving as po-

1. U.S. Bureau of the Census, *Current Population Reports*, Series P-20, No. 235 (April 1972).

2. Everett S. Lee, "Internal Migration and Population Redistribution in the United States" in *Population: The Vital Revolution*, ed. Ronald Freedman (New York: Doubleday, 1964), p. 127.

litical refugees; the second corresponds to the "new migration," predominantly composed of persons from Italy and Eastern Europe.[3] Heavily restrictive legislation passed in 1921 and 1924 greatly reduced the flow of immigrants to the United States, and decline was further accentuated by the Depression of the 1930s. During that decade the average annual number of immigrants was only about 70,000. After World War II the number of immigrants increased somewhat.[4] In 1971 the number of immigrants was 370,000 and the rate of immigration was 1.8 per thousand.[5]

Age is the major differential in migration rates. The highest rates of mobility and migration are for young adults, but there is a secondary peak among very young children. The reason for two peaks is that frequently the migrating unit is a young married couple with small children. In the United States in 1971 about 41 percent of all persons 20 to 24 years old had changed their residence during the past year, and about 16 percent were migrants to a different county. Among children 1 to 4 years old, 28 percent had changed their residence and 10 percent had migrated across a county line. The lowest proportions of movers and migrants were found among the elderly. Among persons 65 years old and over, only 9 percent were movers and only 3 percent migrants. There was little overall difference in the mobility or migration rates by sex.[6] On the other hand, until recent years males have been predominant among immigrants to the United States.[7]

Within the United States, social-class differences in migration are rather small and somewhat contradictory. Persons with a college education are slightly more prone to migration than others, but males with very low income are somewhat more apt to migrate than men with higher income. Self-employment is an important determinant of migration status. In 1971 only 3 percent of self-employed males migrated across a county line during the preceding year, as compared with 7 percent of wage and salary workers.[8] Evidently, persons with their own business or profes-

3. U.S. Bureau of the Census, *Historical Statistics of the United States: Colonial Times to 1957* (Washington, D.C.: Government Printing Office, 1960), pp. 56–59.

4. Ernest Rubin, "The Demography of Immigration to the United States," *The Annals of the American Academy of Political and Social Science* (September, 1966), 367, 15–22.

5. U.S. Bureau of the Census, *Statistical Abstract of the United States, 1972* (Washington, D.C.: Government Printing Office, 1972), p. 91.

6. U.S. Bureau of the Census, *Current Population Reports*, Series P 20, No. 235 (April 1972).

7. Rubin, "The Demography of Immigration in the United States."

8. U.S. Bureau of the Census, *Current Population Reports*, Series P-20, No. 235 (April 1972).

sional practice are at a distinct disadvantage in a new community, since they have to build up a new clientele. On the other hand, many salaried corporation employees are given reassignments and must migrate on pain of losing their job.

Certain major streams of migration deserve to be mentioned either because they have had important historical consequences or because they otherwise exemplify unusual patterns. One of the earliest streams of migration with historical significance was the westward movement of nomadic tribes in Europe and Central Asia coincident with the fall of the Roman Empire. The many tribes that moved westward during this period included those speaking Celtic, Germanic, and Ural-Altaic languages. As the easternmost tribes moved westward, they pushed forward the tribes in front of them. One possible explanation for this extensive migration is that the grasslands of Central Asia dried up. A second theory is that an expanding Chinese empire disrupted the life of the nomadic tribes near its borders and thus provoked the movement of all the other tribes.[9]

The European and African migration to North America, South America, and Oceania has probably had more important historical consequences than any other migratory stream. This flow began slowly after Columbus's voyage to America. It has been estimated that over 60 million Europeans left for overseas points. However, *net* migration was lower, since many of those leaving Europe later returned.[10] The migration from Africa to the New World was almost wholly a forced migration of slaves. The first slaves were brought to the colony of Virginia in 1619, and in the United States the slave trade was not abolished until 1808. During the period of slave trade, about 400,000 Africans were brought to this country.[11] The impact of this migration is revealed by noting that in 1790, 20 percent of the 4 million persons in the United States were blacks.[12]

As we have seen, the migratory stream from Europe to the United States reached its numerical peak in the first decade of the twentieth century. During this time the rate of immigration from Europe into the United States was 9.2 per thousand, and the emigration rate from

9. B. Bury, *The Invasion of Europe by the Barbarians* (London: Macmillan, 1928); Ellsworth Huntington, *Civilization and Climate* (New Haven, Conn.: Yale University Press, 1924); Frederick J. Teggart, *Rome and China: A Study of Correlations in Historical Events* (Berkeley, Calif.: University of California Press, 1939).

10. United Nations Department of Social Affairs *The Determinants and Consequences of Population Trends* (New York: United Nations, 1953), pp. 98–102.

11. U.S. Bureau of the Census, *A Century of Population Growth in the United States: 1790–1900*, by W. S. Rossiter (Washington, D.C.: Government Printing Office, 1909), p. 36.

12. Conrad Taeuber and Irene B. Taeuber, *The Changing Population of the United States* (New York: Wiley, 1958), p. 71.

Europe to the United States about 2 per thousand.[13] Thus in general the transatlantic migration had considerably more effect on the population of the United States than on that of Europe. However, the emigration rate from Europe to the United States varied considerably from nation to nation and from time to time. During the decade of the Irish potato famine (from 1845 to 1854) the emigration from Ireland to the United States was extremely heavy: about 1.4 million Irish emigrated to the United States from a population which had been in 1841 only a little more than 8 million.[14]

In chapter 3 we discussed the extensive process of urbanization that occurred in the wake of the Industrial Revolution in the developed nations. Migration from rural areas was in large part the cause of this urbanization. Whereas in many nations this migration was almost entirely internal, in the United States before World War I much of the urbanization was accomplished by the passage of peasants from Europe. But in a survey conducted in the United States in 1952 it was revealed that twice as many farm-reared adults were then living off the farm as on the farm, and that one of every three adults not living on a farm had been reared on a farm.[15]

In the United States one of the most significant of the migration streams has been, and continues to be from east to west. In many western states only a minority of the resident population has been born in the state. For example, in California in 1970 only about 47 percent of the resident population was born there.[16] However, one must not think of the interchange between east and west as one of high effectiveness. It is a paradox that a higher proportion of persons born west of the Mississippi River have migrated east of that river than have been born east of the river and migrated westward. Specifically, according to the 1970 census, 7.8 percent of all persons born west of the Mississippi were living east of the river, and only 7.2 percent of those born east of the river were living to the west. The paradox is explained when we look at the absolute number of migrants and consider the absolute numbers born on each side of the river. In 1970, 8.9 million persons born east of the Mississippi were living west of the river, and 4.6 million born west were

13.   Calculated from data in *Historical Statistics of the United States*, p. 56, and *The Determinants and Consequences of Population Trends*, pp. 11–13.

14.   R. Dudley Edwards and T. Desmond Williams, eds., *The Great Famine* (New York. New York University Press, 1957), pp. 4, 388.

15.   Ronald and Deborah Freedman, "Farm-Reared Elements in the Nonfarm Population," *Rural Sociology* (1956), 21, 50–61.

16.   U.S. Bureau of the Census, *Census of Population*, 1970, Final Report, PC(2)-2A, pp. 25, 30.

living east, so that the net movement to the west side of the river was 4.3 million, and the effectiveness of the interchange was .32.[17] Nevertheless, since the total population born east of the river was so much greater than that born west of it, the proportion born west and moving east was somewhat higher than the proportion born east and moving west.

Another very significant stream of net migration within the United States has been the northward and westward movement of blacks. This shift began in large scale only during World War I. At that time, northern industrial firms began to recruit labor for jobs which would have normally been filled by newly arrived European immigrants. The movement of blacks out of the South is still continuing. According to the 1970 census, about 24 percent of the total black population born in the South was living in another region, and among those 30 to 34 years of age, about 37 percent were residing outside the region. Of the total black population of the Northeast, 34 percent were born elsewhere—almost entirely in the South; among blacks 30 to 34 years of age in the Northeast, fully 51 percent had been born outside the region.[18]

The migration from Puerto Rico to the mainland United States, of major magnitude since the end of World War II, is of interest because it exemplifies an extremely high rate of out-migration. According to the 1970 census, the combined total of the population of Puerto Rico and of persons in the United States of Puerto Rican birth or parentage was about 4.1 million, of which around 1.4 million were in the United States. Thus 33.9 percent of all Puerto Ricans were on the mainland.[19]

The migration into Israel following World War II is noteworthy because it exemplifies an extremely high rate of in-migration. In 1948, when independence was established, the total population of Israel was 650,000. By 1961, after the influx of more than 1 million immigrants, it had risen to 2.2 million.[20]

Perhaps the world's largest gross interchange in a short time-span took place in India and Pakistan following the 1947 partition of British India and the establishment of these two areas as independent states. This movement is also of interest because it was coerced rather than free. In the face of violence, Hindus and Sikhs in Pakistan were compelled to move to India, and Moslems in India to Pakistan. From 1947 through

17. Ibid., pp. 25–26.

18. Ibid., p. 14.

19. U.S. Bureau of the Census, *U.S. Census of Population: 1970*, Final Report PC(1)-A1, p. 48 and Final Report PC(2)-1E, p. 1.

20. Anthony T. Bouscaren, *International Migrations since 1945* (New York: Praeger, 1963), pp. 89–90; and *United Nations Demographic Yearbook, 1965* (New York: United Nations, 1966), p. 113.

1950, 10 million persons migrated from Pakistan to India, and 7.5 million from India to Pakistan.[21]

DETERMINANTS

In the previous chapter we analyzed the determinants of the desired number of children in terms of a preference system, a price system, and the total amount of resources available for all goals. A similar conceptual scheme can be used to analyze migration. Such a scheme can be used not only when social norms concerning migration are permissive, but also when norms and laws either prescribe or proscribe migration. But in the last two cases we must recognize that there may be very heavy penalties for refusal to migrate or unwillingness to stay.

The preference system describes the relative attractiveness of various places as goals for the potential migrant, compared to other goals which his resources would allow him to pursue. An area's attractiveness is the balance between the positive and negative values which it offers.

Let us first consider some of the positive values which may influence a person or family to migrate. Quite understandably, for many migrants the prospect of a better job is one of the most important. In an analysis of internal migration in the United States, Kuznets and Thomas have shown that the net flow of migration within the United States has been (as one might expect) *away from* those states where average income is low, and *toward* those where it is high.[22] Moreover, studies of international migration have shown that the volume of migration *to* a nation naturally tends to be highest when it is near the peak of a business cycle, and *from* it in times of business depression or famine.[23]

Another positive value which may be achieved by migration is a more favorable climate. Florida, for example, has always had a high rate of in-migration despite the fact that its average income has *not* been high. The sunny skies of California exert a similar pull.[24]

Marriage and the continuation of marital ties also are important

21. O. H. K. Spate, *India and Pakistan: A General and Regional Geography* (New York: Dutton, 1957), p. 119.

22. Simon Kuznets and Dorothy S. Thomas, "Internal Migration and Economic Growth," in *Selected Studies of Migration Since World War II* (New York: Milbank Memorial Fund, 1958), pp. 196–211.

23. Brinley Thomas, "International Migration," in *The Study of Population*, Philip M. Hauser and Otis Dudley Duncan, eds. (Chicago: University of Chicago Press, 1959), pp. 526–28.

24. Kuznets and Thomas, "Internal Migration and Economic Growth."

inducements to migration. In certain of the world's societies, rules of exogamy absolutely compel potential brides and bridegrooms to marry someone from outside their own village; and although no such compulsion exists in our own society, the prospect of marriage quite often necessitates some amount of migratory movement. Too, maintaining marital or family ties is a chief inducement for the wife and children when a family head decides to migrate.

Freedom from persecution has also been an important motive among many religious and racial minorities, as well as for intellectuals. Examples of mass movements of religious or racial minorities include the Puritan settlement of New England, the Jewish migration to Israel, the movement of American blacks out of the South, and the aforementioned interchange of Moslem and Hindu populations between India and Pakistan. Although the desire for intellectual freedom has never resulted in mass migration, some migrations of intellectuals have had important consequences. For example, persecution of intellectuals in Nazi Germany brought to the United States a group of famous scientists whose wartime contributions helped to hasten the Nazis' downfall.

A very common cause of intracounty movement is the desire for more adequate housing.[25] This motive is also the cause of intercounty migration, particularly when the suburbs of a metropolitan area are situated in a different county from its central city.

But migration also creates negative values. A major barrier to migration is that it involves a disruption of interpersonal relationships with kin and old friends. The farther the distance traveled, the greater this disruption, since return visits and contacts become more costly. The importance of this disruption can be measured by the fact that many migrants travel to the same towns or city neighborhoods to which relatives or other people from their town of origin have previously migrated. In addition, the volume of migration from one specific place to another tends to rise once a small nucleus of persons from the place of origin has established itself in the place of destination. The increasing volume of the migratory stream, once a nucleus of persons related in some way has been established, has been termed "chain migration." [26]

If migration involves movement to a new culture, deprivations may

25. Peter H. Rossi, *Why Families Move: A Study in the Social Psychology of Urban Residential Mobility* (Glencoe, Ill.: The Free Press, 1955).

26. John S. MacDonald and Leatrice D. MacDonald, "Chain Migration, Ethnic Neighborhood Formation, and Social Networks," *Milbank Memorial Fund Quarterly* (January, 1964), 52:1, 82–97. See also Oscar Handlin, *The Uprooted* (Boston, Mass.: Little, Brown, 1951), and Morton Rubin, "Migration Patterns of Negroes from a Rural Northeastern Mississippi Community," *Social Forces* (October, 1960), 39:1, 59–66.

also be caused by the necessity to discard old customs and learn new ones, and perhaps even a new language.

Laws restraining the entry or departure of international migrants are of course a very important deterrent to international migration, since very few persons are willing to pay the possible penalties involved in illegal entry or departure. It is true that, in defiance of their own government, a few East Germans have successfully scaled the Berlin wall and escaped to West Germany, and that an unknown number of Mexicans have illegally entered the United States. As a rule, however, relatively few persons ever attempt to disobey laws regarding international migrants, mainly because they are usually easy to enforce.

Most nations are permissive with respect to internal migration. A salient exception in recent years was the Soviet Union under Stalin. However, even then the Soviet government did not have complete success in enforcing its strictures prescribing and proscribing internal movements.

We may now discuss how the price system affects the volume of migration. The price system describes the expenditure of resources which is both a precondition to and a concomitant of migration. For many migrants the price of migration is in large part simply the monetary expense of moving. For self-employed persons it may also include the expenditure of savings in order to sustain a customary living-standard while building up a new business or practice. Since the cost of migration generally varies in direct proportion to the distance traveled, the number of migrants to a given place tends to vary inversely with the distance.

The total resources available for all goals also affects the decision to migrate. If the only drawback to migration is the expense of the move, then an increase in monetary income should increase the probability of migration. The secular increase in monetary income during the last century or more in the developed nations should have increased rates of migration, provided that the value and price of migration had remained constant. The fact that age-specific migration rates have been almost constant in the United States since 1947 may be an indication that the net value of migration is declining. In particular, the incentive of a better job is probably decreasing in importance, since regional disparities in income are being reduced.[27]

CONSEQUENCES OF MIGRATION

We shall now examine the possible consequences of migration for the individual, the area of net out-migration, the area of net in-migration,

---

27. U.S. Bureau of the Census, *Statistical Abstract of the United States, 1972* (Washington, D.C.: Government Printing Office), 1972, p. 319.

and the larger social system which includes areas of net in-migration and net out-migration. Our discussion must of course be in part speculative, since knowledge about these topics is still incomplete.

Before his move, the migrant doubtless will have anticipated a net balance of favorable consequences for himself. Sometimes, however, reality will fall short of his expectations, and dissatisfaction will provoke him to move either to his place of origin or to some other place. Grounds for presuming that many migrants will have considerable difficulty in adjusting themselves to their new environment are provided by studies which show, for instance, that migrants have a higher rate of mental disease than nonmigrants in the place of destination, even when other relevant differences between the two groups have been controlled.[28]

Net out-migration may have several important consequences for an area. It may relieve population pressure and cause the average level of wage and salary income to rise. The resultant rise in income may have a further effect on the area's mortality and fertility. On the other hand, net out-migration may cause the value of land and real estate to decline. Moreover, areas of net out-migration suffer the loss of the investments made to raise and educate children who spend their productive years elsewhere. Since migration rates are selective by age, areas of net out-migration often have few young adults relative to the number of children and aged persons. Certain of these areas may also lose their most intelligent or best educated persons in addition to their most rebellious and nonconforming elements—and for these reasons become unduly conservative.

Net in-migration may also have important consequences. If the area is definitely underpopulated, the resultant population increase may help the area to achieve *economics of scale* (reduction in the cost of goods obtainable by increasing the scale of production and of marketing) and thus raise the general standard of living. Under other circumstances, net in-migration may result in some decline in average wage and salary income. In either case, a net flow of in-migrants will tend to raise the price of land and real estate.

Generally, areas of net in-migration will have a rather high proportion of young adults. They will many times also have a rather heterogeneous and unconforming population, since in-migrants often come from diverse cultural backgrounds. For these reasons, areas of net in-

28. Everett S. Lee, "Socio-Economic and Migration Differentials in Mental Disease, New York State, 1949–1951," *Milbank Memorial Fund Quarterly* (July, 1963), 61:3, 249–68; and Judith Lazarus et al., "Migration Differentials in Mental Disease: State Patterns in First Admissions to Mental Hospitals for All Disorders and for Schizophrenia, New York, Ohio, and California, as of 1950," *Milbank Memorial Fund Quarterly* (January, 1963), 61:1, 25–42. See also Mildred B. Kantor, ed., *Mobility and Mental Health* (Springfield, Ill.: Charles C Thomas, 1965).

migration are often more tolerant of new ideas than are other types of area. It is also possible, however, that a high rate of in-migration fosters social disorganization, or *anomie*. Elizabeth Bott's concepts of *open* and *closed social networks* are useful tools in providing a rationale for this hypothesis. In a closed network a high proportion of a given person's acquaintances know one another; in an open network this is not so. Thus, group solidarity is presumed to be much higher when networks are closed. In the case of a sample of urban English families, Bott showed that open networks were characteristic of individuals who had recently moved into a community, and closed networks were typical of the community's oldtimers. It is also plausible to presume that open networks are more common among non-migrants in areas of heavy in-migration than in other types of areas simply because many of one's neighbors are often new.

Bott suggests that the type of network may affect the husband-wife relationship. Since a too-intense emotional load may disrupt a marriage, a closed social network, in which both husband and wife can seek understanding and companionship not only from the spouse but from many other persons as well, may aid marital stability.[29] This type of network, by strengthening informal social controls, may also be of aid in reducing crime and, by preventing loneliness, may even help to minimize rates of personal pathology. It is perhaps not coincidental that in California, where more than half the population is born out of the state, rates of marital disruption, of most forms of crime, and of suicide all appear to be substantially higher than for the United States as a whole.[30]

For the system comprising both the areas of net inflow and of net outflow, the direct effect of migration is of course to promote a redistribution of population. If migrants have been responsive to differences in job opportunities, this redistribution will further the economic development of the total system. The shift may either increase or decrease the homogeneity of the various subregions with respect to population density. In the United States the recent trend has been toward greater heterogeneity in population density among the small groupings of counties known as State Economic Areas. Moreover, between 1960 and 1970 nearly half the counties lost population although the total population

29. Elizabeth Bott, *Family and Social Network* (London: Tavistock Publications, 1957).

30. For the relevant data, ooo U.S. Bureau of the Census, *Census of Population, 1970*, Final Report PC(1)-D1, pp. 640–51 and Final Report PC(1)-D6, pp. 1298–99; *Statistical Abstract of the United States, 1972*, p. 144; and U.S. Public Health Service, *Vital Statistics of the United States, 1967*, Vol. 2, Part A (Washington, D.C.: Government Printing Office, 1969), p. 1–39.

increase was 24 million persons.[31] However, in other respects migration appears to foster regional homogeneity. Since migrants tend to move from low-income areas toward high-income areas, an important effect is to reduce regional income inequalities. This has been a noteworthy consequence of internal migration in the United States, where the southern states, with low per-capita income and high rates of net out-migration, have gradually come closer to the average income in the rest of the nation. Moreover, migration often helps to reduce regional disparities in other population characteristics as well. Migration of blacks away from the South has gone far toward making the regions of the United States less disparate in racial composition. Consequently, the locus of the problem of black-white relations has broadened to include the entire nation. Migration may also be diluting the Catholic and Jewish concentrations in the northeastern states and the Protestant predominance in the South and West, creating greater similarity between these regions in modes of interreligious accommodations.

31. U.S. Bureau of the Census, *Census of Population, 1970*, Final Report PC(1)-A1, pp. 25, 42.

PART THREE
POPULATION AND SOCIAL STRUCTURE

CHAPTER 7
AGE-SEX COMPOSITION

A population's *age-sex composition*—that is, the number of males and females in each of its age-groups—is determined by two factors. The first is the population's sex ratio at birth. (*Sex ratio* is defined as the number of males divided by the number of females, times 100.) The second is the population's past history of births, deaths, and migrations.

A visual representation of the age-sex composition of an actual population is presented in figure 3, which shows the age-sex composition of the Soviet Union in January, 1959. Two notable features of this graph are the small number of persons of both sexes 10 to 19 years old, and the very large deficit of males relative to females at ages 30 and over. This graph shows a very irregular age-sex distribution—a phenomenon commonly the result either of sharp temporary variations in the birth rate or of sharp and temporary changes in death or migration rates for particular age-sex groups. In the 1959 Soviet distribution, the small proportion of persons 10 to 19 years old was largely the result of the large reduction in the birth rate which took place during World War II, when most men were separated from their families. The extreme deficit of males at age 30 and over in the Soviet Union is the result of the very large losses of military men during World War I, the Civil War of 1917–21, and World War II, and of the severe repressions which occurred during the Stalinist era. In most other nations, there is also some predominance of females at older ages, since typically male mortality is somewhat higher than female. However, in most populations there are more males than females at the younger ages, despite somewhat higher male mortality, because the sex ratio at birth averages around 105.

We have considered the example of the Soviet Union wherein fluctuating birth and death rates have created an irregular age structure. If, on the other hand, fertility, mortality, and migration rates remain relatively constant over time, a more regular age structure results. Let us consider now the types of age structure which emerge when age-specific birth and death rates remain constant over long periods of time. Assume initially a closed population (that is, one with neither in-migration nor out-migration) of one sex only, in which the distribution by age may be of any sort. Beginning with such a population, if birth and death rates at each age remain constant over a sufficiently long period of time, there eventually results a population with a calculable and unchanging rate of growth and with a calculable and unchanging age composition.[1] Such a population, eventuating from the long-term continuation of a given set of age-specific birth and death rates, is called a *stable population*. (A particular subtype of the stable population is the *stationary population;* this is a stable population in which the birth rate is exactly equal to the death rate.) Although the stable population is a mathematical model to which no actual population ever conforms precisely, the model is very useful because many populations are close approximations to it.

Stable populations have a regular age composition. Examples of four types of stable population—each formed by pairing one of two typical peacetime patterns of mortality with one of two typical patterns of fertility—are illustrated in figure 4. Specifically, these four examples are derived by cross-classifying a mortality level with an expectation of life at birth either of 69 years or of 35 years with a fertility level in which the number of daughters per woman of completed fertility is either 1.5 or 3. In the first example, where fertility and mortality are both low, the number of persons in each age-group declines very gradually from the youngest to the oldest age-group. In the second example, where fertility is low but mortality high, the age distribution again slopes down gradually from the youngest age-groups to the oldest. In the third example, where fertility is high but mortality is low, the age distribution slopes down very rapidly from youngest age-groups to the oldest. In the final example where fertility and mortality are both high, the age distribution is again one of rapid decline from the youngest age-groups to the oldest.

---

1.   A. J. Lotka, *Theorie Analytique des Associations Biologiques* (Paris: Hermann, 1939). See also Alvaro Lopez, *Problems in Stable Population Theory* (Princeton, N.J.: Office of Population Research, Princeton University, 1961).

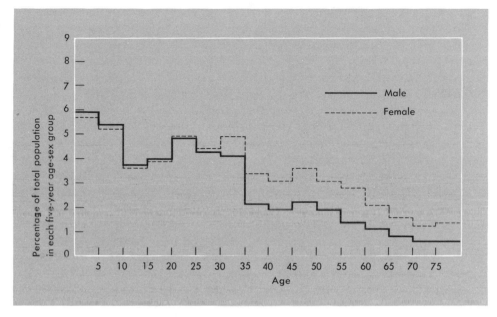

Figure 3 Age-Sex Structures of the Soviet Union, January, 1959. *Source:* James W. Brackett, "Projections of the Population of the USSR, by Age and Sex, 1964–1985," in U.S. Bureau of the Census, *International Population Reports*, Series P-91, No. 13 (Washington, D.C.: Government Printing Office, 1964), pp. 42–44.

These four examples illustrate an important generalization concerning stable populations—namely, that when fertility is high the proportion of the total population in the younger age-groups will be large without regard to the level of mortality, whereas when fertility is low the proportion of the population at young ages will be small, again without regard to the level of mortality.

This conclusion is at variance with much popular thinking. It is commonly assumed that populations with low mortality should have a high proportion of elderly persons, and populations with high mortality a low proportion. Now we see that it is difference in *fertility* rather than in mortality which is the chief cause of difference in age structure. Moreover, the small effect which mortality difference does exert on age structure is contrary to what might be expected, since a normal pattern of low mortality results in a slightly higher proportion of the very young than does a normal pattern of high mortality.

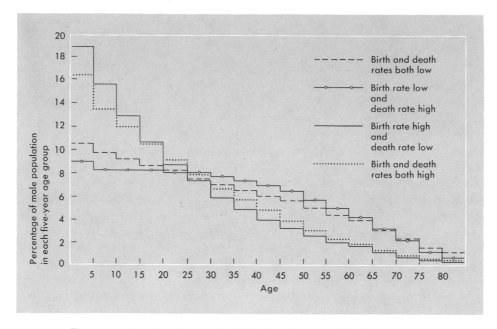

Figure 4 Age Structures of Stable Populations with Differing Birth- and Death-Rates. *Source:* Ansley J. Coale, *Regional Model Life Tables and Stable Populations* (Princeton, N.J.: Princeton University Press, 1966), pp. 184, 212 (mortality levels 8 and 22 cross-classified by Gross Production Rate 1.5 or 3 for West Model males).

CONSEQUENCES
OF AGE-SEX COMPOSITION

We have seen from the example of the Soviet population that age distribution and the sex ratio at each age can be highly irregular. We have also seen that regular age distributions are frequently one of two types: one characterized by a *rapid* decline in number from the youngest to the oldest age-groups (we shall henceforth call this *a young population*), and the other characterized by a *gentle* decline (hereafter termed *an old population*). Variations in age-sex structure, whether of the regular or the irregular kind, may have various consequences for the society in which they occur. Let us now discuss some possible economic, demographic, familial, political, and psychological consequences of such variation.

Perhaps the most important of the economic consequences of differences in age structure is the effect of age structure on the dependency ratio. The *dependency ratio* is defined as the ratio of persons in dependent ages to persons in economically productive age-groups. The lower the ratio, the easier it is for persons in the economically productive ages to support those in the dependent age-group Although the terms *dependent ages* and *economically productive ages* can be variously defined, the definition we shall adopt here is that the dependent ages are the ages under 15 years and 65 years and over; the remaining age groups are economically productive.

What dependency ratio is associated with each of the four age structures shown in figure 4? The first age structure, generated by a pattern of low fertility and low mortality, has a dependency ratio of .607; the second, generated by low fertility and high mortality, has a ratio of .484; the third, generated by high fertility and low mortality, has a ratio of .985; and the last, generated by high fertility and high mortality, has a ratio of .796.

Thus, regardless of whether mortality is high or low, the young population created by high fertility has a much less favorable dependency ratio than the old population caused by low fertility. Moreover, high mortality, paired either with low or with high fertility, produces a slightly more favorable dependency ratio than low mortality similarly paired.

A second economic consequence of difference in age structure relates to the average age of the labor force. In the rapidly sloping age distribution caused by high fertility, the average age of persons within the broad age-group 15 to 64 years will be relatively young; in the gently sloping age structure caused by low fertility the average age will be relatively high. The average age of the labor force may have several consequences. A younger labor force has the advantage that its workers will be more flexible and able to learn new skills more readily. On the other hand, an older labor force is more responsible and experienced.[2] Further research on this topic would be valuable, since as yet we do not have exact knowledge of the magnitude of these various effects.

A third economic consequence of difference in age structure relates to the pattern of consumption. Societies with large proportions of children need to spend relatively large amounts of money on education; societies with larger proportions of elderly persons need to spend more on medical care. Changes in the age composition of a population may lead to changes in the patterns of consumption. For example, currently the United States is experiencing a decline in the total number of its

2.   Robert C. Atchley, *The Social Forces in Later Life: An Introduction to Social Gerontology* (Belmont, Calif.: Wadsworth, 1972), pp. 43–72.

children. As a consequence elementary school enrollment, which totalled about 34 million in 1970, fell to about 32 million by 1972.[3]

An irregular age structure may also have consequences with respect to the supply of labor, which will influence the wage and salary rate for particular age-groups. For example, in the early 1950s in the United States there were relatively few persons 20 to 29 years old, and starting salaries of persons of this age entering the labor force were exceptionally high. According to economist Richard Easterlin, the association between the scant supply of new entrants to the labor force during this period and their high wage and salary level was a causal rather than a coincidental relationship.[4] For the late 1960s and early 1970s an opposite situation obtained, since the number of young entrants to the labor force in the United States was then very large, tending to reduce the wage and salary level of this group.

Variation in age structure will also have demographic consequences. In particular, as noted in chapter 4, a young population will tend to have a much lower crude death-rate than an old population, since mortality is highest at advanced ages. For example, consider the two low-mortality populations illustrated in figure 4: the crude death-rate is 10 per thousand in the old population generated by low fertility, and only 5 per thousand in the young population caused by high fertility. This difference in crude death-rate occurs despite the fact that the death rates at each age are identical for both populations. It is also obvious that the crude birth-rate will be affected either by an abnormal sex ratio or by an unusually large or small proportion of persons of reproductive age. In the United States in the 1950s and early 1960s the crude birth-rate was depressed by the very small proportion of persons who were of reproductive age. Crude rates of migration are also affected by a population's age-sex structure. In particular, since young adults tend to be more mobile than middle-aged or elderly persons, a young population tends to have a higher migration rate than an older one.

Variations in age-sex structure affect the probabilities of marriage for men and women. If we assume that men usually marry women a few years younger than themselves, then the women in any population in which the age structure has a downward slope will have more difficulty in finding mates than will men. This is because there will be more women aged $x - n$ years than men aged x. The problem is of course accentuated for a young population with its very pronounced age-slope.

3. U.S. Bureau of the Census, *Current Population Reports*, Series P-20, No. 247 (February 1973).

4. Richard A. Easterlin, *The American Baby Boom in Historical Perspective*, Occasional Paper 79 (New York: National Bureau of Economic Research, 1962).

In societies with a young population but high mortality, a high proportion of women can marry, but only because a large number of men who have been widowed or divorced remarry women who have never married. However, in such a society a large proportion of the many widows and divorcees will never be able to remarry. On the other hand, in societies with a young population and low mortality, a substantial proportion of women can never marry since the combined supply of young men, widowers, and divorcees is not often sufficient to provide husbands for the large number of young women.

The excess loss of men in war causes additional difficulty for women seeking husbands. The shortage of eligible men can, it is true, be ameliorated through a decline in the age of male marriage, through increasing the proportion of men who will ever marry, or through selective in-migration of males. In countries suffering major losses of men through war, however, the proportion of women who never marry among cohorts of women slightly younger than the men who were of fighting age is usually considerably reduced.

A sudden change in the rate of population growth may also affect the sex ratio at marriageable ages and hence influence marriage probabilities. For example, after World War II the number of births in the United States increased quite suddenly over the number which had prevailed during the war. Since in the United States men marry at about age 23 to women who are on the average age 20 to 21, the marriage market for females is greatly influenced by the relative number of males who are two or three years older. In the United States there were slightly more boys born in 1941–43 than girls born in 1944–46. In contrast, the number of girls born in 1947–49 was 14 percent greater than the number of boys born in 1944–46.[5] Thus, girls born right after World War II and reaching marriageable age in the late 1960s had substantially poorer prospects for marriage than girls born during World War II, who reached marriageable age at mid-decade. However, it is also appropriate at this point to mention that an opposite situation existed in the early 1950s. At that time, because of the declining number of births during the late 1920s and early 1930s, chances for women to marry were excellent, but the chances for men relatively less satisfactory. Moreover, women born in the 1960s and early 1970s will also have excellent chances to marry in the 1980s and early 1990s.

Variations in marriage prospects may have further effects. For example, one may speculate that relatively poor marriage prospects may have influenced the self-image of American females born during the post-

5.   U.S. Public Health Service, *Vital Statistics of the United States, 1963*, Vol. 1, *Natality* (Washington, D.C.: U.S. Government Printing Office, 1964), Sec. 1, p. 3.

war period, and that to preserve feelings of self-worth, many of them made a more favorable evaluation of an occupational career. We do know that a higher proportion of those coming of age in the late 1960s made a serious preparation for one of the higher professions than of those reaching maturity in the 1950s or early 1960s.[6] Moreover, the increasing interest among females in pursuing a career was no doubt a causal factor in the Women's Liberation Movement which burgeoned at this time.

Variations in the proportions of marriageable men to marriageable women also lead to variations in the rate of illegitimacy. In particular, wars which markedly reduce the sex ratio at young ages often cause a substantial rise in illegitimate births. For those nations which participated in World War II, a very high inverse correlation is obtained between the sex ratio among persons 15 to 49 years old in 1949, and the ratio of illegitimate to total births.[7]

Differences in age structure may even affect the relative power of liberals and conservatives within a nation. A higher proportion of all voters will be of advanced years in an older than in a younger population, and there is some tendency for persons to grow more conservative with age (although much of the observed difference in political party identification in the United States by age has resulted because persons who are now elderly were more apt to be Republican when they were young than are more recent cohorts of voters).[8]

It is well known that the morale of the aged is an important problem in the economically developed nations because it is difficult for many older citizens to find meaningful and important roles. If the developed nations had a younger population, the importance of this problem would of course be greatly diminished. However, these nations do *not* have younger populations, and so the problem must be faced in its full magnitude. Furthermore, since economic development and low fertility are very closely associated, it appears that the proportion of elderly persons in the developed nations will tend to remain quite high for some time to come.

6. U.S. Bureau of the Census, *Statistical Abstract of the United States, 1972* (Washington, D.C.: Government Printing Office, 1972), p. 134.

7. David M. Heer, *After Nuclear Attack: A Demographic Inquiry* (New York: Praeger, 1965), pp. 384–88.

8. Matilda W. Riley and Ann Foner, *Aging and Society*, Vol. I, *An Inventory of Research Findings* (New York: Russell Sage Foundation, 1968), p. 472.

CHAPTER 8
POPULATION GROWTH AND ECONOMIC DEVELOPMENT

THE GAP BETWEEN ECONOMICALLY DEVELOPED AND LESS DEVELOPED NATIONS

In the world today a great gulf divides the economically developed nations from the less developed. In 1958 the United States, with only 6 percent of the world's population, produced about 35 percent of the world's economic goods and services; the more developed nations, with only 32 percent of the world's population, produced *in toto* about 82 percent; the less developed nations, containing 68 percent of the world's population, produced a mere 18 percent. The extreme gap between the most developed and the least developed nations is illustrated by the per-capita product in the United States which was some thirty times higher than that in India or China.[1]

The contrast between the developed and less developed nations might be tolerable for the latter if they were completely isolated from the developed nations. Because of modern means of communication and transportation, however, the poorer nations are now more aware than ever of the economic performance of the wealthier nations. This awareness has incited the people and governments of the poorer nations to intensely desire rapid economic development. We see in this desire what has been called the "revolution of rising expectations."

1. Simon Kuznets, *Postwar Economic Growth* (Cambridge, Mass.: Harvard University Press, 1964), pp. 29–33.

111

In this chapter we shall discuss the role of population growth in stimulating and retarding economic development. We shall focus our discussion on the less developed nations. However, we shall also consider the effect of population growth rates on economic growth in the now-developed countries, particularly in those instances where population growth in a developed country may exert an influence opposite from that which it would exert in a poorer nation. We shall examine: (1) two contrasting effects of population growth on costs of production; (2) the effect of changes in population growth rates on the ratio of dependents to wage-earners; (3) the effect of population growth on the volume of productivity-stimulating investment; and (4) the possible effect of population growth on the motivation for economic development.

TWO EFFECTS OF POPULATION GROWTH ON COSTS OF PRODUCTION

Population growth has two contradictory effects on the cost of productive operations. One effect tends to reduce costs, the other to raise them.

As far back as 1776, Adam Smith, in his famous book *Inquiry into the Nature and Causes of the Wealth of Nations,* discussed *economies of scale* (how the cost of production could be reduced by increasing its scale).[2] Henry Ford demonstrated Adam Smith's principles by producing his Model T Ford at a price considerably lower than that charged by his competitors, who did not use mass-production techniques. That large-scale production is often less costly than small-scale production has now been proved in a myriad of instances. If population growth, by expanding the market for goods, allows for an increase in the scale of production, and if an increase in scale reduces average productive costs, then population increase will be a cause of lower production costs. For example, it is quite possible that the past increases in the population of the United States made possible certain economies of scale in American productive and service industries, perhaps particularly in railroad transportation and in heavy industry. Furthermore, currently, Australia and a few other nations with low population density might achieve lower avearge costs through the economies of scale made possible by a further increase in population. However, it should be recognized that there is probably an optimum scale of production and that increasing the scale of operations

2. Adam Smith, *Inquiry into the Nature and Causes of the Wealth of Nations* (New York: The Modern Library, 1937).

beyond a certain point results in higher rather than lower average costs. For example, the streets of American cities are now so overcrowded that there can be little doubt that the average cost of intraurban transport operations would be considerably reduced by a decline rather than by an increase in the scale of vehicular movement.

But a burgeoning population is not the only means by which an escalation of business operations can be achieved. International trade also holds great potential since a large international market may offer as many opportunities for economics of scale as a large internal market. Moreover, the internal market for all but the most necessary goods and services will increase as much through a rise in the nation's per-capita income as by an increase in the number of consumers.

The detrimental effect of population growth on the average cost of production is that every increase in population results in a diminution in natural resources per capita. This point was forcibly brought to the attention of the world by Malthus in his *Essay on Population*[3] and was strongly reiterated by David Ricardo, the most outstanding systematizer among the early nineteenth-century English classical economists. These early economists developed what is called *the law of diminishing marginal returns*. Their discussion revolved about the two factors of production: land and labor. Land, they held, was a fixed factor since the amount of land could in only small degree be altered through human intervention. Labor was a variable factor since each increase in population would result in a rise in the size of the labor force. The interest of the classical economists lay in (1) the total amount of food that could be produced on a given piece of land, depending on the amount of labor that was applied, and (2) the marginal increment in production that could be achieved by applying an additional unit of labor. According to their theory, at the very beginning, when the first few units of labor are applied, the marginal returns are increasing—that is, each successive unit of labor adds more units of product than its predecessor. Thus the classical economists recognized the economies of scale. However, beyond a certain point, they argued, further applications of labor would each earn successively less additional product, until finally an additional unit of labor would result in no marginal return at all.

Malthus contended that the world of his time was subject to diminishing marginal returns from additional increments of labor, and that any increase in population would result in a decline in economic production per capita. That Malthus proved wrong in his prediction of a

3. Thomas Robert Malthus, *Population: The First Essay* (Ann Arbor, Mich.: University of Michigan Press, 1959).

declining living standard was the result of the unforeseen advances in technology which have taken place since his time. There can be no doubt, however, of the overall validity of the classical analysis. As population increases, lands which were previously thought insufficiently productive are brought into use, minerals and fuels which were earlier thought to be too inaccessible or of insufficiently high quality are extracted, and more units of labor are applied to each unit of land or other resources. Under these conditions, and if we assume no advances in technology, living standards are bound to decline once the population exceeds a certain critical size.

What remains at issue is the exact size of population beyond which diminishing returns set in, and the exact relation between each increment in population size and each increment in production. Although this is, as it long has been, a subject for empirical investigation, the difficulties in finding a valid answer are about as great as ever, and so our knowledge in this regard is still very limited. We do know that at present the developed nations and particularly the United States, by far the richest of the major developed nations, have much superiority in natural resources per capita over the less developed nations. For example, in the mid-1950s the United States had about 1.14 hectares (1 hectare = 10,000 square meters, or 2.471 acres) of cultivated land per capita, compared to a world average of 0.49 hectares, 0.39 hectares in India, and 0.19 hectares in China.[4] The United States and most other developed nations also have a great advantage in the magnitude of their energy reserves (or energy potential) obtainable from coal, oil shale, petroleum, natural gas, fuelwood, and water power. In the mid-1950s, the United States possessed 72 million kilowatt-hours of energy potential per capita, the highest of any country in the world. The Soviet Union had 53 million, West Germany 37 million, and the United Kingdom 27 million. However, the world average was only 13 million kilowatt-hours, in China it was 4.5 million, and in India only 1.4 million. Moreover, 53 percent of the population of the world lived in nations with less than 1.9 million kilowatt-hours of energy potential per capita.[5]

Admittedly these data on resources are crude and imperfect. Nevertheless, their inexactness cannot hide the large disparity between nations in per-capita natural resources. From these data, it is obvious that any further population increase in the less developed nations will reduce their already minimal resource base.

4. Norton Ginsburg, *Atlas of Economic Development* (Chicago, Ill.: University of Chicago Press, 1961), pp. 46–47.

5. Ibid., pp. 58–59.

CHANGES IN THE RATE
OF POPULATION GROWTH
AND IN THE DEPENDENCY RATIO

In the previous chapter we discussed how different patterns of fertility and mortality produce differences in the dependency ratio. We pointed out that in stable populations high fertility has a major influence in creating an elevated dependency ratio, and that low mortality has a minor influence in the same direction. Stable populations with high fertility and low mortality therefore have the highest ratio of dependents to productive age-groups.

In their book *Population Growth and Economic Development in Low-Income Countries*, Ansley J. Coale and Edgar M. Hoover have prepared some very interesting projections of how changes in fertility and mortality might affect the ratio of non-earning dependents to earners in India.[6] According to their projection which assumed declining mortality but no change in fertility, the ratio of dependents to wage-earners would rise from 1.51 in 1956 (the actual figure) to 1.71 in 1986. On the other hand, according to the projection assuming the same decline in mortality but also a 50 percent decline in fertility by 1981, the ratio of dependents to wage-earners would have declined to 1.24 in 1986.[7] It is clear from these figures that the level of living in the average Indian family would be greatly improved by such a reduction in fertility, whereas continued decline in mortality might threaten existing living levels merely by increasing the number of persons dependent on each wage-earner.

POPULATION GROWTH
AND CAPITAL INVESTMENT

According to many economists, developed nations with a free-enterprise economy benefit from an acceleration of population growth because such an acceleration helps them avoid business depressions. According to Keynesian economic theory, business depression results when the amount of money which a population wishes to save is greater than that which potential investors wish to invest. It is contended that an

---

6. Ansley J. Coale and Edgar M. Hoover, *Population Growth and Economic Development in Low-Income Countries* (Princeton, N.J.: Princeton University Press, 1958).

7. Ibid., p. 235.

increase in the number of children per family will result in a reduction in intended savings, since an enlarged family will have greater consumption needs. It is further argued that increased population growth will result in larger intended investment because increased capital will be seen to be necessary to provide for the expected increase in total consumption. It is therefore concluded that a rise in fertility will either cure an existing depression or forestall a future one.[8] The "baby boom" in the United States in the years following World War II was thus welcomed by many economists and business spokesmen as a guarantee against severe depression. The argument advanced by these economists has merit, and it is quite possible that reductions in fertility in developed nations with a free-enterprise economy may have detrimental results unless governments act to ensure that consumption is increased in other directions.

A very different relation between population growth and capital investment obtains in the poor nations of the world. Relative to the developed nations, the less developed nations have on a per-capita basis very small amounts of capital. One of their major needs, therefore, is for additional investment. Capital is needed for highways, railroads, communication systems, electric-power generators, irrigation pumps, factories, and machinery. Equally needed is further investment in human beings. A literate populace is necessary even to apply existing technology; a still higher average level of education is necessary before a nation can adapt current technology to special local conditions; and a higher level yet before a nation can be instrumental in pioneering the development of new technology.

On the other hand, because the less developed nations are so short of it, added amounts of capital do more to raise productivity. Economists have estimated that for these nations a given amount of new capital investment will be associated with an increase in annual national income equal to approximately one-third the amount of the capital.[9] In the technical terms of the economist, the *incremental capital output ratio* for these nations would be said to be about 3.

How is this capital raised? Basically, the less developed nations can increase their capital in two ways. Either they must obtain funds from abroad by loan or gift, or they must obtain the money from within the economy by raising total income or by reducing total consumption. Many

8. For the fullest exposition of this argument see W. D. Reddaway, *The Economics of a Declining Population* (London: Allen & Unwin, 1939).

9. Ansley J. Coale and Edgar M. Hoover, *Population Growth and Economic Development in Low-Income Countries*, pp. 181–224. The magnitude of the incremental capital-output ratio will vary according to the broadness of one's definition of capital investment. The broader one's definition, the larger the magnitude of the incremental capital-output ratio.

of the less developed nations do not wish to become excessively indebted to developed nations, nor are the developed nations always anxious to give or lend capital. Therefore, the leadership groups of the less developed nations are usually very much concerned with increasing the level of investment in their nations through internal means.

How does a decline in population growth-rate achieved through fertility reduction affect the ability of a less developed nation to raise additional capital sums to increase its productivity? Two relationships are relevant. First, a decline in fertility will result in fewer dependents per wage-earner, and hence each wage-earner can be either motivated or forced to save a larger proportion of his total income.[10] These savings can then be used to increase the nation's investment in new factories, roads, schools, and so on. Secondly, any nation with a growing population must spend a certain proportion of its invested capital merely to provide the additional population with the same amount of capital equipment per person already enjoyed by the existing population. For example, a growing population will need additional housing, school buildings, hospitals, and factories. Hence, not all of the capital which a nation invests can be spent on capital improvements to increase per-capita productivity and raise the level of living. In sum: The higher the nation's rate of population growth, the greater the amount of capital that will be necessary merely to make provision for the added population, and therefore, the less will be the funds left over for making capital improvements to improve productivity.

Coale and Hoover complete their work by considering how their projected 50 percent decline in fertility might affect: (1) the total amount of capital investment; (2) the proportion of total capital investment applicable to improving productivity rather than providing for population increase; and (3) resultant increase in income per equivalent adult consumer.[11] They assume that 30 percent of any increase in income per equivalent adult consumer will be invested. They also assume that investments made merely to maintain the existing level of equipment per capita of an expanding population will not serve to raise total production—a reasonable assumption since during the period of their projection the size of the labor force will not be materially affected by fertility reduction. They do not assume any declining returns caused by increasing scarcity of natural resources per capita.

According to Coale and Hoover, in the population with declining

10. Governments force savings and investment through taxing the populace and using the proceeds for government-sponsored capital investment. This is the usual method fo financing investment in the Soviet Union and other Socialist nations.

11. In calculating the number of equivalent adult consumers, men 10 and over were given a weight of 1, children under 10 a weight of 0.5, and women 10 and over a weight of 0.9.

fertility, income per equivalent adult consumer would gradually rise relative to that in the population with unchanging fertility. After ten years (i.e., in 1966), average income per consumer in the population with declining fertility would be only 3 percent higher than in the population without fertility change. However, by 1976 it would be 14 percent higher, and by 1986, 41 percent higher. Assuming fertility reduction, income per consumer would be 95 percent higher in 1986 than it had been in 1956; assuming no fertility reduction, it would be only 38 percent higher.[12] All of these projections imply that fertility reduction would have a very substantial effect on the future course of economic development in India and other poor nations.

POPULATION GROWTH AND THE MOTIVATION FOR ECONOMIC DEVELOPMENT

Most of our previous discussion has pointed out various detrimental effects of a high rate of population growth, and particularly of a high birth rate, for economic development in the poorer nations. We shall now examine an argument that these various detrimental effects may be offset by the influence of a high rate of population growth in stimulating the motivation for improved productivity. The chief exponent of this argument has been the economist Albert Hirschman, who argues that the population pressure resulting from a high rate of population growth will lead to counterpressures designed to maintain or restore the nation's traditional level of living. This counter-pressure will take the form of increased motivation to undertake a new organization of economic activities based on a more advanced technology. Once a society has taken the crucial step of discarding traditional economic activity, it can then make the additional effort needed to increase the per-capita level of living, even despite the continuing growth in population.[13]

Hirschman's argument is of course very similar to that of Durkheim, which we discussed in chapter 1. It would be difficult to deny Hirschman's contention that productivity-increasing activities take place under conditions of rapid population growth. However, the crucial question for present-day policy-makers is whether a decline in the rate of population growth through fertility reduction in the now less-developed nations

12. Coale and Hoover, *Population Growth and Economic Development in Low-Income Countries*, p. 280.

13. Albert O. Hirschman, *The Strategy of Economic Development* (New Haven, Conn.: Yale University Press, 1958), pp. 176–82.

would bring about a reduction in their motivation to undertake productivity-increasing efforts. Hirschman has produced no empirical evidence to show that this would occur.[14] Moreover, it is at least plausible to argue that all of the poorer nations are now highly motivated in favor of economic advance simply because the difference between their own level of living and that in the developed countries has (as we have already seen) been made manifest by modern methods of communication and transportation. On the other hand, Hirschman's argument can be supported in part by the possibility that a reduction in mortality may have a very beneficial influence on motivation for increasing the productivity of economic activities, a point we considered in chapter 4.

Another argument, which claims that motivation in favor of increasing economic productivity may be endangered by programs of population control, is that of David McClelland. He argues that the supply of potential entrepreneurs—that is, persons with a high motivation to achieve innovations in economic activity—may be limited if a fertility-reduction campaign is accepted most eagerly by the middle socio-economc strata, wherein McClelland believes a disproportionate number of potential entrepreneurs are bred.[15] However, McClelland's caveat may be ignored as long as fertility-contrtol programs achieve acceptance from the lower social strata in greater proportion than from the middle and upper strata.

14. To the contrary, Hirschman even argues that the adoption of birth-control techniques may serve to teach a populace that the environment *can* be controlled and hence aid it in coping with the tasks of development. See Hirschman, *The Strategy of Economic Development*, pp. 180–81.

15. David C. McClelland, *The Achieving Society* (Princeton, N.J.: D. Van Nostrand, 1961), p. 424.

CHAPTER 9
POPULATION AND POLITICAL POWER

We may define the *political power* of a nation or group as the ability to influence other nations or groups to engage in policies which they would not otherwise undertake. This power may be exercised through: (1) providing rewards for compliance with one's goals; (2) threatening the use of force for failure to comply; and (3) the actual use of force when compliance has not otherwise been induced. Population variables influence the relative power both of nations in international politics and of groups engaged in political conflict within a nation. However, the influence of population variables on power is not always a simple one. In particular, it would be wrong to postulate that political potency can always be enhanced by an increase in population size. We shall presently discuss why this is so.

POPULATION AND POWER IN INTERNATIONAL AFFAIRS

Although there is without question a positive correlation between the size of a nation's population and the potency of its influence in international affairs (certainly none of the nations with a very small population is a great power), it is only a rough one. For instance, most persons would agree that the United States is the most powerful nation in the world, yet it is exceeded in population by China, India, and the Soviet Union. There would also be general agreement that the Soviet Union is the second most important power in the world, but the population of the USSR is less than that of either China or India. Perhaps the most striking recent illustration of the imperfect correlation between population size and power in international affairs was the 1967 victory of Israel, with only about 2.5 million population, over the Arab opponents whose combined population totaled about 100 million.

Clearly, population size alone cannot explain variations in international power. Probably five variables are necessary to explain a nation's force in world affairs: (1) *population size,* (2) *income per capita,* (3) the *possession of natural resources* specifically necessary *for warfare,* (4) the degree of *governmental motivation* to achieve international goals, and (5) the *efficiency* of government *in mobilizing resources* to attain these goals.[1]

Population size is important for two reasons. First, a large population is necessary if a nation is to have a large body of men in military service. Secondly, it is important because from the productive effort of each member of the labor force a certain amount can be siphoned off to pay for the cost of a military establishment, foreign aid, and other expenditures which enhance the power of the nation. If this amount is constant for each member of the labor force, then the effort which can be expended to maintain or increase the nation's power will vary directly with the size of the labor force. Moreover, the larger the population the larger the labor force, and hence, under the condition stated above, the potential resources available for increasing the nation's power will vary directly with the size of the nation's population.

The amount of productive effort which may be extracted from each member of the labor force and devoted to aggrandizing the nation's power may not, however, be constant, and income per capita is thus an important variable in explaining variation in national power. The higher the per-capita income, the lower will be the proportion of all income which must be spent on the absolute necessities of life. Hence, the proportion of each individual's income which can be spent to increase the power of the nation will vary directly with the level of per-capita income.

A nation will have greater military power to the extent that it possesses on its own soil the resources such as petroleum, coal, and iron ore which are specifically necessary for maintaining a military establishment.

Nonetheless, a nation which is potentially powerful because of a large population, high per-capita income, and requisite natural resources is not actually powerful unless it uses its potential resources efficiently. Nations with governments both highly motivated to exercise power in

---

1. In this exposition I am following closely (but not exactly) the thinking in Kingsley Davis, "The Demographic Foundations of National Power,"' in Morroe Berger et al., eds. *Freedom and, Control in Modern Society* (New York: Van Nostrand, 1954), pp. 206–43, and Katherine Organski and A. F. K. Organski, *Population and World Power* (New York: Alfred A. Knopf, 1961).

international affairs and skilled at doing so will have an advantage over nations which are either less highly motivated or unskillful in using the resources they have mobilized.

Table 5 shows the twelve nations having the largest population, the highest per-capita income, and (by way of a ranking of productive capacity) the greatest total production of steel. It is apparent from this table that population size and per-capita income are not well correlated: of the twelve nations of largest population, only the United States and West Germany are included in the dozen having the highest per-capita income.

Of the available single indicators of national power, aggregate steel production may be the most valid (although not invariably accurate). A high level of steel production obtains only when population is large and per-capita income is reasonably high. Moreover, the level of steel production is also somewhat dependent on governmental motivation in favor of international power, since a sizeable steel industry is a prerequisite for large-scale armaments manufacture. In terms of total steel production, the United States in 1970 was the most important world power; the Soviet Union ranked second. Although these two nations were among the top four in total population, of the top twelve nations in population, only six would rank among the top dozen in power, as-

Table 5   The Twelve Nations with Largest Population, Highest Per-capita Income, and Greatest Steel Production, circa 1970

NATION	1972 POPULATION (IN MILLIONS)	NATION	1970 PER-CAPITA GROSS DOMESTIC PRODUCT (IN $)	NATION	1970 STEEL PRODUCTION (IN THOUSANDS OF METRIC TONS)
China	786	USA	4,734	USA	119,308
India	585	Kuwait	4,189	USSR	115,889
USSR	248	Sweden	4,055	Japan	93,322
USA	209	Canada	3,676	West Germany	45,040
Indonesia	129	Denmark	3,141	United Kingdom	28,316
Japan	106	Switzerland	3,135	France	23,773
Brazil	98	West Germany	3,034	Italy	17,277
Bangladesh	80	Luxembourg	2,960	China	17,000
Pakistan	67	Norway	2,944	Belgium	12,611
West Germany	59	Australia	2,916	Poland	11,480
Nigeria	58	France	2,901	Czechoslovakia	11,480
United Kingdom	57	Belgium	2,633	Canada	11,200

Sources: Population: Population Reference Bureau, 1972 World Population Data Sheet (Washington, D.C.: 1972); Per-capita Gross Domestic Product: United Nations, Yearbook of National Account Statistics, 1971 (New York, 1973), Vol. 3, pp. 3–7; Steel Production: United Nations, Statistical Yearbook, 1971 (New York, 1973) p. 288.

suming steel production to be an accurate indicator thereof. Hence, population size and power are apparently only roughly correlated.

If population size and political power are not highly correlated, it follows that a nation which wishes to increase its power relative to other nations should not necessarily encourage an acceleration of its population growth. There are two reasons why an acceleration of population growth may not augment a nation's power. First, an increased growth-rate made possible by a rise in fertility can produce additional military manpower only after a lag of some twenty years following the birth-rate rise. Secondly, a high rate of population growth may be very detrimental to the nation's ability to raise its per-capita income. For nations such as China, India, Bangladesh, Pakistan, and Indonesia, wherein the level of per-capita income is exceedingly low, the best method of increasing national power may be to curb population growth drastically and thereby facilitate the rise of per-capita income. On the other hand, nations such as the United States, with very high per-capita income, might suffer a decline in power if their population, relative to that of other nations, were to be considerably reduced.

Although an acceleration of population growth may not always be an optimum strategy for increasing national power, most governments have in the past assumed that it is. Sometimes this policy may have been justified. For example, the French government, stung by vanquishment in the Prussian War of 1870 and near defeat in World War I, resolved to increase the French birth rate to match that of Germany and instituted a system of financial aid to families.[2] Under other conditions, pro-natalist policies may be unwise. For example, Stalin prohibited legal abortion in the Soviet Union in 1936, probably because he was afraid of Hitler's armies and wished to raise the birth rate to provide more military manpower. Following the prohibition of abortion, the birth rate did rise. However, this increase in the birth rate probably lowered the proportion of women in the labor force and no doubt reduced the funds which could have been spent in expanding heavy industry. Moreover, the additional male babies born because abortion had been prohibited provided no increase in military manpower to repel Hitler's invasion in 1941.

POPULATION AND INTRANATIONAL POWER

In a democracy where one man has one vote it would seem obvious that groups with large populations would have more power than groups

---

2.   David V. Glass, *Population Policies and Movements in Europe* (Oxford: Clarendon Press, 1940), Chs. 3 and 4, and Joseph J. Spengler, *France Faces Depopulation* (Durham, N.C.: Duke University Press, 1938).

with a small number. Certainly many minority racial, religious, and ethnic groups have often assumed that they could relieve themselves of persecution if only they could increase their number sufficiently to gain greater voting power. In the United States it has been suggested that elements within the Roman Catholic Church may have encouraged large families among Catholic parishioners in order to gain the Church greater political strength and counter Protestant-sponsored policies considered inimical to the Catholic interest.[3]

In many cases a larger population *has* provided the minority group with an increase in political power. In the early days of the United States, Roman Catholics suffered a great deal of political persecution at the hands of the overwhelming majority of Protestants. As their numbers increased, the Catholics found themselves in an ever more favorable political position, and in 1960 one of their number, John F. Kennedy, finally was elected President. The tremendous increase in the proportion of Catholics in the total U.S. population over the past 100 years has been caused by both very heavy immigration from abroad and a somewhat higher Catholic birth rate than that of the rest of the nation's population.

The relation between the two trends we have just discussed is probably one of cause and effect. However, an increase in population is not the only road to greater power for a minority group. The case of the American Jewish group is instructive. Jewish fertility has been less than that of any other religious group in the United States. On the other hand, individual Jews have made great strides in advancing their socio-economic status, so that at present American Jews have a higher average income and a generally higher occupational and educational status, than either Catholics or Protestants.[4] In all probability, Jews have increased potency in the United States not through an increase in number (currently they constitute only about 3 per cent of the population[5]) but because so many individual Jews have gained influential positions in the society.

It is interesting to note, moreover, that American blacks are most persecuted where they form the largest proportion of the population. From the standpoint of civil rights, the relative position of the American black is at its worst in Mississippi, Alabama, and the other Deep South states wherein blacks form a relatively large proportion of the total popu-

3. For a discussion of Roman Catholic encouragement of large families see Judith Blake, "The Americanization of Catholic Reproductive Ideals," *Population Studies* (July, 1966), 20:1, 27–43.

4. Sidney Goldstein, "Socioeconomic Differentials among Religious Groups in the United States," *American Journal of Sociology* (May 1969) 74:6, 612–31.

5. U.S. Bureau of the Census, *Current Population Reports*, Series P-20, No. 79 (2 February 1958), p. 6.

lation, and at its best in those northern and western states with relatively small black populations. A major reason for this situation may be the fact that the socio-economic status of individual blacks is so low in the Deep South. The principle of "one man, one vote" is meaningless in states where blacks can be kept from the polls by economic threats. Moreover, the vote alone will not mean power unless blacks have enough education to understand their own interests and sufficient finances to voice their views effectively. If American blacks wish to achieve a greater measure of power, their optimum population policy may be the encouragement of small families to allow close attention to the education and upbringing of each child. In this way blacks may raise their socio-economic status more rapidly, and through the attainment of higher status gain a large share in forming national, state, and local policies.

CHAPTER 10
POPULATION
LEGISLATION
AND POLICY

Change in population size, geographic distribution, composition, and process may all be influenced by governmental decrees and legislation. Some of the legislation affecting population is intentionally designed to influence one or more aspects of a nation's population. However, much of the legislation affecting population has some other goal as its primary aim. Only the former can be called population policy, but we cannot neglect the latter since its total effect on population may be even greater than that of the legislation consciously designed to have an impact on population.

The ultimate *effect* of population legislation may be on size, geographic distribution, or composition. The *mechanism* to achieve any one of these effects is a change in one of the three population processes: mortality, fertility, and migration. Any legislation affecting a population process will of course have an impact on the rate of change in population size. In addition, laws which induce change in mortality, fertility, or migration differentials will also affect population distribution and composition. It will therefore be convenient to divide our discussion of legislation according to whether there is an attempt to influence mortality, fertility, or migration.

LEGISLATION AFFECTING MORTALITY

Although governments generally place a high value on the preservation of human life, they have other values to consider, and these sometimes take precedence over the maximum preservation of life. For example, almost all governments place the independence of the nation above the protection of human life, and many have also considered imperial aggrandizement to be a higher value. As a result, throughout human history wars and armed conflict have resulted in millions of deaths not only to fighting men but to civilians as well. Mankind has increasingly felt the inhumanity of war, however, and in the twentieth century has attempted to control its outbreak through the mechanism of international organizations. The first such organization, the League of Nations, was not successful in preventing World War II—mainly because it was not taken seriously by many of its member nations, and partly because the U.S. refused to join it. The second international organization, the United Nations, has enjoyed a qualified success. That is, since its inception following World War II, it has been able to help stave off encounters among various great powers but has failed to prevent a rash of smaller but very serious conflicts.

Almost all nations have attempted to reduce mortality among their own people by means of public health programs. These are measures for environmental sanitation, inoculation against infectious disease, and regulation of foods, drugs, and sanitary facilities. Although these measures cost relatively little money, their impact on mortality has been extremely great.

Many of the developed nations, including Great Britain, France, West Germany, Austria, Sweden, the Soviet Union, Australia, and New Zealand have also instituted governmental programs of medical care. In these nations either the government establishes medical clinics which provide the public with largely free care, or it makes a large contribution to the payment of patients' medical and hospital bills.[1]

Unlike most of the other developed nations, the United States does not have a general governmental program of free or subsidized medical care. Nevertheless, gradually the federal government has been assuming more and more responsibility in this area. Since 1946, the federal government, under the Hill-Burton Act, has subsidized the construction of hospitals, and for a long period it has appropriated large amounts of money for medical research. In 1965 Congress passed an amendment to the Social Security Act with two very important titles relevant to federal participation in medical care programs. Title 18 provides for the establishment of the *Medicare* program, whereby the hospital and medical

1. For a cross-national description of state-operated or state-subsidized medical care programs, see Matthew Lynch and Stanley Raphael, *Medicine and the State* (Springfield, Ill.: Charles C. Thomas, 1963), and Helmut Schoeck, ed., *Financing Medical Care: An Appraisal of Foreign Programs* (Caldwell, Idaho: Caxton Printers, 1962).

expenses of all persons 65 years old and over are in large part "covered" by the federal government. Title 19 establishes the *Medicaid* program, under whose terms each state, with the help of federal financing, is to provide free medical care for persons established as medically indigent according to a means test. This 1965 legislation obligates the federal government to large expenses for medical care without imposing a pattern of extensive government controls over the actual rendering of medical services.[2]

Government expenditures on health programs have probably had two principal effects on differential mortality. In the first place, they may have done more to reduce death rates among infants and children than among older adults. Thus their direct effect has probably been to cause the total population to be somewhat younger. The second probable effect has been to reduce social-class differentials in mortality. Since poor persons cannot generally afford adequate medical care, governmental programs of medical care probably do more to reduce death rates among the poor than among the well-to-do.

LEGISLATION AFFECTING FERTILITY

Legislation with a conscious attempt to influence fertility is of very long standing, and until recent times almost all of it was pro-natalist. The Code of Hammurabi, enacted in the twentieth century B.C. in Babylon, is the first recorded attempt to elevate fertility by means of legislation.[3] Pro-natalist policies were also enacted in Rome during the reign of Caesar Augustus, somewhere between 18 B.C. and 9 A.D. The *Lex Papia et Poppaea*, for instance, contained various provisions designed to encourage marriage and the raising of children: fathers were given preference in public office according to the number of children in the family, and mothers of large families were given the right to wear distinctive clothes and ornaments. According to Glass, the main intent of the laws was to encourage births not in the general population but rather among the aristocrats, who apparently were not reproducing themselves in sufficient numbers to please the government. However, the aristocrats chose not to let the government order their conjugal behavior, and the laws proved both unenforceable and ineffectual. They were abolished

2. For a detailed description of the Medicare and Medicaid programs see Arthur E. Hess, "Medicare: Its Meaning for Public Health," *American Journal of Public Health* (January, 1966), 56:1, 10–18, and Ellen Winston, "The New Medical Assistance Program," *Public Health Reports* (October, 1966), 81:10, 863–66.

3. David V. Glass, *Population Policies and Movements in Europe* (Oxford: Clarendon Press, 1940), p. 86.

entirely when Christianity, which placed a higher value on celibacy than on marriage, became the religion of Rome.[4]

Pro-natalist legislation was also enacted in France and in Spain during the seventeenth century. In Spain, men who married early or who had a large family received partial or full exemption from taxes. The French legislation was similar to the Spanish, but provided in addition that any of the nobility who had ten or more living legitimate children were henceforth to receive annual pensions. There is some doubt, however, whether the Spanish legislation was ever put into effect, and the French legislation was soon repealed.[5] The seventeenth-century Spanish and French pro-natalist policies had been established because, in the case of Spain, the government feared the military consequences of an absolute loss in population, and in the case of France, a loss relative to population in other nations. In Spain the population had declined from about 10 million in 1500 to about 6 million in 1700.[6]

During the eighteenth and early nineteenth centuries, the actual increase in European population largely stilled the demands for pro-natalist legislation. Pro-natalist sentiment revived in many European nations coincident with the fertility decline of the late nineteenth and early twentieth centuries. Pro-natalist legislation has probably been carried to its fullest extent in France, where, as previously mentioned, defeat by Prussia during the war of 1870 and the terrible losses of World War I caused the government to resolve that the French birth rate should match that of Germany. But such legislation has been important at one time or another in almost all of the European nations.

One of the principal components of modern pro-natalist legislation in France and other nations has been the program of family allowances. A *family-allowance program* may be defined as any program in which monetary payments are made to parents on behalf of their children without regard to individual financial need. According to this definition, many other nations beside France have such programs, including Australia, Austria, Belgium, Brazil, Bulgaria, Canada, Chile, Czechoslovakia, Finland, the German Federal Republic (West Germany), Great Britain, Hungary, Iceland, Ireland, Italy, Lebanon, Luxembourg, the Netherlands, New Zealand, Norway, Poland, Portugal, Romania, Spain, Sweden, Switzerland, the Union of South Africa, Uruguay, the USSR, and Yugoslavia.[7]

4. Ibid., pp. 86–90.

5. Ibid., pp. 91–95.

6. United Nations Department of Social Affairs, *The Determinants and Consequences of Population Trends* (New York: United Nations, 1953), p. 9.

7. James C. Vadakin, *Family Allowances: An Analysis of their Development and Implication* (Miami, Fla.: The University of Miami Press, 1958), pp. 41–46.

The French family-allowance system evolved gradually. Beginning in 1918, family-allowance schemes were voluntarily organized by various industries; each company within the industry contributed to an industry-wide equalization fund, which in turn distributed the family-allowance payments. Legislation in 1932 nationalized the system of family-allowance payments, and according to the new French law all industrial employees were to be given cash allowances for each dependent child. In 1939 the French system was further enlarged to include workers in all occupations.[8] In 1961, family-allowance payments in France were equal to 5 percent of the total national income and were a substantially higher proportion of national income than the family-allowance payments in any other major nation.[9]

An increase in the birth rate was also the main object of family-allowance programs introduced into Germany by Hitler, into Italy by Mussolini, and into the Soviet Union by Stalin. In the Soviet Union a munificent program for families with three or more children was enacted in 1944. This legislation closely followed the staggering population losses which the nation had suffered during the first years of World War II. However, in 1948 the benefits were cut in half, and after that date the impact of the program was further diluted by the very substantial increase in the Soviet wage level. In 1944 the monthly payment to a family after the birth of the fifth child had been about 51 percent of the average wage, whereas in 1964 it was worth only 12 percent. It is obvious that the Soviet government was much less concerned about increasing its birth rate in 1964 than it was twenty years earlier.[10] Since 1964 many Soviet demographers have expressed renewed concern that the birth rate in the Soviet Union was too low. As of 1972, however, there had been no change in official policy with respect to the family allowance program.[11]

In many of the nations with family-allowance programs the main aim has been social welfare rather than population increase. Since the parents of large families often do not have enough income to provide adequately for their children, family-allowance payments help to equalize the position of children from large families. In Sweden, for example, the main purpose of the family-allowance program has unquestionably been that of social welfare.[12] Nevertheless, it is doubtful that intent makes any

8. Glass, *Population Policies and Movements in Europe*, pp. 99–124.

9. David M. Heer and Judith G. Bryden, "Family Allowances and Fertility in the Soviet Union," *Soviet Studies* (October, 1966), 18:2, 153–63.

10. Ibid.

11. David M. Heer, "Recent Developments in Soviet Population Policy," *Studies in Family Planning* (November, 1972), 3:11, p. 257–64.

12. Glass, *Population Policies and Movements in Europe*, pp. 312–38.

difference; family-allowance payments probably have much the same effect on fertility whether the intent is pro-natalist or the desire to foster child welfare.

Legislation restricting birth control may also help to raise fertility. The motivation for passing such legislation is often pro-natalist; on the other hand, a very important attitude sustaining such legislation is the belief that the free availability of birth-control information and devices encourages sexual promiscuity. In various nations laws have been passed restricting not only abortion but also contraception. Until 1967 the most restrictive legislation against contraception was in France. A law enacted in 1920 prescribed imprisonment for anyone engaging in birth-control propaganda, divulging means of birth control, or facilitating use of methods to prevent pregnancy. An important loophole was that the condom could be legally sold if the sale was for protection from venereal disease only. Nevertheless, the law placed severe limitations on the establishment of clinics whose specific aim was to foster family planning.[13] In the United States very restrictive birth-control legislation was in effect in Connecticut and Massachusetts as late as 1965 and 1966. Since 1966, dissemination of contraceptive information and the sale of contraceptive appliances have been legal throughout the nation.

Although abortion is still illegal under most circumstances in a very large number of nations, marked shifts in public attitudes have occurred in recent years in many countries resulting in dramatic liberalization of prohibitory legislation. In 1967 the English Parliament enacted new legislation allowing abortion on broad social indications.[14] Various American state legislatures enacted liberalized abortion legislation in the late 1960s and early 1970s; perhaps the most important of these legislative changes was in New York State allowing abortion by a licensed physician on any grounds within the first twenty-four weeks of pregnancy.[15] In congruence with the shift in public opinion on this issue, the U.S. Supreme Court ruled on January 22, 1973, in *Roe* vs. *Wade* that during the first trimester of pregnancy the decision to have an abortion must be left solely to a woman and her physician. After the first trimester the Court decreed that regulations "reasonably related to maternal health" were permissible (such as a regulation requiring that abortions be performed in a hospital). However, legislation prohibiting abortion was deemed constitutional only for the rare instances where the

---

13. Ibid., pp 159–62; "Rapport sur la Regulation de Naissances en France," *Population* (July–August, 1966), 21:4, 647–48.

14. Daniel Callahan, *Abortion: Law, Choice and Morality* (New York: Macmillan, 1970) pp. 142–43.

15. Association for the Study of Abortion, *ASA Newsletter* (Summer 1970), 5:2, 2–4.

fetus has capacity for life outside the mother's womb and the abortion was not necessary to preserve the mother's physical or mental health.[16]

In the United States and other nations there are many laws which probably have pro-natalist consequences even though their main intent is doubtless one of furthering welfare. In the United States perhaps the most important of this kind of legislation is the federal income-tax law. According to the law, single persons are subject to a higher tax-rate than most married persons, since married couples may average their income and each spouse pay a tax on this average income rather than on his own income. Furthermore, the law allows each taxpayer a $750 exemption for each of his dependent children. Finally, a substantial tax deduction is given to holders of a home mortgage, who may deduct from their taxable income the interest they pay. Since a large mortgage is more frequent among family heads with children than among other taxpayers, this provision may also have pro-natalist consequences. In the United States the income-tax laws of the various states also tend to favor family heads with children over other taxpayers. The selective-service law in the United States may also have had an impact on the birth rate, since fathers were declared to be draft-exempt.

Although legislation restricting fertility is of much more recent origin than its opposite, within the last few years such legislation has assumed very great importance in many areas of the world. An early example of anti-natalist legislation was a decree passed in 1712 in Württemberg (now part of West Germany) prohibiting marriage unless ability to support a family could be proven.[17] Nevertheless, anti-natalist legislation was of little general consequence until after World War II.

In the postwar period, Japan was the first nation seriously to undertake an anti-natalist policy. Following the devastation of the war, living standards in Japan had fallen to 52 percent of the prewar average. Furthermore, Japan had been stripped of her territorial possessions in Manchuria, Korea, Taiwan, and Micronesia, and as a result was forced to receive 6.6 million repatriates and demobilized soldiers from abroad. In 1949 the House of Representatives of the Japanese Diet expressed its official belief that means should be taken to reduce the birth rate. In the previous year Japan had legalized induced abortion for reasons of maternal health, provided the applicant received the approval of a local committee. In 1949, in accordance with the new anti-natalist policy, legislation was enacted to allow abortion for economic reasons. In 1952, a further amendment to the law allowed abortion at the discretion of only

16. "United States Supreme Court Issues Sweeping Decision on Abortion," in *Family Planning/Population Reporter* (February, 1973), 2:1, 1–5.

17. Glass, *Population Policies and Movements in Europe*, p. 98.

one doctor and authorized midwives and nurses to give guidance in conception control. As a result of these legal changes, the reported number of induced abortions increased greatly from less than 250,000 per year in 1949 to annual totals of more than one million in 1953 and later years. Since 1955 the number of abortions has declined as the proportion of population practicing contraception has increased, and in 1964 it was less than 900,000. Coincident with the legalization of abortion and the official encouragement of contraception, fertility in Japan declined dramatically. In 1947 the gross reproduction rate had been 2.20, but since 1957 the gross reproduction rate has averaged around 1.0 or slightly lower.[18]

In recent years many other nations, particularly in Asia, have developed family-planning programs. As of 1973 the nations of more than 10 million population which had family-planning programs included Afghanistan, Algeria, Bangladesh, Ceylon, Chile, Colombia, Egypt, India, Indonesia, Iran, Iraq, Kenya, Malaysia, Mexico, Morocco, Nepal, North Vietnam, Pakistan, the People's Republic of China, Philippines, the Republic of China (Taiwan), South Africa, South Korea, South Vietnam, Sudan, Tanzania, Thailand, Turkey, Uganda, the United States of America, and Venezuela.[19] Let us consider a few of the programs in detail.

Communist China has been markedly ambivalent about its fertility policy, vacillating several times with respect to whether it has wanted to discourage fertility. However, as of 1972 the Chinese government was attempting several anti-natalist measures, including the discouragement of early marriage, provision of facilities for contraception and sterilization, the legalization of abortion, and even the denial of additional rations to children in large families. The Chinese government has published no data concerning the effectiveness of any of these measures.[20]

The Indian government, as early as 1952, adopted a national policy

18. Minoru Muramatsu, ed., *Japan's Experience in Family Planning—Past and Present* (Tokyo: Family Planning Federation of Japan, 1967), pp. 27, 69, 83–101.

19. Dorothy Nortman, "Population and Family Planning Programs: A Factbook," *Reports on Population/Family Planning* (September, 1973), No. 2 (5th ed.); Calman J. Cohen, "Mexico Lays Base for Nationwide Family Planning Program," *Population Dynamics Quarterly* (Winter, 1973), 1:1, 2–4.

20. Leo A. Orleans, "The Population of Communist China," in Ronald Freedman, ed., *Population: The Vital Revolution* (New York: Doubleday, 1964), pp. 227–39; Irene B. Taeuber and Leo A. Orleans, "Mainland China," in Bernard Berelson, ed., *Family Planning and Population Programs* (Chicago, Ill.: University of Chicago Press, 1966), pp. 31–54; and John S. Aird, "Population Policy and Demographic Prospects in the People's Republic of China," in U.S. Congress, 92nd, *People's Republic of China: An Economic Assessment* (Washington, D.C.: Government Printing Office, 1972), pp. 220–331.

in favor of family planning—but little was actually done until the advent of India's Five Year Plan in 1961. Since 1961 the financial expenditures of the program have increased severalfold. The Indian program envisions the establishment of a family-planning unit headed by a female physician for each rural area of about 75,000 persons and each urban district of about 50,000. In each family-planning unit a "block extension educator" is supposed to organize educational meetings on family planning and work with voluntary family-planning workers. Auxiliary nurse-midwives connected with each unit are trained in family planning and are expected to provide advice to pregnant women and new mothers while carrying out their regular duties. The principal methods of birth control encouraged at these units are vasectomy, condom, and IUD insertion. In many of the Indian states a small bonus is granted to both men and women who consent to a sterilizing operation and to women who accept an IUD. Since 1966 there has been a sharp shift away from the IUD toward the male methods of vasectomy and condom. As of 1972, however, the family-planning program had not yet been fully implemented, and there was as yet no firm indication that the portion already implemented had had any substantial effect on fertility. But if the program's magnitude continues to increase at the same rate as in the recent past, before very long its impact will probably begin to increase correspondingly.[21]

The family-planning program in Taiwan has been one of the most successful of the recent contraceptive programs. An island-wide program with unofficial government backing was begun in 1964 following a local program conducted in the city of Taichung. Initially, the IUD was the only contraceptive made available. Physicians in private practice were provided with IUD's and were paid about 75¢ for each insertion, from funds accruing from the interest on counterpart loans from the U.S. Agency for International Development (AID). An additional 75¢ for IUD insertion had to be paid by the patient. In 1967 oral pills were added to the offerings of the government program and in 1970 the condom. Field workers in each local community promote family planning, and a limited use is made of the mass media for this purpose. By 1972 more than half the married women 15 to 44 years of age were estimated to be current users of contraception.[22] The program in Taiwan

21. United Nations Department of Economic and Social Affairs, *Report on the Family Planning Programme in India*, Report No. TAO/IND/48 (20 Feb. 1966); Stanley Johnson, *Life without Birth* (Boston: Little, Brown, 1970) pp. 173–224; and Nortman, "Population and Family Planning Programs."

22. *Family Planning in Taiwan, Republic of China, 1965–66* (Taichung: Taiwan Population Studies Center, 1966); Johnson, *Life Without Birth*, pp. 68–92; and S. M. Keeny, ed., "East Asia Review, 1972" *Studies in Family Planning* 4:5, 119.

has been accompanied by a significant decline in fertility. In 1963, the year before the program began, the total fertility rate was 5.4, but by 1971 it had declined to 3.7.[23]

During the decade of the 1960s the United States government altered its attitude toward family planning. In February, 1965, AID announced that it would henceforth entertain requests from foreign nations for technical assistance in family planning.[24] By fiscal year 1968, it was extending help to twenty-six nations and its total spending for family and population planning amounted to 34.7 million dollars.[25] This amount rapidly increased, and by fiscal 1971 AID funding in this area was 95.9 million dollars, an amount equal to more than 5 percent of all AID obligations.[26]

Although for a number of years various state and local health departments in the United States had offered family-planning services, until recently the federal government had given no specific support. It was not until January, 1966, that the United States Department of Health, Education, and Welfare proclaimed its willingness to make funds available to state and local agencies for this purpose.[27] It is probable that this federal subsidization of family-planning programs has had significant impact among the poorly educated, who tend to be inadequately informed about birth-control methods and particularly about the newer methods such as the oral contraceptive and the IUD.

Fertility policies, if successful, will have a major impact on the age composition of a nation. Pro-natalist policies will tend to produce a young population, and anti-natalist policies an older one.

Governmental programs to influence fertility probably affect social-class differences in fertility, too. One may speculate that family-allowance programs have their greatest impact among low-income groups since the supplement for child-rearing awarded to low-income families is a comparatively higher proportion of their total family income. Furthermore, it may be presumed that restrictive laws concerning birth control prob-

23.   *1965 Taiwan Demographic Fact Book, Republic of China* (Taipei: Department of Civil Affairs, Taiwan Provincial Govt., 1966), pp. 226–27; *1971 Taiwan Demographic Fact Book, Republic of China* (Taipei: Ministry of Interior, Republic of China, 1972), p. 501.

24.   "Statements on Population Policy," *Studies in Family Planning*, No. 16 pp. 8–9.

25.   *Population Program Assistance* (Washington, D.C.: Agency for International Development, 1969).

26.   Phyllis Tilson Piotrow, *World Population Crisis: The United States Response* (New York: Praeger, 1973), p. 178.

27.   "Statements on Population Policy," p. 8.

ably have their greatest effect in low-income groups, since married couples of higher socio-economic status can probably more easily evade them. Thus, consistent pro-natalist policies may encourage fertility among the lower socio-economic strata more than they do in the higher. On the other hand, anti-natalist programs which advertise the availability of birth-control devices and which subsidize their cost may ultimately discourage fertility within the lower strata to a greater extent than within the upper strata. Because of the possibility of this differential impact by social class, government legislation concerning fertility may greatly influence the genetic composition of a population. Further research to quantify this apparent effect will be of great value.

LEGISLATION AFFECTING MIGRATION

Migration legislation runs a very wide gamut. Laws concerning international immigrants and emigrants vary from complete prohibition to positive encouragement. Although in general the laws of most nations concerning internal migration are permissive rather than either prohibitory or encouraging, in certain countries governmental control over internal migrants has been vigorously exercised.

In the seventeenth and eighteenth centuries a mercantilist ideology, which saw a large population as the key to national wealth and power, encouraged many of the governments of Europe to attempt to prohibit emigration and to encourage immigration. In the late seventeenth century, the French Minister Colbert enacted legislation prescribing the death penalty for persons attempting to emigrate or helping others to emigrate anywhere except to a French colony. In 1721, Prussia passed a similar law, and the Prussian Emperor Frederick the Great invested state funds to subsidize the settlement of immigrants. In Russia both Tsar Peter and Tsarina Catherine subsidized colonists from abroad—mostly from Germany.[28]

The nineteenth century, influenced by the economic doctrines of *laissez faire*, was the great period of unrestricted international migration. During this century the European governments freely permitted emigration, and the newly independent United States of America welcomed millions of immigrants.

After World War I, governments again took a more active role in policy relating to international migration. The major events in this connection were the changes in U.S. immigration laws in 1921 and 1924 which greatly restricted the number of immigrants to the United States,

28.   Glass, *Population Policies and Movements in Europe*, pp. 94–96.

establishing a quota for each of the countries outside the Western Hemisphere. Furthermore, each of the nations of northwest Europe was given a much larger quota relative to its population than those of southern or eastern Europe. This was done even though in the immediately preceding years rates of emigration from southern and eastern Europe had been much higher than from northwest Europe. The justification made at the time for the quota differentials was the presumed greater ease with which immigrants from northwest Europe could assimilate themselves.[29]

By the 1960s, a changing climate of opinion with respect to the inferiority or superiority of different ethnic groups made it possible for President Kennedy to advocate the abolition of the discriminatory national-origins quota system, and a law accomplishing this was enacted in 1965 under the Johnson administration. The 1965 law called for the abolition of the national-origins quota system as of July 1, 1968—but nevertheless imposed an overall annual quota of 170,000 immigrants from outside the Western Hemisphere and 120,000 from within it (exclusive of immediate relatives of United States citizens). This legislation grants preference to persons with relatives already in the United States, to persons with needed occupational skills, and to refugees.[30]

Some nations, while placing severe restrictions on immigrants in general, make use of positive inducements to encourage immigration from *selected* nations or groups. Australia, for example, has a national policy of attempting to attract an annual number of a certain type of immigrant equal to 1 percent of her total population. In many cases she even subsidizes their cost of transport. Since she maintains very tight restriction against immigrants from Asia, most of her new population comes from Europe.[31] Canada also subsidizes some new immigrants—for example, from the Netherlands—while placing severe restrictions on the immigration of nonwhites.[32] A similar policy of subsidizing selected immigrants only is in effect in Israel, which has committed itself to encouraging the immigration of Jews from anywhere in the world.

Restrictions against emigration are currently exemplified in the

29. Helen F. Eckerson, "Immigration and National Origins," *The Annals of the American Academy of Political and Social Science* (September, 1966), 367, 4–14.

30. Edward M. Kennedy, "The Immigration Act of 1965," *The Annals of the American Academy of Political and Social Science* (September, 1966), 367, 137–49.

31. Anthony T. Bouscaren, *International Migrations Since 1945* (New York: Praeger, 1963), pp. 105–8, and R. T. Appleyard, "The Economics of Immigration into Australia," Paper No. WPC/WP/71, delivered at the United Nations World Population Conference, Belgrade, Yugoslavia, 1965.

32. Bouscaren, *International Migrations Since 1945*, pp. 141–44; and William Petersen, *The Politics of Population*, pp. 301–22.

Soviet Union. Except in rather special cases, citizens of that nation have not been allowed to establish residence abroad.[33] Although the restrictions apply to all citizens of the Soviet Union, they have been particularly disturbing to Soviet Jews wishing to emigrate to Israel. As of 1973 some, but not all, Soviet Jews were being allowed to leave.[34]

The USSR is also a prime example of a nation which has exerted considerable control over internal migration. Even though policy was greatly liberalized after Stalin's death, the government, being the principal employer, still is able to promote in-migration to certain areas (such as Siberia) both by positive inducements and by compulsion, and to restrict voluntary in-migration by limiting the number of job openings in other areas. In practice, however, the actual movement has not always coincided with that planned. For instance, many persons who go to Siberia, are able to return because managers of enterprises in Moscow, Leningrad, and other western areas often succeed in hiring a larger number of employees than have been assigned them according to the terms of the government's comprehensive plan for the geographic distribution of labor.[35]

Although the United States has neither legislative restrictions on internal migration nor subsidies to encourage it, various types of governmental actions influence the flow of internal migrants here. For example, a governmental decision to grant a military contract to a particular corporation or to establish a military base in a particular location will influence the direction of migratory flow. In addition, area redevelopment programs for economically depressed areas, such as that for Appalachia, reduce the number of out-migrants below what would otherwise occur.

It is obvious from the examples already cited that governments

33. James W. Brackett, "Demographic Trends and Population Policy in the Soviet Union," in U.S. Congress, 87th, *Dimensions of Soviet Economic Power* (Washington, D.C.: Government Printing Office, 1962), p. 549; Frederick A. Leedy, "Demographic Trends in the U.S.S.R.," in U.S. Congress, 93rd, *Soviet Economic Prospects for the Seventies* (Washington, D.C.: Government Printing Office, 1973), p. 451.

34. The *New York Times:* 5 May 1973 (editorial), p. 11; 10 May 1973, p. 65; 13 May 1973, p. 13.

35. Warren W. Eason, "Problems of Manpower and Industrialization in the USSR," and Demitri B. Shimkin, "Demographic Changes and Socio-economic Forces within the Soviet Union, 1939–1959," in *Population Trends in Eastern Europe, The USSR, and Mainland China* (New York: Milbank Memorial Fund, 1960), pp. 79–80, 230–37; Murray S. Weitzman et al., "Employment in the USSR: Comparative USSR–US Data," in U.S. Congress, 87th, *Dimensions of Soviet Economic Power* (Washington, D.C.: Government Printing Office, 1962), pp. 633–41; and James W. Brackett and John W. DePauw, "Population Policy and Demographic Trends in the Soviet Union," in U.S. Congress, 89th, *New Directions in the Soviet Economy* (Washington, D.C.: Government Printing Office, 1966), pp. 621–25.

have been as much concerned with regulating migration differentials as they have with controlling the absolute volume of migration. Many governments have sought to reduce ethnic heterogeneity by promoting immigration only from nations considered to be relatively similar in culture and racial composition. Many have also placed a premium on certain occupational skills. For example, the 1965 immigration legislation of the United States gives a definite preference to professional workers. As a result, the United States has been accused of perpetrating a "brain drain" from the rest of the world.

THE EFFECTIVENESS
OF POPULATION POLICY

Governments throughout the world are becoming more aware of the consequences of population processes and are increasingly adapting population-influencing policies. The United States does not yet have a population policy, but President Nixon's appointment of the Commission on Population Growth and the American Future represented a first step in this direction, and there is no doubt that the Commission's recommendation to legalize abortion[36] had an important effect on the Supreme Court's 1973 decision in this regard.

Governments enact population policy with the idea that it will have a certain effect. But how are they to know that what they intend will actually come about? Ideally, the effects of a population policy should be measured by means of a controlled experiment. In the simplest form of such an experiment, areal units would be randomly divided into two groups, and the policy would be administered only to the areas within one of the two groups. Analysis of the differences between the two groups would then reveal the effects of the policy. The approximate impact of a policy may also be investigated by the statistical analysis of a so-called natural experiment. If areas exist to which the policy has been applied, and other areas exist to which it has not been applied, then a statistical analysis in which other presumably relevant variables are controlled will give some indication of the policy's actual effects. The least satisfactory way of determining the effect of a population policy is by deductive reasoning alone—that is, by imagining the results of the policy according to our general understanding of human behavior and in the light of our command of logic.

On the whole, empirical research to examine the effects of population policy has been rather infrequent. Although on a number of oc-

---

36. The Commission on Population Growth and the American Future, *Population and the American Future* (Washington, D.C.: Government Printing Office, 1972).

casions controlled experiments have been conducted to measure the effect on mortality of certain public-health policies, there have never been any to measure the effectiveness of any pro-natalist policy; nor has the impact of a pro-natalist policy ever been studied by means of a thorough statistical analysis of existing policy variation. For the most part, the effect of these policies has only been estimated from deductive arguments alone.

In the late 1960s a sharp debate arose regarding the adequacy of family-planning programs alone to reduce worldwide birth rates to a sufficiently low level. The noted demographer Kingsley Davis argued that the real problem was not that of eliminating unwanted births but that persons were motivated to want too many children. Davis further maintained that family planners, in implying that the only need was a perfect contraceptive device, avoided discussion of the possibility that "fundamental changes in social organization" were necessary prerequisites of achieving a sufficiently low level of fertility.[37]

A few controlled experiments have been done on the effect of organized birth-control campaigns. One of the earliest of such experiments, conducted in the Punjab state of India before the advent of the IUD and oral contraceptives, showed the campaign to have no measurable effect on fertility. A later Indian study, also conducted before the advent of the newer contraceptives, did show the campaign to have reduced fertility. However, the cost per prevented birth (including the cost of publicity and education) was extremely high.[38] In 1963 an elaborate experiment was conducted in a city in Taiwan to measure the effectiveness of varying degrees of intensity in disseminating information about the IUD and other contraceptives. This study provided valuable data both on the frequency of IUD insertion and on the monetary cost per insertion, depending on the intensity of the information campaign.[39]

Since in so many nations a continuation of high fertility militates against a rise in living standards and may eventually lead to higher mortality and a reduced level of living, a clear knowledge of the most efficient ways to reduce fertility is imperative. As we have seen, there has been some experimentation concerning the direct impact of organized birth-control campaigns. However, much further experimentation is necessary. For example, we need to know more about the relative effec-

37. Kingsley Davis, "Population Policy: Will Current Programs Succeed?", *Science* (10 November 1967), 163, 730–39.

38. "India: The Singur Study," and "India: The India-Harvard-Ludhiana Population Study," in *Studies in Family Planning*, No. 1 (July, 1963), pp. 1–7; and "Needed: Standardized Data from Action Programs," *Studies in Family Planning*, No. 12 (June, 1966), pp. 13–16.

39. "Cost Analysis of the Taichung Experiment," *Studies in Family Planning*, No. 10 (February, 1966), pp. 6–15.

tiveness of different types of contraceptives, the best means of communicating accurate birth-control information, and optimal ways of organizing family-planning services.

Moreover, if the availability of a perfect means of birth control will not of itself be sufficient to reduce fertility to the desired level, we must also obtain further knowledge concerning possible policies which will motivate couples to bear fewer children. Many fertility-control policies which go beyond family planning are possible, including such relatively extreme direct measures as substantial monetary incentives for having fewer children, individual child-bearing quotas, and marketable licenses for babies (a system in which a nationwide quota on average childbearing would be established, but individuals would be free to buy and sell childbearing licenses from other individuals and thus, if willing to pay the requisite price, be free to have as many babies as they wanted). Furthermore, certain changes in social structure can be instituted, such as the introduction of a social security system, programs to induce a decline in infant and child mortality, or a rise in the status of women, all of which may lead indirectly to a substantial decline in fertility.[40]

The effectiveness of some of the policies which go beyond family planning can be determined through experimentation. For example, to ascertain the effect of a reduced level of infant and child mortality on fertility, we could design a study in which a greatly improved maternal and child health service was provided for certain randomly selected experimental areas while the existing inadequate service was retained in control areas. Controlled experiments could also be used to investigate the impact of a program providing monetary incentives for couples who have refrained from bearing more than the number of children considered appropriate to the needs of society.

Other changes in social policy which might have a depressant effect on fertility probably cannot be studied by means of controlled experiments. Such changes probably include the legalization of abortion, and the introduction of social-security laws, compulsory education, and legislation restricting child labor and raising the age of marriage. Nevertheless, the effects of at least some of these can be studied by the statistical analysis of natural variations.

If fertility-control programs are to be maximally effective, much more of this type of research must be undertaken. Clearly, in the years ahead the professional student of population has an important role to play in evaluating actual and proposed population policies.

---

40. For a very detailed description of the various policies which have been advocated see Bernard Berelson, "Beyond Family Planning," *Science* (February, 1969), 163, 533–43.

SELECTED
REFERENCES

The following constitutes a selected list of some of the more important works in the field of population study.

An encyclopedic survey of population studies is contained in Philip M. Hauser and Otis Dudley Duncan, eds., *The Study of Population: An Inventory and Appraisal* (Chicago, Ill.: University of Chicago Press, 1959).

Major works on the history of population growth include: A. M. Carr-Saunders, *World Population: Past Growth and Present Trends*, 2nd ed. (London: Frank Cass, 1964); United Nations, *The Determinants and Consequences of Population Trends* (New York: United Nations, 1953); David V. Glass and D. E. C. Eversley, eds., *Population in History* (Chicago, Ill.: Aldine, 1965); David V. Glass and Roger Revelle, eds., *Population and Social Change* (London: Edward Arnold, 1972); W. S. Rossiter, *A Century of Population Growth from the First Census of the United States to the Twelfth: 1790–1900*, reprinted edition (New York: Johnson Reprint Corp., 1966); Conrad Taeuber and Irene B. Taeuber, *The Changing Population of the United States* (New York: John Wiley, 1958); and E. A. Wrigley, *Population and History* (New York: McGraw-Hill, 1969).

Malthus's earlier and later views on the relation between population growth and increase in the means of subsistence are found respectively in Thomas Robert Malthus, *Population: The First Essay* (Ann Arbor, Mich.: Ann Arbor Paperbacks, 1959), and "A Summary View of the Principle of

Population," in Thomas Malthus et al., *Three Essays on Population* (New York: Mentor Books, 1960), pp. 13–59. Other important volumes on the relation between population and resources are Harrison Brown, *The Challenge of Man's Future* (New York: Viking Press, 1954); Georg Borgstrom, *The Hungry Planet* (New York: Macmillan, 1965); Donella Meadows et al., *The Limits to Growth* (New York: Universe Books, 1972); *The World Food Problem: A Report of the President's Science Advisory Committee*, Vols. 1 and 2 (Washington, D. C.: The White House, 1967); and Alfred Sauvy, *General Theory of Population* (New York: Basic Books, 1969).

Important books on population distribution include John I. Clarke, *Population Geography* (Oxford: Pergamon Press, 1965); Philip M. Hauser and Leo F. Schnore, eds., *The Study of Urbanization* (New York: John Wiley, 1965); and Gerald Breese *Urbanization in Newly Developing Countries* (Englewood Cliffs, N.J.: Prentice-Hall, 1966).

Two of the important works on mortality are Louis I. Dublin et al., *Length of Life: A Study of the Life Table* (New York: Ronald Press, 1949), and *Population Bulletin of the United Nations*, No. 6 (1962). Social class differences in mortality are considered thoroughly in Evelyn M. Kitagawa and Philip M. Hauser, *Differential Mortality in the United States* (Cambridge, Mass.: Harvard University Press, 1973). David M. Heer's *After Nuclear Attack: A Demographic Inquiry* (New York: Praeger, 1965) describes some of the consequences of hypothetical population losses in the United States during and as a result of a nuclear war.

Among the many important works concerned with fertility and family planning are *Population Bulletin of the United Nations*, No. 7 (1965); Wilson H. Grabill et al., *The Fertility of American Women* (New York: John Wiley, 1958); Charles F. Westoff et al., *Family Growth in Metropolitan America* (Princeton, N.J.: Princeton University Press, 1961); Norman E. Himes, *Medical History of Contraception* (New York: Gamut Press, 1963); Bernard Berelson, ed., *Family Planning and Population Programs* (Chicago, Ill.: University of Chicago Press, 1966); Pascal K. Whelpton, et al., *Fertility and Family Planning in the United States* (Princeton, N.J.: Princeton University Press, 1966); Clyde V. Kiser et al., *Trends and Variations in Fertility in the United States* (Cambridge, Mass.: Harvard University Press, 1968; Ronald Freedman and John Takeshita, *Family Planning in Taiwan* (Princeton, N.J.: Princeton University Press, 1969; S. J. Behrman et al., *Fertility and Family Planning: A World View* (Ann Arbor, Mich.: University of Michigan Press, 1970);

Stanley Johnson, *Life without Birth* (Boston, Mass.: Little, Brown and Co., 1970); Larry Bumpass and Charles Westoff, *The Later Years of Childbearing* (Princeton, N.J.: Princeton University Press, 1971); and Norman Ryder and Charles Westoff, *Reproduction in the United States: 1965* (Princeton, N.J.: Princeton University Press, 1971).

Among the major books on migration are Marcus Lee Hansen, *The Atlantic Migration, 1607–1860: A History of the Continuing Settlement of the United States* (Cambridge, Mass.: Harvard University Press, 1941); Everett S. Lee et al., *Population Redistribution and Economic Growth: United States, 1870 to 1950*, Vols. 1, 2, and 3 (Philadelphia: American Philosophical Society, 1957, 1960, and 1964); and Henry S. Shyrock, Jr., *Population Mobility within the United States* (Chicago, Ill.: Community and Family Study Center, University of Chicago, 1964).

The most significant book on the relation between population growth and economic development is Ansley J. Coale and Edgar M. Hoover, *Population Growth and Economic Development in Low-Income Countries* (Princeton, N.J.: Princeton University Press, 1958). Other important discussions are found in Harvey Leibenstein, *Economic Backwardness and Economic Growth* (New York: John Wiley, 1957), and Stephen Enke, *Economics for Development* (Englewood Cliffs, N.J.: Prentice-Hall, 1963).

The relation between population and political power is most extensively discussed in Katherine Organski and A. F. K. Organski, *Population and World Power* (New York: Alfred A. Knopf, 1961). The most comprehensive discussion of European population policies is David V. Glass, *Population Policies and Movements* (Oxford: Clarendon Press, 1940). Important viewpoints concerning population policy for the United States are contained in The Commission on Population Growth and the American Future, *Population Growth and the American Future* (Washington, D.C.: Government Printing Office, 1972).

Major studies of national populations include Kingsley Davis, *The Population of India and Pakistan* (Princeton, N.J.: Princeton University Press, 1951); Irene B. Taeuber, *The Population of Japan* (Princeton, N.J.: Princeton University Press, 1958); Frank Lorimer, *The Population of the Soviet Union: History and Prospects* (Geneva: League of Nations, 1946); Donald J. Bogue, *The Population of the United States* (New York: The Free Press, 1959); Irene B. Taeuber and Conrad Taeuber, *People of the United States in the 20th Century* (Washington, D.C.:

Government Printing Office, 1971); and Leo Orleans, *Every Fifth Child: The Population of China* (Stanford, Calif.: Stanford University Press, 1972).

Three of the chief works on demographic methodology are George W. Barclay, *Techniques of Population Analysis* (New York: John Wiley, 1958); Mortimer Spiegelman, *Introduction to Demography*, rev. ed. (Cambridge, Mass.: Harvard University Press, 1968); and Henry S. Shryock, Jacob A. Siegel, and associates, *The Methods and Materials of Demography*, Vol. I and II (Washington, D.C.: Government Printing Office, 1971).

The most important English-language periodicals devoting all or most of their contents to population are *Demography, Population Index, Population Studies, Social Biology, Studies in Family Planning, Family Planning Perspectives, International Migration Review, Population Bulletin of the United Nations, United Nations Demographic Yearbook,* and the *Current Population Reports* of the U.S. Bureau of the Census.

INDEX

F

Family
mortality decline and,   57
religion and,   125
Family-allowance program,   130–32, 136
Family and Kinship in East London (Young and Willmott),   40
Family planning,   132, 134–36, 141–42. *See also* Contraception
Famine,   52
Feather River project,   23
Fertility,   18–20, 59–86, 107–8, 115–19, 141–42. *See also* Birth rate(s); Reproduction
age-specific birth rates,   60–61, 104–5
comparison of in different populations,   60, 62–65
differentials,   60, 62–68, 75
economic development and,   13–16, 116–17
ethnic groups and,   67, 125
general fertility rate,   60
gross reproduction rate,   60–61, 63, 76
in Hutterite community,   11, 62–63
income and,   63–67, 75, 117–18
industrialization and,   14–15
involuntary causes, affected by,   70–72
of Jews,   62, 125
legislation and,   129–37
measurement of,   59–62
mechanisms affecting,   68–73
men,   59–61, 66, 70
period total rate,   61
religion and,   67–77
social class differences in,   65–66, 136–37
in stable population,   104–5
total rate,   60–62
urbanization and,   14–15, 64–66
voluntary causes, affected by,   69–73
women,   11, 59–67, 70
Finland, rate of population growth,   5
Fleming, Sir Alexander,   55
Food,   19–25. *See also* Subsistence, means of
animal sources,   23
increase in production of,   19, 20, 24–25
marine sources,   24
urbanization and,   35
Ford, Henry,   112
Fossil fuels,   9, 25–26, 114
France
abortion,   73
family allowance program,   130–31
medical care,   128
pro-natalist policy,   124, 130, 132

G

Galton, Francis,   80
Genetics,   79–83
Genovese, Catherine,   41
Germany, importance of potato to,   9. *See also* East Germany; West Germany
Glass, David V.,   129
Goldschmidt, Walter,   7
Gorer, Geoffrey,   56
Great Britain
abortion,   73, 132
energy,   114
fertility,   15
importance of potato to,   9
medical care,   128
rate of population growth,   5
transport relationships,   32
Greece, fertility in,   63
Guatemala, nutrition in,   52–53

H

Health education,   52–55
Hill-Burton Act,   128
Hirschman, Albert O.,   118–19
Hominidae,   3, 4, 8. *See also* Man, definition of
Homo sapiens,   3, 4. *See also* Man, definition of
Hoover, Edgar M.,   115, 117
Hungary
abortion,   73
rate of population growth,   5
Hutterites,   11, 62–63

I

Immigration,   89–95, 137–38, 140. *See also* Migration
Immunization,   52, 54
Incaparina,   24, 52–53, 55
Income
decision to have children and,   74–75
fertility and,   63–67, 75, 117–18
per capita, nation's power and,   122–24
suburbanization and,   37
Income-tax laws, 133
India
age at marriage in,   69
crude death-rate, decline of,   51–52
energy,   114
expectation of life at birth,   51
family planning,   134–35, 141
fertility,   63, 118
groundwater,   22
income per capita,   124
land per capita,   114

XCOM 2

RESURRECTION

RESURRECTION

GREG KEYES

INSIGHT
EDITIONS

San Rafael, California

Dedicated to my brother-in-arms,
Charles Lawton Williams.

PROLOGUE

"OUR SATELLITES CAME down like so many shooting stars," he told Ivan. "What few we managed to get up in the first place. We had no idea what we were dealing with."

"But you tried," Ivan said. "You fought."

He dredged up a rasping, humorless chuckle. "Yes. We fought. And most of us died."

He regarded Ivan critically across the crate that served as his dinner table. The battered lawn chair and three-legged stool he and Ivan were perched on rounded out his wealth in furniture, unless you counted the ragged futon in the clapboard-and-sheet-metal shack behind him.

Ivan seemed very young, very enthusiastic. So much so that at first he worried the fellow was acting, was another collaborator tracking down what little remained of XCOM. But there was something about him that was convincing.

Besides, he didn't have much to lose. If Ivan wasn't what he seemed— well, he wasn't going to be taken alive. And it would be over.

He took another drink of what he charitably thought of as whiskey. He remembered a time when he had savored a good Highland single malt or American rye. Back then, he would spend half an hour sipping a single shot. Now, he had to make do with whatever rotgut he could find. But then again, these days he only cared about the impact of the drink.

"What do you want from me, son?" he asked.

"There are many like me," Ivan said. "Many with the will to fight the aliens, to win our world back. But we need leaders, men and women who were there. Yes, the aliens beat you, but—"

"The aliens didn't beat us," he snapped, half-surprised at his own sudden anger. Still inside of him, after all these years and a determined campaign to deaden it.

"Sir?"

He took another drink, a long one.

"So you have people willing to fight," he said. "That's great. But you need much more than that. We had it all—an international coalition to fund us, the best scientists and engineers in the world, highly trained soldiers, air-craft, excellent leaders—everything. We shot two of them down; did you know that?"

"No, sir," Ivan said.

"Well, we did. We were making headway on cracking their technology, developing the tools we needed to beat them. Our losses were heavy, yes, but we believed we had a chance. I believed."

"Then . . . what happened?" Ivan asked.

"The coalition caved on us, that's what. Gave us up. I'm not sure which country went first—it's not like they did it to our faces. But in the end they cut us off. The aliens hit our headquarters and major facilities in a coordi-nated strike. Someone gave them our locations."

"Why?"

"Panic," he grunted, taking another drink. "They were afraid that if we kept fighting, the aliens would exterminate us all."

"Do you think they would have?" Ivan asked.

He snorted. "They could have done that from the beginning. Instead they were conducting small raids, abducting people, spreading fear. I think they got exactly what they were after. A compliant population of sheep."

"I'm no sheep, sir," Ivan said. "My comrades aren't sheep. My father was an XCOM squaddie. He died fighting them in Minsk."

"What was his name, your father?"

"Sasha Fedorov."

"I remember him. He was a good man."

"I didn't know him," Ivan said. "I was still in my mother's womb when he died."

Ivan hesitated for a moment, seeming to sit up straighter in his seat. "Sir, will you help us?"

"Haven't you been listening? We had all of Earth's resources at our fingertips. And we lost. What have you got?"

"Heart, sir. Determination."

"Heart. Determination. That and this bottle of whiskey might be able to get you drunk enough to forget the whole thing. Ninety percent of the human race is perfectly fine with the way things are now. More than fine, from what I can tell. Who are you even fighting for?"

"The abductions haven't stopped, sir," Ivan said. "Thousands go missing every year."

"Right. he said wryly, "And for the most part—you call yourselves 'Natives,' right? You get the blame for that. The people swallow that right along with the rest of ADVENT propaganda and that god-awful stuff they're feeding people now."

"CORE, sir."

"Yeah. CORE. 'Reclaimed protein'. That should raise a few eyebrows. Reclaimed from what? But it doesn't. People eat it. And those weird vegetables . . ." he shook his head.

"There are more of us than you think," Ivan said. "And many more who just need a little hope. You can give them that hope, sir."

"No," he said. "I can't. Because there isn't any. The war ended twenty years ago. More people head into the New Cities every day." He took another swallow. "Now kindly get the hell out of here. I'm bored with this conversation."

"It took me a long time to find you, sir," Ivan said.

"Yes, thanks for that," he said. "It means I have to move again. Go. Leave all of this. I'm not asking again."

Ivan reluctantly stood, and for a moment the young man looked just like his father from almost two decades earlier.

For an instant, something hitched within him, and he remembered how he'd felt back then.

The pride. The purpose.

The Commander.

It was a fuzzy memory, and as he watched Ivan disappear into the Peruvian cloud forest, he began taking larger gulps in the hopes of eras-ing it entirely.

Part I
Natives

"From what little I've seen of their technology . . . if the aliens were intent on conquering Earth, there's not much we could do to stop them. I'm guessing they have something else in mind."

—DR. RAYMOND SHEN, XCOM CHIEF ENGINEER

CHAPTER 1

AMAR JERKED BACK reflexively as a ferromagnetic slug translated a few cubic centimeters of concrete wall into vapor and white-hot spalls that scattered tiny plumes of smoke on his body armor. He'd gotten a glimpse of her position, though. At least it looked like a "her."

His earphone crackled.

"KB?" It was Thomas, his squad leader.

"Heartbroken, Chief," Amar replied, wiping the sweat trickling down from his unkempt mop of black hair. "I thought she was the one, but she's just like all the others—trying to kill me on the first date. About thirty meters, Chief, and I think another one over your way."

"That's a damn ugly woman if you ask me," piped up another voice. That was Rider, off to his left. "You're better off without her. Kakking jabbers. What're they doing way out here?"

"There are at least six of them," Thomas said. "We need to roll up this side before they can encircle us."

"I've got you covered, KB," Rider said. Playtime was over.

"Moving up," he said.

Rider's assault rifle started chattering, and Amar slipped from behind the wall, hammering across the kudzu-covered concrete toward a pile of overgrown rubble. He was almost there when Rider's fire stuttered off, and an armored head appeared from the other side of the debris. He yelped and dove, but then Rider fired again. He heard the telltale sound of a bullet striking metal as he squatted.

"Took the bait," Rider said. "Don't know if she's down."

"Took the bait?" Amar yelped indignantly. "I was the bait! You used me for bait!"

"Damn fine bait, too," she replied.

Off to his right, he heard Chitto's shotgun boom once, twice. Then a general conversation of arms began.

Amar took a deep breath, let it out, and jumped up.

The jabber was waiting for him. He heard the whine of the mag rifle firing even as he pulled the trigger. In that very long moment, he saw Rider's shot had glanced from the black, insectile mask, scoring it deeply. He saw the muzzle of the magnetic rifle pulling into line with him and holes appearing in the jabber's armored chest as his weapon spit bullets into it.

Then he was standing there, looking at a dead jabber.

"Jabber" wasn't what they called themselves, of course, or what most people called them. To the majority of people on Earth, they were ADVENT police, peacekeepers, protectors. Supposedly they were citizen volunteers, but Amar had never known anyone who had volunteered. He had never met anyone who knew anyone who had volunteered. And they spoke an odd language amongst themselves that wasn't Hindi or German or Malay or—according to Chitto—Choctaw or any other Earthly language. Which was why Amar and his squad called them jabbers.

As Amar watched, the mag rifle exploded. It wasn't much of an explosion—no danger to him—but the weapon was now useless. They always did that, which was too bad. It would be nice to have one of the damned things. Or better, a few hundred.

"KB?" Rider asked.

"Got her," he said, feeling his pulse beating in his temples. His fingers were starting to tremble. So close . . . "You rang her bell pretty good," he said. "Couldn't draw a bead on me."

"You're welcome," she said.

"Come join the party."

He glanced back quickly and saw her slip over to his right and up.

"I'll just—" she began, then yelped, "*Chips!*"

"Rider? What is it?"

He looked over his shoulder and saw Rider spin to her right. As she fired, a red burst from a mag rifle slammed into her chest. She dropped and rolled behind the remains of a wall, her breath whistling over the radio connection.

"Rider!" Everything seemed to shine with a peculiar golden light. Rider couldn't be shot. She'd never been shot. Not even a scratch, in the three years he had known her. Luckiest person in the squad.

"KB?" Thomas demanded. "What's happening?"

He saw Rider's assailants now, two of them, advancing quickly toward her position.

Thomas's headcount had missed some—not surprising given that these guys had had plenty of time to get in place as they arrived, and that all the kudzu and honeysuckle made things thicker than the jungle he had grown up in.

There were more out ahead of him. If he turned his back to help Rider . . .

He didn't have a choice.

"Falling back, Chief," he said.

He fired at the oncoming troopers as he ran for Rider's position. One looked like the trooper he'd just taken down, clad in mostly black armor with a little red on his mandible. The other was bigger, heavier, a walking shield. It projected a faintly luminous energy field that the smaller trooper took care to remain within.

Amar hit the shield bearer three or four times without apparent effect. Mag rounds jetted past him as he ducked down with Rider.

She was panting heavily, and her eyes were wide. The projectile had pierced her armor, but there was no blood—the heat had cauterized the wound, which looked terribly deep. Her always-pale complexion was now bone white, and sweat plastered stray strands of red-gold hair to her forehead.

"*Verdamme*," she gasped. "That's gonna sting in the morning."

"Just stay down," he said. He peeked over the wall and was greeted by another blast. He shifted and fired again, but they kept coming on. He needed to grab Rider and retreat, find a more defensible spot. . . .

Too late he realized that Rider had staggered to her feet and was trying to flank the shield bearer to get a clear shot at the trooper.

19

"Rider!" he yelled.

"I'm dead already, KB," she shouted. She took her shot but was drilled by mags once, twice. She and the trooper dropped almost simultaneously.

"So there, son of a bitch," she said. Or at least he thought that's what she said. It was so faint. . . .

No, no, no! She was okay. DeLao could patch her up. He just had to take care of this thing. . . .

Amar emptied his clip into the shield bearer, scrambling back, watching it take aim, knowing he was next and there was nothing he could do about it.

Then it rocked back. Amar saw a neat hole had appeared in its mask before it collapsed.

"Toby?" he gasped.

"Yes," the sniper replied. "You're clear on the right. More bad guys up ahead, though. I've got a captain at one o'clock."

"Thank you," he said. "Rider—"

"I saw," he said. "Busy now."

Amar scrambled over the debris to where Rider had crumpled to the ground.

She wasn't okay, and DeLao was not going to patch her up. There was no longer a soul behind Rider's sapphire eyes.

His throat tightened. Rider had been in the squad when he joined it two years ago. She was sarcastic and funny and profane and sometimes a real pain in the ass. She told wild stories about her youth in Utrecht; she was a terrible singer but insisted on singing anyway. She was fiercely loyal to her friends.

And suddenly she wasn't any of that.

Deal with it later. Or die now.

He ran back up to his previous forward position.

"Chitto," he heard Thomas say. "You're with KB now."

That was bad news. Chitto was as green as they came. This was the first action she had seen, and nothing about her suggested to him that she was up to the job.

"Yes, Chief," Chitto said. He thought he heard a quiver in her voice.

He noticed another jabber trying to move around.

"Oh, no," he whispered, furious. "You most certainly do *not.*"

***

Amar's chronometer said the skirmish lasted just over an hour, but it felt like twenty by the time the last shots were fired and the squad began cautiously sweeping the area to make certain all of the ADVENT forces were dead. His arms felt like lead, and his knee hurt like hell, though he couldn't remember how he'd banged it.

When Thomas was satisfied, she called them to rest. They had walked into the situation with eight soldiers; now they were seven.

It could have been much worse.

But that didn't make him feel any better about Rider. He kept expecting for her to walk up, clap him on the shoulder, and ask how badly he had soiled himself this time.

Now that he had the opportunity to have a leisurely look around, Amar realized that the rubble they had been fighting in was the bombed-out ruin of some sort of complex. About a fourth of the main structure was still standing, two walls forming a corner and a roof. The guts of the three-storied building were open to the air. All of it was blanketed in a sea of vines and leaves.

The squad had been on its way to Gulf City to raid for supplies when Captain Thomas had heard a faint signal on her radio. It was an SOS, in the current code, and the source of the transmission was nearby, so they had followed it. The signal had abruptly gone quiet just before they came under fire.

"The question is," Thomas said, "whether the signal was legitimate or whether it was sent to lure us here."

Thomas was the real veteran of the group. She'd fought with XCOM back in the day, which he figured probably put her at about forty. She had blunt features and dirty blond hair pulled back into a braid, but she kept a few centimeters of her forehead shaved. She had a burn scar on one cheek and was missing half of her left ear. He had seen her take down a jabber with nothing but a knife.

"If it was a trap," Toby said, a frown on his dark features, "that's pretty bad news. It means they've broken our encryption."

"Well," Thomas said, "why don't we just go see? We don't have that long before dark. I'm guessing the signal came from over there." She gestured at the remains of the building.

He heard DeLao groan. Amar knew why—he didn't feel like taking another step, either.

"Arthritis acting up, old fellow?" Amar said, trying to lighten the mood, as he usually did. But it came out weird and flat, and he wished he hadn't said anything.

***

As they moved up to the battered structure, they encountered a few more dead jabbers. Amar prodded one of them and rolled it over, making certain it was dead.

Even in the oppressive heat, he felt frost on his spine.

The trooper's mask had come off—whether she had pulled it off while dying or the force of the explosion that killed her had loosened its fastenings, he couldn't tell. But he could see her face.

The lower part of her face looked human—her lips and cheekbones were familiar enough. Her nose was broad, with very little separation from her forehead, but was still within the realm of human variation. But her ears were oddly flattened against her hairless skull, and there was nothing at all human about her large, silvery eyes. They were set too far apart, almost on the sides of her head, and contained no orbs or pupils.

He felt like he was going to vomit.

For twenty years the aliens had been playing with human DNA. This was one result. Had she begun life as fully human and then been altered?

No one could be sure about that.

***

When they reached the ruin and entered the only passable hall, they started finding equally dead humans.

They'd made a stand here, obviously, and given their numbers and those of the enemy dead, they had fought well.

To his relief, Amar didn't recognize any of them. They were armed and armored in the same ragtag fashion as his bunch, at least at first glance, wearing whatever ancient bits of body armor they could find and filling the gaps in their gear with patches of Kevlar, cold hammered sheet metal—whatever was at hand. Most of their weapons were decades old.

But upon closer inspection, these guys looked as if they had new gear. New as in months old instead of twenty years.

Still, it hadn't saved them.

"This one's alive!" DeLao said, kneeling and reversing the Mexico City Red Devils cap that held his frizzy brown hair in check.

The man was sitting, propped against a wall just past a turn in the corridor. He was alive, but only barely so. DeLao already had his medical kit out, but Amar doubted they could do much for the fellow beyond easing his pain.

Thomas knelt next to DeLao.

"What happened here, son?" she asked the soldier. "What's your name?"

He looked up at her with pale gray eyes. His lips moved, but nothing came out.

"Here's another live one," Chitto said. Her voice was quiet—she was always quiet. She had moved farther down the hall—too far, actually. She had a frown on her round face, and her wide lips were pressed tight. To Amar, she looked as if she might lose it at any moment.

They had picked Chitto up in an illegal settlement in a contagion zone just a few days before. The squad had been on another mission but ran across her people being rounded up by ADVENT troopers. After they finished off the jabbers, Chitto had asked if she could volunteer. Thomas said yes, and the plan was to take her to a haven for training. Instead, like a bad dream, trouble kept finding them, drawing them farther and farther from their intended goal.

"Wait for the rest of us, Chitto," Amar said, cautiously moving up to her position. "We have to watch each other's backs. You can't just wander off when I think you're in place."

"Yeah, okay," she said.

Amar looked down at the man she'd found.

The fellow was young and wiry, with narrow, pleasant features, and he was unconscious. He wasn't wearing any armor, and he didn't seem to actually be wounded. The cause of his insensible state was likely the dead ADVENT soldier a few feet away who had been armed with a stun lance, the weapon used to break up crowds and protesters—and to take live prisoners. It looked something like a sabre or a long billy club with a knuckle guard and could deliver a powerful neurological shock.

"Hey, buddy," Amar said, kneeling and patting his cheek.

The man stirred and, with a little more encouragement, opened his eyes, which were pale blue.

"What's . . . what's going on?" he asked. He had a slight accent that Amar guessed was probably Scottish.

"That's what we're wondering," Thomas said, as she arrived. Dux lumbered back to the rear, while Nishimura padded lithely to the end of the corridor. Even in her armor Nishimura seemed tiny, almost birdlike, but she was as deadly as anyone Amar had ever known—and far more dangerous than most.

"Sergei?" the man said, suddenly trying to sit up.

"If you mean the man down there, he didn't make it," Thomas told him, nodding at the young man DeLao had been working on.

The man closed his eyes and sighed.

"That's unfortunate," he said. "Did anyone else . . ." He looked around at them. Thomas shook her head.

"They're all dead," she said.

He seemed to absorb that for a moment, his lips pressed together hard enough to turn white. His Adam's apple bobbed.

"Who are you guys?" he finally asked.

"We picked up an SOS," Thomas said, instead of answering his question. Her blue-eyed gaze stayed steady on the fellow.

"Yeah, that was me," he told her. "I managed to rig up a spark-gap generator and use the steel beams in the compound as an antenna. It didn't have much range, but more than our short-range units at least. You must have been close." His eyes shifted. "You broke the encryption. You're Natives."

"Holly Thomas," the Chief said. "We're out of Felix, at least for the moment."

Felix was the code name for their base. She waited to see what his reaction would be.

"Felix," Sam said. "Outside of Gulf City. I've heard of you guys. Hacked their propaganda system, right?"

"Well, that was our tinkers," Thomas said. "We're more on the shoot-and-loot end of the business."

"Lucky for me," he said. "You can call me Sam. But I can't tell you my cell. It's classified."

"What are you doing here, Sam?" She gestured at the dead trooper. "What were *they* doing here?"

"I'm an analyst," he said, as if that explained everything. He slowly stood up. "This is an old XCOM facility. Not one of the larger ones. I came here looking for data."

"Data," Thomas repeated, dubiously.

"The central facility was destroyed," he said. "Utterly. Pulverized into dust and then blasted again for good measure. But XCOM wasn't stupid enough to keep all of their eggs in one basket. Or, in this case, data in one mainframe. They had backup servers in a closed network. A private mini-cloud. One of the servers was here. Or rather, beneath here. We had just discovered the way down when the ADVENT attack began."

"How did they find you?" Thomas asked.

"I wish I knew," he said. "Colonel Dixon and the rest—they killed the first bunch, but when it was over, Dixon was dead, and there were only five of us left. By the time I found what we came for, reinforcements had shown up and penned us in. I rigged the radio, and we tried to hold them off for as long as we could. Then it got down to just Sergei and me. The cuss there with the stun lance did me." He nodded at the dead trooper. "Did you guys get him?"

"He was dead when we got here," Thomas said.

"Must have been Sergei, then," Sam said. "You must have shown up in the nick of time." His face fell, and he glanced down the hall at his fallen comrades. "For me, anyway."

"We were ambushed," Amar said, starting to feel angry at Sam without knowing exactly why. "We lost someone."

"I'm sorry about that," Sam said. "But believe me, he didn't die in vain. None of them did."

"She," Amar corrected.

Nobody said anything for a moment. Sam stood there, looking uncomfortable.

"So you found something," Thomas said, breaking the silence.

"Yes," Sam said. "Something amazing. Something that will change everything."

"And what's that?" Thomas asked.

"I can't tell you," he said. "It's classified."

"Classified? Classified by who?" Thomas demanded.

"I can't—"

"Tell me that," she snapped. "Right." She turned away from Sam. "We need to roll, *now*. More reinforcements are probably on the way. Sam, you're coming with us. We'll drop you off at the closest refuge."

"No," Sam said, suddenly more animated. "No! You have to come with *me*! I have to show them what I found, or this really will have all been for nothing. I'll never survive on my own."

"No kidding," DeLao grunted.

Nishimura chuckled at that and pushed a few long, fine strands of black hair back up under the camouflage bandana she wore.

"We already have an assignment," Thomas explained, a bit impatiently.

"This is more important," Sam insisted.

"I have no way of judging that," Thomas shot back.

Sam pursed his lips and nodded.

"Fair enough," he said. "May I have a word with you in private, Captain?"

Thomas paused a minute, then gestured toward the outside of the building. Amar watched them walk out of earshot. They stood there for a moment and then came back.

"We're taking him," Thomas said.

"Why?" DeLao demanded. "What did he say?"

"A name," she replied. "Just a name."

CHAPTER 2

THE SQUAD HAD arrived on the scene in a battered Humvee and an ancient pickup truck. Both vehicles were now smoking wrecks, the first casualties of their encounter with the ADVENT.

The ADVENT soldiers had arrived in a flying transport, but as tempting as it seemed, experience had proven it was a bad idea to try and commandeer one. Their controls did not respond to human hands. On a few occasions, some very clever Natives had gotten around that using sophisticated hacking gear, at which point the vehicles had begun broadcasting a silent alarm and tracking signal, which on one occasion had led to the discovery and destruction of an entire resistance cell. The one instance Amar had ever heard of in which the tracking mechanism was disabled, the vehicle had instantly flared white-hot, vaporizing everyone inside and within ten meters of it. ADVENT weapons and armor were equally useless once separated from their bearers.

So they left the transport alone and double-timed it out of there on foot. Amar tried not to think of Rider lying in the kudzu, cold and alone, but if they stayed long enough to bury her, they would likely need burying themselves. In any case, the ADVENT would return her and the other dead humans to their next of kin using DNA analysis, along with a heaping dose of propaganda concerning what had happened to them. The aliens liked things tidy.

**

They alternated between a fast walk and a slow run, following the cracked asphalt of an old state road through what had once been pasture and fields but were now twenty years along toward becoming forest. The aliens had returned much of the world to wilderness, luring most of the population into the New Cities they built on the ruins of the ones they had razed in the conquest.

Vast areas between the population centers were closed to human traffic, and entry into them was forbidden due to something the aliens rather loosely called the *contagion*. Whether it was a disease or some sort of bioagent or nothing of the kind wasn't known to the resistance. Yet, whatever it was, the aliens were scared of it. The road they were on was just inside one of the forbidden areas, and as night fell, Amar felt the presence of the unknown lurking somewhere in the darkness.

When it was finally full night, they slowed to an easier pace. The moon rose, a little more than half full, so they didn't need to use their torches. Night birds called in the distance as frogs and insects provided a chorus.

"KB, right?"

Amar had seen Sam coming up from the corner of his eye, so he wasn't surprised. But he wasn't pleased, either.

"Amar," he corrected. "I'm KB to my friends."

Sam's cheerful expression didn't falter.

"Okay, Amar," he said. "Look, I really am sorry about Rider."

So he had asked someone who had died. That was something at least. But Amar still had a bitter taste in his mouth.

"Yeah," Amar said. "But it was totally worth it, right?"

"I didn't mean to be glib," Sam said. "Dixon, Sergei, those guys with me— they knew what we were doing. They understood the risks and the possible gains. You guys didn't. You were just trying to help someone you didn't know. That was noble. I'm sorry any of you suffered for it."

"Yet you've drafted us to go along with you and still won't tell us why."

"I wish I had the authority," he said. "Thomas understands."

"Yeah," Amar replied.

He hoped Sam would go away, then, but he continued to walk beside him.

"So help me out," Sam said, after a moment. "I didn't know Rider, but I'd like to know who I'm with now. Thomas isn't all that talkative. I was hoping you could fill me in."

"I'm not all that talkative, either," Amar said. "And I'm not a social director." He instantly regretted it—the fellow seemed sincere enough. And he knew what Rider would have done.

But Sam was finally getting the message and dropping back.

Damn it, Amar thought.

"Well," he said, lifting his chin toward Chitto, only a few meters away. "That's Kathy Chitto, some fresh meat we picked up in—what's that place called, Chitto?"

Chitto turned her broad face toward him. She had what his mother would call a moon-face, with dark, expressive eyes. Her jet black hair was cut short, with bangs in the front. She was on the short side, with broad shoulders.

"Conehatta," she replied.

Sam nodded as he caught back up.

"Right," Amar said. "Just a few days from here. We were headed up to—" He stopped abruptly. They hadn't discussed how much to tell this guy about their own operations.

Sam was studying Chitto's moonlit features.

"Are you a Native American?" he asked.

"I'm a Native," Chitto said. "Like you."

"Sure," Sam said. "But—"

"Choctaw," she said with a sigh. "Okay?"

"Noted," Sam said.

Amar wondered if he had misjudged Chitto. Her reply to Sam was the nearest thing to grit he had seen from her.

Amar pointed ahead. "Tomas DeLao, the guy with the baseball hat and crooked nose—he's from Acapulco. Trained as a physician before he fell in with the resistance. The tall, very dark guy that looks like he has a bowl on his head is Toby Ayele. Born in Israel but grew up mostly in North American shantytowns. Sharpshooter. Stay on his good side, or you'll never hear the bullet. The red-headed ogre next to DeLao is Blake Duckworth, but we just call him Dux, which he likes because it's apparently the Latin word for 'duke.' He won't say where he's from, for some reason. He sounds American, though, maybe Midwestern. The woman on point is Alejandra Nishimura, from one of the settlements outside of New Lima."

"And there's you."

"There's me," Amar allowed. "Mama Tan's little boy."

"So why do they call you KB? What's that?"

"Kampung boy," he replied.

Sam stared at him blankly.

"Kampung is what we call the settlements in Malaysia," Amar explained. "A kampung boy is someone who grew up in a kampung. It can mean salt of the earth—or something like a redneck or a hick, depending on who's saying it."

"Got it," Sam said.

"There was this famous cartoon, years ago—"

He broke off as Nishimura raised her hand to signal a halt, then pointed to cover. Amar ducked into the thorny scrub on the side of the road, double-checking his weapon.

For a long, still moment, Amar didn't hear anything but an owl in the distance and the steady whir of crickets. But then, as the quiet settled, he made out the very faint tinny sound of amplified speech, punctuated by a sort of rushing noise.

After a moment he saw Toby stand, raise his rifle, and put his eye to the scope. Then Thomas and Nishimura appeared beside him. They all gazed off in the same direction as Toby. Thomas gestured for the rest to move up.

The landscape was almost uniformly flat, but here and there small slopes developed, the remnants of natural levees formed by the river's flooding. From that slight elevation, looking beyond the still water of an oxbow lake, Amar saw a line of orange flame. As he watched, a jet of fire appeared and set more trees to burning. A second spume of liquid fire jetted at the other end of the line, and another.

"It's ADVENT," Toby said. "I can make their silhouettes out through my scope."

"Yeah," Dux said. "But what the hell are they burning? And why in the middle of the night?"

"Maybe it's something that only comes out at night," Chitto murmured, more to herself than to the rest of them.

"The contagion?" DeLao whispered.

"Doesn't matter," Thomas said. "That's not our mission. Come on, let's move out."

They continued on, and soon the flames were no longer visible. But the wind shifted and brought with it the scent of burning wood.

And something else. Amar didn't know what it was, but it wasn't like anything he'd ever smelled before.

The night was good cover, but he was glad when the sun came back up.

***

Around midday Thomas called a halt next to the remains of a country store that had probably been abandoned twenty years before the invasion. From any distance—and, importantly, from above—it looked like a mound of kudzu vines. Nishimura chopped through the creeping tendrils with the long, wickedly sharp blade that served as both her machete and sword, and they finally had a chance to rest.

"We're about a kilometer from the Greenville settlement," Thomas said. "Amar, Chitto, take an hour's rest. Then I need you to go down and see if it's safe. We need supplies, and we need vehicles."

"We have a contact there?" Amar asked.

"We do," she said. "I haven't been able to get through by radio, but that doesn't necessarily mean anything. Then again, it might, so be careful."

"I don't need to rest," Amar said. "I can go on in."

"Take a nap," Thomas said. "I don't need you all woozy-headed; I need you thinking straight."

He agreed, and using his backpack as a pillow, he fell asleep almost the moment his body came to rest on the rotting wood floor.

***

They were on patrol, back on the West Coast, almost a year ago. They were all together, joking, talking nonsense. DeLao was talking about this time a guy he knew set a slap-trap and then ended up tripping it himself that night when he got up to pee. Nishimura countered with a tale about a man who once tried to buy her from her mother for six chickens and some ice.

And then they fell strangely silent.

"This isn't right," Amar said. "Something is missing."

The others didn't reply. They just kept marching silently along.

"Really," Amar said. "There's supposed to another story. Something about rigging up a shoe—"

"It was a kakking boot," Rider said. "I set up a boot to swing down and kick my brother in the face when he opened the door."

"That's it!" he said. "Rider!"

"Who?" Nishimura asked, a puzzled expression on her delicate features.

"Rider," Amar insisted. "You know. She's right back there."

He turned to point, and there she was, her dead eyes looking at nothing, her mouth slightly ajar, gaping holes in her armor . . .

He jerked awake, panting wildly, unsure of where he was.

"Bloody hell," he grunted after a moment. Reluctantly, he lay back down, hoping for some dreamless sleep.

CHAPTER 3

AMAR DID NOT feel refreshed when Chitto woke him. He felt hungover without the benefit of actually having been drunk. But he rose and—casting a longing look at his weapons and armor—started out with her on the road to Greenville.

To most people, the New Cities seemed like a great deal. They were clean and neat, and they came with a whole list of benefits. No one went hungry in the cities. No one died of malaria or the flu or a random staph infection, and even the diseases of old age could be staved off with the advanced gene therapy that the aliens had developed. More people moved to the cities every day.

But the aliens didn't force anyone to move. And there were people who didn't care to move to the cities, who still didn't trust the aliens and their propaganda, who remembered that their planet had been taken by force. The independent, the stubborn, the paranoid; natural outsiders and clannish groups holding to themselves, like Chitto's people. All of these and more chose to live outside of the places the aliens had so carefully prepared.

And the aliens allowed it, so long as they didn't build their towns in forbidden areas. But they did nothing to make life in the settlements easy or pleasant.

Parts of the old town still stood—the courthouse, a church here and there, an old strip mall. But most of the settlement was either recently constructed or had come in on wheels. Trailers and RVs accounted for much of the living space, some solitary, with their own little yards walled off, some formed into compounds. Shacks of sheet metal, chicken wire, bamboo, cinderblocks, and other sundry materials had been marshaled to form mostly simple, but sometimes weirdly complex structures. One house on the outskirts was entirely covered in Mardi Gras beads and small plastic dinosaurs, glued into elaborate but mysterious patterns. Mysterious to Amar, anyway. Another was surrounded by wind chimes made of tire irons and frying pans.

If nothing else, the settlements had personality.

Almost every roof sported solar arrays, so they had power. A sniff of the air, however, proved they weren't doing as well in the sanitation department.

To Amar it felt like home, even though his kampung was thousands of miles away, in a tropical climate, where people spoke different languages. While the details were dissimilar, the feel was the same. Settlement life was settlement life, wherever you were.

And the biggest fact of settlement life was the ADVENT. They appeared suddenly, often for no clear reason. They searched warm bodies and houses. They arrested people who were never seen again. Sometimes weeks would go by without a patrol showing up. Sometimes half a hundred would arrive and stay for two weeks.

Given the number he saw at the moment, it looked like the latter was happening here. Greenville was under full occupation.

"Well," Chitto said, "this doesn't look safe at all."

"Yeah," Amar said. "You want to wait here?"

She seemed to think it over.

"No," she finally said.

"Good," he said. "So if they question us, we've just come from your settlement—what is it again?"

"Conehatta," she said.

"Does that mean something?"

"Yes," she replied. "It means Gray Skunk."

"Izzit? That's kind of a funny name for a town."

She shrugged. "I didn't name it."

"So we're looking for a relative of yours," he said. "From Gray Skunk. Is that plausible?"

"We could be looking for my uncle John," she said. "He disappeared a while back."

"That'll work. Uncle John has a medical condition, and we're going to try to talk him into moving into Gulf City for treatment."

"He won't go," Chitto said.

"That doesn't matter," he said, starting to become impatient with her. "We just need a reason to—" He stopped when he saw the slightest curve of her wide mouth.

"Oh," he said. "You *do* have a sense of humor."

As they wound their way through the mazelike settlement, Amar began to feel naked without his armor and weapons, but they were looking to avoid attention, and humans weren't supposed to go around armed to the teeth—or at all, for that matter. Not unless they were ADVENT.

He tried not to look at the troopers for fear his expression would betray him. The memory of Rider's dead face was a raw wound within him, and he was afraid they might see that. Some of the ADVENT were said to be able to read minds, and although he was skeptical of that, it would be foolish to test that hypothesis at the moment. So he tried to think about kittens and flowers and move along as quickly as wouldn't seem suspicious.

Ahead, a few of the troopers were removing debris that had been placed in front of one of their billboards, which was scrolling images of beautiful, happy people living it up in Gulf City. Meanwhile an old woman was wailing as several jabbers dismantled the wall of old carpet she had erected to hide her chicken coop. Livestock of any sort was now illegal—supposedly something to do with the contagion—but that didn't stop people from trying to keep animals.

They reached their destination, an old Greyhound bus, without incident. Its windows were papered over, and COLD BEER was painted across the length of it in large block letters.

Inside it wasn't as dark as he had imagined it would be; the paper was translucent and of various colors, giving the place a sort of rainbow feel. The few characters hanging out on the stools at the bar, however, didn't have any rainbow connections whatsoever.

He and Chitto settled on two of the mismatched seats. The bartender, a young man with dreadlocks, dark skin, and darker tattoos glanced their way.

"Yeah?" he said.

"I guess I'd like a cold beer," Amar said.

The man didn't say anything, but he went to the single tap and filled a plastic cup. The cup bore streaks and patches of color on it suggesting it had once advertised something, probably a movie for kids. He poured the second beer into a mason jar.

"Who wants the fancy one?" he asked.

Amar pointed at Chitto, whereupon they learned that the "fancy one" was the mason jar.

The beer not only wasn't cold, but Amar wasn't sure it was even beer.

"I love a cold beer," he said. Then he waited to see how the man would respond.

The fellow stared at him for a second.

"That's about all we have right now," he said, nodding vaguely toward the front door. "You see how it is."

"Yeah," Amar said. He glanced at Chitto.

"So we're looking for her Uncle John," he told the man. "I don't guess he's been in here? John Warren."

He didn't know what her uncle's last name actually was, but Warren was their black market contact in Greenville.

"He was here," the man said. "He didn't like the beer."

"Do you know where he went?" Amar asked.

"How are you with directions?" the fellow said. "I don't have anything to write them down on."

"I can remember," Amar assured him.

"These directions are a little . . . redneck. Can you deal with that?"

Amar smiled. "I think so."

He listened carefully and then nodded.

"Thanks," he said.

"Don't forget to pay for the beer," the man said.

"Right." He reached into his pocket and plunked a small package on the counter. The bartender took it and quickly slipped it somewhere Amar couldn't see.

Back outside, the images on the billboard had changed. It now showed dead bodies, and with a growing sense of horror, Amar realized that they were the Natives who had been with Sam. They had been stripped of their armor and dressed in settlement-style clothing. He suddenly understood what was coming and tried to turn away, but it was too late. There was Rider in a faded denim jumper, crumpled among them.

". . . the work of unknown dissidents," the voiceover was saying.

Amar felt a wet sting in the corners of his eyes. The thought of them handling her, making her part of *this*, this lie . . . the indignity of it all . . .

"Let's get out of here," he rasped. "Now."

How he managed to hold it together until they were clear of ADVENT eyes he didn't know, but back in the woods he broke and wept like he hadn't since childhood. Chitto hung back, giving him a little space and making sure they weren't followed. When he thought he was capable of holding a conversation again, he waved her up.

"I think we're okay," she said. "Nobody behind us."

"Yeah. Thanks."

They walked in uncomfortable silence for a few moments, which Chitto uncharacteristically broke.

"Did you understand his directions?" she asked.

He tilted his head yes.

"He said to take a left at old man Renfro's back fence," she said, a little indignantly, "and to go about half a mile to the east of Tallaboga Creek."

"Don't your people give directions that way?" he asked.

"Sure, to people who grew up in the area and know where things like that are. Do you know where old man Renfro's back fence is?"

"No," he said. "It doesn't matter. That was all a smokescreen. Only the numbers were important. Third left, third right, third big tree, half a mile, nine-mile creek, first big pile of tires, and so on."

"Oh," she said. "Coordinates."

So she wasn't stupid. That was good.

"Exactly," he said.

"What did you give him for the beer?" she asked.

"Penicillin," he said. "Worth a lot on the black market."

"You trust him?"

"Trust is all we have," Amar replied. "Some of these guys have fewer scruples than others, but they're all businessmen. If you do bad business, word gets around and eventually you're not in business anymore. And they need us, too, to carry their goods through the more dangerous places or 'liberate supplies' from ADVENT outposts. So do I like that they gouge their own people? No. But with the aliens running things, it's the only economy the settlements have."

***

On foot, it took three days to reach their destination. This time, at least, they didn't walk into an ambush. ADVENT ground transports were quieter than internal combustion vehicles, but they still heard it coming in time to hide in the dense vegetation that crowded up to the road.

"This road only goes one place, so far as I can see," Thomas said. "I don't think it's a coincidence that ADVENT is here. What do you think, KB? Did he set us up?"

"I thought he was honest, Chief," he told Thomas. "If he wanted to turn us in, all he had to do was yell."

"Sure," DeLao said. "But then everyone in town would know where his loyalties lay. How safe would he be after the jabbers were gone?"

Thomas fingered the nub of her left ear, a sign that she was conflicted.

"Amar has pretty good instincts about this sort of thing," she finally said. "With this much ADVENT presence in the area, they may just be busting every illegal settlement they can find, and this place is definitely over the line." She shrugged. "We'll know when we get there."

There wasn't much to the place: part of a ruined corrugated metal building, four shipping containers that had been welded together to form a square, and a few smaller shacks arranged on what had once been a parking lot. Also in sight were two pickups, a minivan, and a pair of ADVENT ground transports. The troopers themselves didn't seem to be in any particular state of readiness. Four were visible, but there were likely more inside.

They were looking at all of this from the relatively dense forest surrounding the clearing.

"Toby, do you see a spot?" Thomas asked.

They were close to the river, and the landscape was flatter than ever. There were plenty of trees, though.

Toby had other ideas.

"Over there," he said, extending his lanky arm. "The bridge."

Amar hadn't spotted it, but now that the sharpshooter pointed it out, he could see the concrete supports. It wasn't the main bridge that crossed the river—that was gone—but rather a smaller one to take the road over swampy ground bordering the river.

"That's about three hundred meters," Thomas said.

"Yeah," Toby said. "That's about what I make it."

"Okay," Thomas said. "Go get in position. I can't spare anyone to watch your back."

"Understood," Toby said. He turned and trotted off through the woods.

"KB, Chitto," Thomas continued, "work your way around to the other side of the clearing, about eleven o'clock. When Toby's first target goes down, we'll lay down fire from here. Nishimura, you're over there at two o'clock. You all know the drill."

"Got it, Chief," Amar said.

Amar had barely settled into position when he heard a metallic thud and saw one of the troopers crumple almost gracefully to the ground. Predictably, the others scrambled for cover. Two ran directly into the rocket Dux launched at them. Two more turned and sprinted straight for him and Chitto, trying to get around behind the containers.

He was waiting for them to come into range when Chitto's shotgun boomed. The troopers, surprised but unhurt, unloaded into the trees. Amar ducked further behind the pine, but the mag rounds punched right through it.

Alamak, he gritted. *Bloody hell!*

He rolled out and opened up on the nearest, but both suddenly broke and ran toward transports. One of them went down like a sack, another victim of Toby's eagle eye, but the other made it and was joined by a couple from the building. One of them had the flattened helmet and red sash of a captain.

The door closed, and the vehicle jerked into motion. A grenade exploded next to it but didn't slow it down.

Amar stared after the retreating transport.

"What?" Chitto said.

"I've never seen them give up so easily," he said.

"Easily? We killed four of them."

"Yeah. And by the way, next time you're ready to give away our positions to the enemy, please wait until they're close enough for that boom stick to actually hurt them, okay?

She nodded, her round face darkening a little.

They moved up the container house.

Amar kept his weapon aimed at the front door, sure there had to be some trick in this, but then Nishimura stuck her head out.

"All clear," she said. "But there's someone in here."

CHAPTER 4

SHE WAS YOUNG, probably no more than twenty. Her light brown hair was clipped just below her ears, and she wore a belted yellow smock and dark green pants.

DeLao was already examining her, and Amar hoped she wasn't dead. She didn't look much like a smuggler, and he wondered what she was doing here.

"Gather supplies, quickly," Thomas said. "DeLao, what about her?"

"She's fine," he said. "It looks like they gave her something to make her go night-night."

"Do you think they were abducting her?" Thomas asked.

DeLao shrugged. "I don't think they were escorting her to the prom. I might know more when I finish examining her. What I can tell you—"

"Tell me later, if she's not about to explode or something. We've got to acquire supplies and get out of here before those others set up an ambush or call in an air strike or whatever it is they're up to. I don't trust this situation. Make her comfortable in the van. Amar, she's your charge."

"Right, Chief," he responded, wondering how he had somehow become the point man for rookies and the unconscious.

It took less than half an hour to get the vehicles packed up and on the road. The bridge that had once crossed the river wasn't there anymore. During the invasion, the aliens had blown every bridge they came across to limit ground transportation, and most of them hadn't been rebuilt, because ADVENT was still very much invested in controlling transportation and movement. They likewise destroyed rail systems, although in that case they had replaced some of them with their own trains. If they went south, they would be heading toward Gulf City and probably the other ADVENT vehicle, which wasn't at all in their best interest. According to Sam, southwest was the direction they ultimately wanted to go, but they couldn't until they found a river crossing. There was a rumor that someone was running a ferry over to Helena, and that was north, and so north they went, across miles of more flat delta landscape, through the rusting and rotting remains of towns that had been on the wane even before the aliens declared the area off-limits.

They had been on the road less than an hour when the girl awoke with a scream. She was lying on the backseat behind him, her eyes pitching around the interior of the van.

"Hey," Amar said. "Calm down. You're okay."

She sat up, but her gaze kept shifting, settling briefly on Chitto, DeLao, and Dux, who was driving, before returning to him. He noticed she was feeling the back of her shoulder and wincing.

"What happened?" she asked. She had a deeper voice than he had expected. Throaty. "Where am I?" Her eyes were a really startling green color, like jade.

"We found you at a smugglers' compound," he replied. "You were kind of out of it. Do you remember how you got there?"

Her eyes widened. "Smugglers' compound?" She shook her head. "I don't remember anything like that." She frowned. "You're not smugglers, are you?"

"No," Amar said, although he knew that was not entirely true. Why make things complicated? She needed reassurance.

"So what's the last thing you remember?" he pressed, gently

"I was in Greenville," she said. "That's a settlement."

"I know," Amar replied. "I've been there."

"I went into this bar—the one in the bus. Do you know it?"

Amar told her he did.

Her eyebrows scrunched together. "Maybe I drank too much," she said. "Or maybe . . ." She suddenly looked horrified. "These smugglers," she said, "do they . . ."

"Traffic in humans?" Amar finished. "No. That doesn't happen, ADVENT propaganda to the contrary."

"Unh-unh," DeLao shot back from the front. "It wasn't about that. Check your left shoulder."

"It hurts," the girl said. She pulled her collar down, revealing a crudely stitched incision.

"My implant," she said, blinking in confusion.

"Implant?" Dux grunted, and then proceeded to swear colorfully for about thirty seconds, his sunburnt face flushing bright red. For Amar, it all suddenly made sense—her haircut, the way she dressed. She was not only clean; she had a flowery scent about her.

This was no settlement girl. She was from one of the New Cities. Not everyone in the cities had identification implants, but to receive gene therapy and advanced medicine, you had to have one.

She had that panicked look again.

"What's your name?" Amar asked, trying to ease her back down.

"Lena," she said absently, still craning her neck to stare at her wound. "Lena Bishop."

"Lena, where are you from?"

"I'm from Gulf City," she said. "I guess you figured that out. Who cut out my implant? Why?"

"The smugglers," Amar said. "They probably thought you were a spy. You . . . sort of were."

"What are you talking about?" she demanded. "I just wanted a drink."

"Yes, but when you have one of those things under your skin, they can track you, maybe even see what you see, hear what you hear. So, in a lot of settlements, when someone comes in from the outside, they don't ask questions. They just cut it out of you."

She looked at them all in horror. "Who are you guys?"

"The good guys," DeLao said.

"DeLao," Dux cut in. "Did you make sure it's really out?"

"Of course," DeLao said. "No lump, and the magnetometer didn't pick up a signature. Ran it over her whole body."

"My whole body?" Lena said.

"Nothing inappropriate," DeLao assured her. "I'm a doctor."

"I think that's enough," Dux snapped. "Finish debriefing her with Thomas."

It was unwise to drive at night, so when twilight came they pulled onto a dirt road and followed it until they found a good campsite. Amar helped establish a perimeter while Chitto sat chatting laconically with Lena. When everything was secure, Thomas called a meeting, reviewing the girl's story—first without her, then with her. There didn't appear to be any inconsistencies.

"What were you doing in a settlement, anyway?" she finally asked Lena. "Ghetto tourism?"

Lena looked around nervously. "I think . . . " she began, checked herself, and then started again. "I think I was looking for you guys."

"And what do you mean by that?" Thomas asked.

"The . . . you know. The resistance."

"Huh," Thomas said.

"That's who you are, right? I mean, you have all of those guns. That's hard to miss. And you're hiding in the woods. You were at a smugglers' compound . . ."

"Never mind us," Thomas said. "Why were you looking for the resistance?"

"To join them. You. To fight ADVENT."

**

Amar took the first watch. Lena stayed up with him, which was convenient since she was—in part—what he was watching.

"Where are you from?" she asked. "Not from around here, given your accent."

"What do you mean?" he said. "You have the accent, not me."

He smiled to let her know he was kidding, but she didn't seem to get it, and he realized that he couldn't actually feel a smile on his face. It probably looked more like a grimace.

"Sorry," he said. "Just a little . . ." He gave up. "I'm from a settlement in Malaysia," he finally told her.

"Your English is excellent," she said.

He shrugged. "I've been speaking it since I was a kid, along with Malay, Mandarin, and Tamil."

"Ah," she said. "Just put my big ol' foot in my mouth, huh?"

"No worries," he replied.

"I always do that," she said. "My sister Jules used to say I couldn't talk my way out of . . ." She didn't finish, and her smile vanished. He didn't press. A lot of people joined the resistance because someone they knew had gone missing—with or without explanation. That had been the case with him.

"So tell me about where you're from," she said.

"Well," he said, "it's near a place that used to be called Kuantan. It's on the ocean, and there are lots of palm trees and monkeys. Not a lot to tell, really."

"But it was a settlement?"

"Oh," he said. "Yes. Not a big place. Picture Greenville with palm trees and monkeys."

She looked down. "I'd rather not remember Greenville, thanks," she said.

"Understandable," he said. "They shouldn't have done that to you."

She closed her eyes and smiled.

"Thanks," she said. She sighed. "I'm tired. What's your name?"

"KB," he told her, after a moment's hesitation. "You can call me KB."

"KB, if I sleep right over here, will you make sure I'm okay? Will you keep me safe?"

"Yeah," he replied. "I can do that. It'll be fine."

She lay down on the bedroll they had commandeered for her back at Warren's depot. In minutes, she was asleep. She was still asleep when Chitto spelled him, and he took his own rest next to her, but a half meter away.

***

Amar woke with something cold pushing against the side of his head.

"Don't move, KB," someone whispered. No, not someone—Lena. He cracked his eyelids and saw she had the muzzle of Chitto's shotgun pressed against his temple.

"You're going to get up real slow," she said. "And we're going to go over to that truck, and you're going to get in and drive."

Wow. He had been stupid, hadn't he? But Chitto was supposed to have been on watch.

"Drive it yourself," he said.

"I would love to do that," Lena replied, "if I had the faintest idea how to drive that ancient tetanus trap. But being civilized, I don't."

"You're going to get yourself killed," Amar warned her. "Really, this isn't a good idea. I don't know what your problem is—"

"Well, you'd know all about that, wouldn't you?" she said. "About people getting killed. About killing them. Get up."

"Trouble, KB?" Chitto asked, mildly.

"Chitto, how the hell did she get your gun?"

"I guess I fell asleep on watch," she replied.

"Shut up," Lena hissed. "If you wake the others, I'll really have nothing to lose. I'll die, but you two will go first."

"But," Chitto said, "I did take all of the shells out before I fell asleep. You know. Just in case someone was pretending to be asleep and waiting for a chance to arm herself."

"You're bluffing," Lena said.

Amar slapped the barrel away from his head and then took hold of it. He scrambled up and pushed the butt against Lena, hard, and she fell back.

He heard the hammer click. Nothing happened.

She had just tried to kill him.

Amar drew his pistol.

"This," he informed her, "is loaded."

Everyone was stirring now, coming over to see what was happening. Lena climbed unsteadily to her feet. She was plainly terrified but trying not to show it, and not doing a very good job.

"Was it you?" she demanded. "The bombing in the Helena settlement? Or another bunch of murderous scumbags?"

"What are you talking about?" DeLao snapped.

"You know damn well what I'm talking about," Lena said. "Eight innocent people died. One of them was my sister."

Amar recalled the billboard in Greenville, Rider dressed in civilian clothing.

"There was no bombing at Helena," he said. "That was propaganda. A lie. The dead they showed were *our* dead. Native dead. Really, do you people believe everything the aliens tell you? When you get your implant, do they take out part of your brain as well?"

"My sister was not one of you," Lena exploded.

"Really?" he asked. "What was she doing in Helena?"

"She . . . she was a doctor. She went to help people, to try to bring them into the city. The ones with cancer and tuberculosis, with diseases nobody has to die of anymore. And you assholes killed her."

"Why would we bomb civilians?" Amar asked. "Human civilians?"

"I don't know," Lena said. "I'm not a sociopath." She stood straighter, a look of defiance on her face. "You people drugged me, kidnapped me, and cut me open, and now you expect me to just swallow any bullshit you toss my way? What now? Are you going to kill me now, in your war on clean water and good healthcare?"

"It's starting to sound real damn tempting," Dux muttered.

"No," Thomas said. "We're going to show you something."

***

A flight of ADVENT drones delayed their departure the next morning, so by the time they got started it was already getting hot. Their vehicles didn't have functioning air conditioning—other than open windows—and probably hadn't for decades. Twice they had to stop and clear debris from what remained of the road, and in one place a meandering stream had cut a channel right through the highway, forcing them to spend three hours chopping trees to form a makeshift bridge. It was nearly sundown when they reached the ferry.

If Sam hadn't been with them, Amar doubted they would have ever known the boat was there. It was docked underneath part of the bridge that had once spanned the river, protected from sight by canebrakes and strands of willow that Amar thought must have been deliberately planted as screens. The ferryman lived on his boat, an old barge he had fitted out with a biodiesel engine. He was an older man, knobby and gangly, and as bald as an egg. He had about five days' worth of gray stubble on his face. He regarded them all with a great deal of suspicion until he noticed Sam.

"I remember you," he said. "Cocky young fellar. But these ain't the ones you came with."

"No," Sam allowed, "we had some unexpected trouble."

"I'm sure sorry to hear that," he said. "Big trouble, or little trouble that you walk out of but go a different direction?"

"Big trouble, I'm afraid," Sam said.

"Damn. Can't say how sorry I am. That's rough." He sized the rest of them up.

"Come on over to the lounge," he said.

The lounge was the area around the control cabin, which had been decorated with tiki statues of various sizes, some cut from palm trunks, other made of driftwood and even plastic, the latter dating from a distant age. Island scenes had been painted on the cabin walls, and some wicker chairs surrounded a table.

"I'm Captain Simmons," he told them, as they settled into the chairs. "Y'all want some coffee?"

Amar remembered the last time he'd had coffee. It had been almost two years ago, on the long trip from New Guinea to the southern coast of Mexico, a little settlement named Puerto Arista. It hadn't been that good, and he didn't have high hopes for whatever Captain Simmons had brewed up, especially as it came out in vintage tiki glasses. But he couldn't hide his amazement when he tasted it.

"I know," Simmons said. "Had some guys come through a few weeks ago. This is what they paid me in."

"Nice of you to share it," Sam said. "You never know when someone will come through with something this good again."

"The E.T.s may get me tomorrow, for all I know," Simmons said. "Or I might have a good old-fashioned heart attack. I always thought coffee was best shared in company, and being stingy never made a man one whit happier. Relating to that, I've got a stew going, if you're hungry."

"That's very kind," Thomas said. "But the sooner we can cross the river, the better."

"Then you have time," Simmons said. "There have been enough air patrols today I don't fancy crossing until night."

So they relaxed a bit as Captain Simmons went to fool with his stew. Fireflies began to drift up across the river.

The stew wasn't as good as the coffee; it seemed like it had been cooking for days and had a little of everything in it. But it was filling and hot.

"Don't you want some?" Simmons asked Lena.

Amar watched the exchange. She had refused food all day. She had to be starving.

The captain pushed a little bowl of the stuff toward her. Reluctantly, she took it and the proffered spoon.

"Thank you," she said. It was the first word she had spoken since the previous night. She took a tentative bite, then another.

"This is really interesting," Lena said. "How did you get it to taste like this?"

"What do you mean?" Simmons said.

"It just doesn't taste like CORE," she said. "I know they say it's like an empty palate, that you can make it taste like anything at all, but to me there's always this taste on the back of your tongue, and you know what it is. I'm not getting that here."

Everyone stared at her for a few seconds, and then Dux let out a belly laugh, and everyone else joined in. Lena frowned and her cheeks reddened.

"What are you all laughing at?" she demanded.

"There's no CORE in this, honey," Simmons said. "Some squirrel, and a little rabbit, some mudbugs, and I think a little nutria is still in there. . . ."

Lena stared at her bowl.

"This is animal meat?" she gasped.

"Well, yeah," he replied.

"Oh, god." She dropped the bowl and lurched toward the side of the boat.

"Stay with her, KB," Thomas ordered.

Amar was already on his feet. He didn't think she was faking, but she was not one with whom to take chances. He kept his eyes trained on her as she heaved her guts into the river for fear that she might jump or push him in.

"What is wrong with you people?" she managed, when she was finally done.

"We eat what we can out here," Amar said. "There's no CORE in the set-tlements. Besides, who even knows what CORE is? 'Reclaimed protein'? Reclaimed from what?"

"It's safe," she said. "It's nutritious. No one has to kill it."

"It's bland," Amar said. "It's boring. And it's what the aliens want us to eat. That's enough to put me off it right there."

She wiped her mouth on her sleeve. "Why?" she asked. "Do you really think things were better before they came? There was war everywhere, and famine, and crime!"

"We still have all that," he said.

"But you chose it! There's no crime in the cities, no hunger."

"Because you're *kept*," he said. "Like a herd of cows. And why do people herd cows?"

"They don't anymore," she said.

"Right," Amar said. "Because cows have been replaced."

She just stared at the water, sweat beaded on her forehead.

"Look," he said. "I don't know if the world was better before they came. But it was *ours*. Our fate was in our own hands."

"Pretty shaky hands, from what I know," she muttered.

"A lot of what you know isn't true," Amar said.

CHAPTER 5

THEY CROSSED IN the dark and debarked their vehicles underneath the other end of the ruined bridge. Helena had an actual resistance outpost, and a radio exchange between the cell captain and Captain Simmons confirmed that there was no active ADVENT presence in the town.

The old town of Helena had been largely destroyed by flooding, and many of the new structures were built on stilts, reminding him even more of home. The night was young, and people were out enjoying the slightly cooler air that sundown brought. Someone was projecting an old movie on the side of a Winnebago, and Amar smelled popcorn. Some kids were playing football in a clearing by the river. Helena seemed a little cleaner than Greenville; the smell of frying fish and hush puppies were enough to overwhelm the stench of sewage.

"Okay," Thomas told Lena. "Start asking."

"What do you mean?" Lena replied.

"There was a bombing here, right?" Thomas said. "People died. You were on your way here for a reason."

"Yes," she said. "I wanted to see it. See where she died. I wanted to try to understand."

"Go to it, then. Amar will see to your safety while I meet with the local Natives. The rest of you—take the night off, but stay on your toes. Keep your earpieces in."

Lena looked around for a bit and then walked over to a stand where two teenagers were selling watermelon juice. It turned out they were expected to have their own cups, and when they didn't Amar had to spring for a pair of plastic tumblers.

"Where are y'all from?" one of them, a girl with uneven, blackened teeth, asked.

"We just came from Greenville," Amar said.

"That's a long way," the boy said. "I've never been that far."

"Why are your teeth like that?" Lena asked.

The girl recoiled. "Ain't too polite, are you?"

"So you came up from Greenville," the boy persisted. "Were you there for the bombing?"

"What?" Lena said her brows arching up.

"Yeah," the boy said. "A bunch of people killed, according to the vid stream. Of course, my daddy says the vid stream ain't worth much. Says a hognose snake knows more about the world than folks that watch that."

"No," Lena said slowly. "The bombing was here. My sister was killed in it."

"In Helena?" the boy said. "Weren't no bombing. Hell, what's there to bomb in Helena?"

"But . . ." Lena trailed off, uncertainly. "Did you know a woman named Jules Bishop? Looked a little like me, two years older, with blonde hair?"

"Jules Bishop?" The two looked at each other. "Peculiar woman," the girl said. "From Gulf City. She used to help out at the school, but she ain't been around there for a year or two."

"Where is the school?" Lena demanded.

"It ain't open right now."

"Where?"

***

The school overlooked the river, a single-room building surrounded by a porch and mounted on pilings so it stood well above the waterline. There were no lights on, but two men were passing a bottle between them. One was Sam.

"I figured someone would direct you here sooner rather than later," Sam said. "But I wanted you to get here on your own."

The other man was little older than Sam, maybe thirty-five. He had a narrow face set in sorrowful lines. He stood up and stared at Lena.

"God," he said, "you look like just her."

Lena looked back and forth between the two men.

"Okay," she said. "I'm not doing this. For all I know, one of you crossed the river early and set this all up for my benefit. I don't know why you would bother, but I'm not—"

"She was my wife," the man said.

Lena closed her eyes. "I'm. Not. Doing. This."

Amar felt his fuse sputtering up its end. Did Lena think she was the only person in the universe who had lost someone? Who did she think she was?

"Right," he said. "I swam over here and coached the whole town to lie. I'm bloody amazing that way." He swept his arms about. "Helena isn't all that big. Did you see anything that resembled a blast radius? Really, what is wrong with you?"

"We corresponded," Lena erupted. "Don't you think she would mention a husband?"

"No," the man said. "Jules wouldn't. My name is Laurent Gerox. ADVENT has been searching for me for years. Jules wanted to make certain they didn't find me through her. Any communication you had with her was recorded and analyzed—if not before she joined the resistance, then certainly after."

"This is all absurd."

Laurent sighed. He put his hands on his knees. "She liked the little things," he said. "A funny turn of phrase. The color of the sky on a clear morning. Cherries—she really loved cherries."

"Stop it," Lena said.

"Her favorite color was aquamarine, and she was very firm about it—not blue, not turquoise, not teal—aquamarine. If you ended a sentence with a preposition, she would always correct you. She once told me that when you were little, you were afraid that some sort of monster lived under your tub. A sewer snake? No, that wasn't it. Something like that, though."

"Slewer snake," Lena said. Her voice was thick, and tears had begun slowly tracing down her face. "That's how I said it, and it stuck."

"She was in my detail," Sam said softly. "She died protecting me. We had to leave the bodies, and this is what ADVENT does. It lies. All of the time. About everything."

"Why?" Lena asked softly. "Why?"

"Because," Laurent said, "they have something to hide. Because if people knew what they were really up to, more would rise up against them."

"What are they really up to, then?" Lena asked.

Sam cleared this throat. "That we don't actually know," he said.

"My sister died for that?" she said derisively. "For 'We don't really know?'"

"Yes," Laurent said.

"Then she was an idiot," Lena said. She turned and walked away.

"She'll be okay," Laurent said. "I'll see that she gets back to Gulf City, if that's what she wants."

"Good enough," Amar said. As long as she wasn't his responsibility anymore, he was happy.

***

They were still flush with fuel and supplies when they left Helena. Now that they were across the Mississippi, they could turn south toward their as-yet-unnamed destination. Their path carried them deeper into a contagion zone than Amar would have liked, but he didn't see anything out of place. Everything looked very much as it had on the other side of the river. The few aircraft they saw were very high and far away.

That night they parked the trucks inside an old farm building of some sort. Dux and Toby began unpacking, and a few minutes later they were again treated to the big man's impressive vocabulary of obscenities.

Amar trotted over to see what was happening, and there was Lena, looking up at the redhead with a defiant glare in her eyes. She had apparently stowed away on one of the pickups by crawling under the tarp.

Before Dux got too out of hand, Amar took Lena by the elbow and escorted her to the edge of the camp.

"Why?" he demanded. "Laurent said he would take you back to the city. Or you could have stayed there."

"You're not telling me everything," she said. "Until you do, you're stuck with me."

***

Thomas put Lena under Chitto's guard and called a meeting, out of earshot of the two. Dux got his opinion out immediately.

"We should leave her here," the big man said.

"It's a long walk back to Helena," Amar felt he should point out.

"That's her problem. She'll be fine if she sticks to the road."

"Sure," Nishimura said, slapping at a mosquito. "If a snake doesn't bite her. Or a cougar. Or whatever the aliens are scared of doesn't get her. Or an ADVENT patrol, for that matter. Leaving her here alone might be a death sentence."

Thomas agreed. "I'm not going to leave her in a contagion zone."

"We can't take her any farther," Sam said. "It's too dangerous."

She turned to Sam. "It's time you told us where we're going."

"It's classified," he began.

"Do not tell me that again," Thomas snapped. "Conditions change. We adapt. That's what you *do* when you're in the field. Obviously your old squad knew where they came from. So now we're your escort. You haven't gotten new orders because it's not possible, right? Are you in contact with your superiors?"

"No," Sam admitted.

"So you adapt," she snapped. "Where the hell are we going?"

He took a deep breath and settled his shoulders. Then, reluctantly, he began to speak.

"There is a base," he said. "Near here. Not just any resistance base. An XCOM base."

To Amar, he might as well have just said they were going to meet Sun Wukong, the Monkey King, or Ravana, lord of the Rakshasa. Or King Arthur.

XCOM was a thing from legend—another time, another world, even.

"I don't find that likely," Nishimura said. "After all these years? Where have they been? Why haven't we heard from them?"

"The time wasn't right," Sam said. "The world wasn't ready. But soon . . ."

"The name you mentioned," Thomas said. "You're sure?"

"I am completely certain," Sam replied. "You don't know me that well, but I hate to lie. It almost makes me physically ill to lie."

"So instead you don't tell us anything at all," DeLao complained, pulling off his ball cap and fanning himself with it. "Where is this base? You say it's only about a day away. That puts it somewhere just outside of old Houston—basically jabbertown central."

"It's safe," Sam said. "When we get there, we'll be safe. Then this whole mess will be out of my hands, and you can take your concerns up with someone much more highly placed than me. Okay? But we have to lose Lena."

"Not here," Thomas decided. "Somewhere closer to the coast, where she has a better chance of being found."

"What if she doesn't want to be found?" Amar said. "What if she wants to join up? You let Chitto in pretty easily."

"Chitto isn't a brainwashed New City brat," Dux said. "Who knows what she's got kicking around in that brain can of hers?"

"My point is this," Sam said. "If she goes with us much farther into this, letting her go isn't going to be good enough. Do you understand? I'm serious. This is for her own good."

"She stays with us until we're out of the contagion zone," Thomas said. "There are settlements outside of Houston. We'll leave her at one there." She glared at Dux. "And next time, we'll check the vehicles before we pull out."

***

Midmorning the sun shone hot and bright, but in the west it was beginning to darken. The trees along the highway first shivered and then began to sway in sporadic buffets of wind. Rain began, like liquid gold in the sunlight.

"Devil's beating his wife," Chitto murmured. They were in the pickup, and Amar was driving.

"What?" Amar said.

"When it's raining and the sun is still out," Chitto explained, "we say the devil is beating his wife."

Amar thought about that for a second, wondering when he'd had this conversation before. "We used to say the fox is marrying the crow," he said.

"That doesn't make any sense," Chitto opined.

"And yours does?" he retorted. She shrugged.

Then, he remembered. "Rider used to say it was a 'chicken carnival,'" he recalled, "which makes even less sense."

"Uh-huh," she replied as the rain began to hammer so hard the ancient wipers could no longer clear it.

"I'm not her, I know," Chitto said, after a moment, "but I will watch your back as best I can."

Amar nodded, feeling his breath tighten. "Thanks," he said, as the wind tried to yank the truck from the road.

"I wonder," Chitto said, "why they don't just call it 'sunny rain.'"

"Oh, yeah," Amar remembered. "*Hujan panas.* Some people back home do call it that."

"See, that makes sense," Chitto said. He nodded his agreement.

But by then it wasn't sunny rain anymore. Clouds darker than soot rolled over them, and thunder began pounding their ears. They were forced to slow to a crawl, the taillights of the minivan ahead of them the only thing Amar could see. Then they stopped entirely for fear of driving into something too deep.

They needn't have bothered—the deep came to them. First, Amar felt a sort of tug. Then the wheel turned in his hand. The yellow water outside was rising very quickly, he saw. Then the truck lifted and turned half around.

"Oh, crap," Chitto said.

It wasn't like sea waves, coming and going. This just kept coming, now horrifyingly quickly. The truck raised completely from the road as water began to gush in from the floorboards and seams of the doors.

Then something hit them—a log, another car, he didn't know, but the truck began flipping over, driver side down. His window shattered, and water poured in as the truck continued to roll.

After that, he only remembered water churning everywhere as he gasped for breath, clawing his way out of the window even as the truck turned again. He couldn't tell up from down anymore. All he could feel was a pull like the strongest riptide he'd ever experienced.

Then his head struck something, and he blacked out.

CHAPTER 6

WHEN HE CAME to, something was hanging onto him from behind. He struggled wildly, in a total panic, as lightning limned everything in white and thunder exploded in the same instant, leaving his ears ringing and a long red stripe on his retinas.

He realized then that it wasn't just ringing in his ears. Someone was talking to him. After a moment, he understood that it was Chitto, and that she was behind him, holding his face up out of the water, not dragging him into it. She was holding onto something else with her other arm.

"Your armor," she gasped. "Get if off, or we'll both go under."

He fumbled at the catches, his fingers dulled by cold. The water pulled at him like a sea monster's claw, and he heard Chitto groaning behind him. Finally the breastplate came off, but Chitto lost her grip on whatever she had a hold of, and they were borne off by the flood, branches and deadfall tearing at their exposed flesh.

After what seemed like forever, the current lessened, and they fetched against something. Together they crawled up onto a bank that rose a few feet from the flood. The rain lessened, and thunder growled on, but only in the distance. The water rose another six centimeters and then began to subside.

"Thanks," he managed.

"It's all good," Chitto said.

"Except the bit where we just lost everything," he said. "Weapons, supplies, the truck."

"Nitpicker," Chitto replied.

But he was right. When it was clear enough to look around, the truck was nowhere to be seen—nor was there any sign of the rest of the squad.

***

Before nightfall they found a road running generally south, although they couldn't be certain it was the same highway they had been on earlier. Amar was relieved to discover that both of them still had their sidearms, and so they weren't completely helpless. But he felt like a walking bruise, and his every joint and juncture felt aflame, chapped by his wet, stiff clothes.

Making camp involved little more than finding the highest, driest place they could to take turns sleeping. They still had their radio transceivers, but they were short range, and there was nothing but static on the frequencies they used.

The night was wet, hot, and miserable, and he didn't get much in the way of sleep, but in the gray hours before morning, his radio finally started talking to him—not with a human voice, but with the dots and dashes of Morse code. The signal repeated six times, then gave way to static.

"Did you get that?" Chitto asked. "I haven't had time to learn the code."

"Yeah," he said. "We've got a rally point."

***

In the truck, the longleaf pine and oak that was reclaiming the land blurred into a continuous screen, obscuring the contents of the young forest. On foot, you saw more. The rusting cars, the crumbling churches, the faded billboards, water towers proclaiming the names of towns few remembered ever existing.

Oakdale was one such town. The sign cheerfully declaring they were entering it was still there, peeking through the understory.

"Rally point is about a kilometer ahead," Amar told Chitto. "Near the old town center."

They had covered about half that distance when his radio started prattling again, this time urging him to approach with caution. It came a bit belated, because by that time he could hear the screams.

Oakdale wasn't like Greenville and Helena, settlements that ADVENT grudgingly tolerated. Oakdale was far too deep in a contagion zone. It should have been empty, and from the looks of it, it had been until recently. It was poor even by shantytown standards, consisting of a handful of tents, some tarps thrown over the holes in the roofs of existing buildings, and a few small solar arrays. Also glaringly present were two ADVENT aerial transports. The troopers were rounding the settlers up and marching them—or, in some cases, carrying—them into the transports.

And not all the captives were settlers: Toby, DeLao, and Lena were among them.

"Shit!" Chitto yelped, and then her pistol went off. He spun around and saw she was shooting at a jabber only a few meters away. It had a stun lance in its hand. Chitto fired again but came nowhere near hitting the thing. From the corner of his eye, he saw another one charging up on his right like a berserker.

He jerked his pistol up and fired twice. The first bullet hit the jabber in the neck and the second right in the face. He was turning to fire at the second when he felt a searing pain in the back of his shoulder. His whole body spasmed, and he dropped his pistol as he fell to the ground. It felt like his blood had been pumped out and replaced with lava. Groaning, he rolled, reaching for the fallen weapon, but he knew there was no time. He heard Chitto firing wildly. The trooper raised her lance.

Then her head came off. Dazed by the pain, he watched curiously as it bounced on the ground, and the body that had once worn it dropped to its knees.

Nishimura grinned down at him, her small mouth bent in a devilish grin, her eyes bright beneath her sable brows, and then she was off again, bloody sword gripped in one hand.

He picked up his weapon, trying to ignore the agony that had been burned into his flesh, but it took a few moments to regain his motor skills. He knew he was lucky that he hadn't passed out, but somehow it didn't feel that way.

When he did manage to get up, he saw that more fighting was going on near the transports, but he couldn't make out the details. Nishimura was no longer in sight, but she'd left another corpse behind her—the jabber who had stabbed him.

He glanced at Chitto, who looked a little shaken. "You got it together?" he asked.

"Yeah," she said. "Sorry."

"Don't be sorry," he told her. "Just keep your head. See that brick building up there? Move up. I'll cover you."

She was about halfway there when a mag blast speared toward her, narrowly missing her shoulder and cutting a sapling in half. He saw the jabber and began firing at it. It was about twenty meters away, so his first shot missed. His second bullet connected before the trooper crouched down behind a tree. Chitto made it to the building and fired at it from two meters away. He saw chips fly from a nearby oak.

No wonder she had been issued a shotgun. Chitto had terrible aim.

The jabber stood up again, and he shot it twice more. It staggered back, and then Amar heard a burst from an assault rifle. The trooper shuddered and went down.

Amar saw Dux about ten meters off to his right, giving him a thumb's up.

In a few more minutes it was over. There had only been eight jabbers to begin with, and most had been armed with stun lances. They hadn't expected heavy resistance, and probably no resistance at all, not from a group this small and impoverished.

He gradually sorted out what had happened as DeLao looked over his wound and the rest tried to sort some semblance of order into the panicked settlers.

Toby, DeLao, and Lena had reached the rendezvous first and found it occupied. They didn't know they had walked inside the ADVENT perimeter and had been surprised pretty much the way he and Chitto had, only there had been no Nishimura to pull their asses out of the fire. Thomas, Dux, and

Nishimura arrived next, and had been working out a strategy when he and Chitto showed up.

"Took a ding out of your scapula," DeLao told him. "Nothing that'll kill you right away."

Dux was in worse shape. At some point in the final moments of the battle, he had taken a glancing hit on his gut. He still had his armor, and it had saved his life, but bits of it had vaporized and blown through one of his lungs. He was bearing up for the moment, but it was the sort of wound that would definitely not get better on its own or with the resources they had. They now had another reason to find Sam's XCOM facility.

"Mister."

He glanced up to find a boy of perhaps seven years looking at him. He was thin and had a couple of gaps in his teeth.

"Yes?"

"Thank you for what you done."

"It's okay," he said.

The boy continued to stand there.

"Are y'all going to stay with us?" he asked.

Amar looked around. "No," he said. "We can't. We have something we have to do a long way from here."

"Well, can I come with you then?"

"I bet your mom and dad wouldn't want that," Amar said.

"They ain't got no say in the matter," the boy replied. "They got took last year."

Amar swore silently and then swayed to his feet. "Do you guys have a leader?" he asked.

"I reckon that would be Mr. Deloach over there," the boy told him.

Deloach was thirty-something. He had a mane of dirty blond hair and arms that looked as if they had been made of wire and rubber.

"You're Deloach?" Amar asked.

"Yes, sir," Deloach said. "We're awful grateful for what you've done here."

"That's great," he said. "But you need to get these people—these kids—to one of the settlements. It's not safe out here."

"Don't much care for the settlements," the man said. "Can't hear myself think."

"A boy just told me his parents were taken last year," Amar persisted. "Where was that?"

"Down in Atchafalaya Basin," he said.

"Another contagion zone."

"I ain't lettin' no damn aliens tell me where I can and cannot live," Deloach snapped.

"I understand that," Amar said, starting to heat up. "I just killed two of their troopers. You think I'm on their side? But understand, when they find you out here, they do not take you to a settlement. They do not take you to a city. They take you, and no one ever sees you again. Ever."

"I got news for you," Deloach said. "The settlements ain't safe, either."

"It's better than being out here," Amar said. He turned away, disgusted, and nearly ran into Lena, who was standing there with tears running down her face.

"It's real, isn't it?" she said. "Everything you've been saying."

"You think?" he said, and brushed by her.

***

None of the vehicles operated after the flood. The other pickup had a broken axle, and the van was likewise totaled. The others had managed to salvage some of the supplies and weapons, but once again they were on foot. Fortunately, according to Sam, they could probably walk it in two days. He was right, but they were two very long, hot days of biting flies, mosquitoes, and leeches. They saw a cottonmouth big enough to eat a cat. A big cat. Everyone else seemed pretty impressed, but Amar had grown up with cobras.

ADVENT patrols grew more frequent as they approached the Gulf of Mexico, so they stayed adjacent to the road rather than on it when they could.

Dux couldn't walk by the end of the first day, so they built a litter and took turns carrying him. Amar noticed that Lena took a turn like everyone else.

When she was done, he walked up beside her.

"Hey," he said.

"KB," she said. She hesitated and then plunged on.

"I'm sorry about the other night," she said. "I wouldn't have . . . I pulled the trigger by accident when you hit me."

"That's fine," he said. "I never met a pretty girl who didn't try to kill me at some point."

She fingered her mud-streaked hair and glanced at her filthy clothes.

"That was supposed to be a joke," he said.

"The part about me being pretty, or about girls trying to kill you?" she asked.

"Never mind," he said. "It's just something I used to say."

"Anyway," she said. "I'm sorry." She looked up at him, and her green eyes caught him. He held her gaze for what felt like too long.

He finally looked down, feeling embarrassed.

"In your position, I probably would have done the same thing," he said.

"You came up to me, just now," she said. "Did you have something to say?"

"Yeah," he said. "I wanted to tell you that for someone who grew up in a city, you're hanging in there pretty well. You're kind of tough."

"If you could be inside of my skin for a while, you wouldn't think so," she said. "But thanks."

***

On the evening of the second day, they reached the settlement of Sunflower. Toby and Nishimura went in to see if it was safe, and they were all in by dusk. What passed for a doctor there said he couldn't do much more for Dux than make him more comfortable.

And there was Lena. Amar found her sitting near a patch of bare dirt, where some girls were skipping rope. He mentally braced himself and then sat down beside her. She had washed up and traded her clothes for a pair of brown pants and a stained blue shirt.

"Why did you stow away back in Helena?" he asked her. "Why didn't you just stay there or go back to Gulf City?"

She didn't look at him, and for a while she didn't say anything.

"I had to know what my sister died for," she said. "I wanted to understand. I still do."

He nodded. "Okay," he said. "Do you?"

"I don't know."

"Then you don't," he said, as gently as he could. "And you can't come any farther with us."

"Why not?"

"Right now, if ADVENT picks you up, you can't tell them anything all that important," he said. "In another day, that will change."

"And you'll have to what—make sure I can't talk?"

He sighed. "Something like that."

"I see." She sounded cold. He didn't blame her.

"Just make it easy on yourself," he said. "Stay here. They'll take care of you until you figure it all out."

***

But the next morning, she was there, stubbornly lifting one end of Dux's litter.

Sam frowned and glanced at Thomas, who shrugged. Amar expected an argument about it, but instead they started on.

About a kilometer down the road, however, things came to a head, when Sam drew his sidearm and pointed it at Lena.

"Okay," he said. "Turn around and walk back the settlement. You'll be fine. They'll take care of you."

Lena looked pale. Amar could see her lip quivering. But she didn't move.

"Why here?" she asked. "Why did you let me leave the settlement with you? Is it because you wanted to be out of earshot of Sunflower when you shot me?"

"Nobody has to get shot," Sam replied. "But you aren't going another step with us."

"But if I do?"

"I'll do what I have to," he replied.

Lena was about a meter to his right. Amar stepped to place himself between her and Sam.

"What the hell is this, KB?" Sam demanded.

"I'm not going to watch you kill an unarmed human," he said. "And if you are who you say you are—and belong to the organization you say you do—you won't do it."

"You don't understand," he said. "If you knew what I was protecting—"

"It wouldn't change anything," Amar interrupted. "I still wouldn't let you shoot her."

"Put your gun away, Sam," Thomas said. "That's an order."

"I don't answer to you," Sam replied.

"Today you do," she said.

Amar kept his gaze locked on Sam's. He felt strange, almost serene, and each breath seemed to go on for a century.

Sam lowered the gun and looked past him at Lena.

"I can't promise anything once we get there, Lena," he said. "The decision won't be in my hands anymore." He nodded his head toward Thomas. "Or theirs."

"I understand," she said.

"I really hope you do."

***

Half an hour later they reached the densely vegetated banks of the Sabine River. Across the water the remains of an old oil refinery slept beneath a blanket of rust. The aliens had power sources that had rendered fossil fuels relatively useless for that purpose, although some petroleum was still used in manufacturing plastics and such.

Was this really where the XCOM base was? Hidden in this ruin? So close to the coastal cities? He could see three aircraft at the moment, although none were directly overhead. How could they possibly have avoided detection for twenty years?

Sam was talking to someone on his radio. It seemed that this was the place.

"Well?" Thomas said.

"In a moment," Sam replied.

It was a long moment. Amar watched across the river, looking for a door to open, someone walking toward them. . . .

A cormorant sitting on a stick in the water suddenly took wing. Amar was wondering what had startled the bird when he realized the stick was growing taller, and then he understood that it wasn't a stick, but a pipe of some sort.

Then something large emerged, gunmetal gray, flange-shaped, and now the water was mounding, as if a whale was surfacing.

Or a submarine.

"*Asu!*" Nishimura gasped.

"What she said," DeLao said.

"Ladies and gentlemen," Sam said, "I give you the Elpis."

Part II
The Elpis

"*The mouse-deer may forget the trap, but the trap will not forget the mouse-deer.*"

—MALAY PROVERB

CHAPTER 7

THE ELPIS HAD old bones. The bulk of her dated to the first decade after World War II, nearly a hundred years ago, when diesel submarines were state of the art. But the atomic age was unfolding and as nuclear subs became the front line in underwater technology, the older vessels were gradually refitted or retired to shipyards, museums, and scrapheaps.

"It would have been easier to obtain a nuclear sub, actually," Sam told them. He was obviously excited about and proud of the ship.

At the moment they were in a conference room, waiting to be debriefed, and Sam—always talkative—was now practically blabbering. It was possible he was in part trying to repair his mistake in threatening Lena. No one in the squad really trusted her, but Natives did not kill humans, and threatening to do so had lost him any goodwill he might have gained since conscripting them.

So now he was trying to impress them with the amazing place where they now found themselves, to show them that his attempts to protect it were justified or at least understandable.

Amar was impressed, but he wasn't yet convinced.

However, Sam was still working on it.

"The thing about a nuclear sub," he was saying, "is it emits neutrinos, and the aliens are very good at tracking neutrino sources. It doesn't occur to them that anything dangerous to them could run on technology this old. But there's more here than meets the eye. . . ."

He didn't finish the lecture, because the door opened, and Sam bounded to his feet. Thomas was close behind him.

The man in the doorway was on the frail side, nearly bald, with mere wisps of gray hair along the fringes of his skull. But behind his wire-rimmed glasses his eyes were lively and intelligent.

As he stepped into the room, he was followed by a much younger fellow with a shock of red hair and an expression that was probably meant to be neutral but which to Amar seemed somehow disapproving.

"Dr. Shen!" Thomas said. It was the most excited he thought he had ever seen her.

"You look familiar," the old man said, studying her intently. His lips curled in a little smile. "Thomas, yes? Holly Thomas?"

"I'm flattered you remember me, sir," she said.

"You were one of the Commander's favorites," he said. "Because you were one of our best. I'm so glad you're still with us. Gladder still that you have joined us here on the Elpis."

"I think it was only because I mentioned your name that Captain Thomas agreed to escort me here," Sam said.

Shen's features fell a bit as he surveyed the rest of the squad. "Sam, is it true that you are the only survivor of your expedition?"

"Yes, sir," he said. "We were ambushed by ADVENT troopers. Captain Thomas and her squad saved my life and escorted me back to the Elpis."

"How convenient that they were nearby," the red-headed man said.

A look of irritation flashed across Thomas's face, but she quickly mastered it.

"When Sam told me that you were still alive, sir, it seemed too good to be true." She paused, looked at the floor, then raised her gaze again. "Sir, is the Commander . . ."

Shen shook his head. "There has never been any word of him, and I have searched, believe me. But there is also no conclusive proof that he is dead—so there is always hope, you know. Elpis."

"Sir?"

Dr. Shen smiled.

"Do you remember the ancient Greek story of Pandora's box? How she was given a chest but forbidden to open it? But of course she couldn't resist, and when she finally broke the seals, all of the sorrows, disasters, diseases, and misfortunes that plague us now escaped. When she finally managed to close it, only one thing remained in the box: Elpis. Hope." He waved his arms around the ship. "This is our Elpis. The Commander may be missing, but others have survived. I've spent many years trying to find them, to recover data, to gather new information. To rebuild XCOM. And I believe we are very near succeeding."

He took a seat, and the red-headed man sat beside him.

"So, as the rest of you have no doubt gathered, my name is Shen, Raymond Shen. I had the honor of being chief engineer back in the old days. This is our ship's captain, Ahti Laaksonen."

"Good day, all," Laaksonen said.

Sam made a round of introductions, and then Shen got down to business.

"Sam, what do you have to report?"

"Hold up," Laaksonen interposed. "Sam, what have you told them already?"

"Only that I was looking for something in the old facility. But not what."

"Then perhaps the three of us—Dr. Shen, you, myself—ought to review your findings before making them available to men and women we know very little about." He nodded to Thomas. "No disrespect intended. But we must be very careful."

Thomas's expression was unreadable.

"As Dr. Shen wishes," she said.

The old man looked them over. "Captain Thomas, it's been a long time, but I have no doubts about you. Do you vouch for your people?"

Thomas nodded toward Lena. "Ms. Bishop is a civilian, sir. We found her in ADVENT custody and brought her along for her own protection. If you're going to tell us anything classified, I suggest she be removed from the conversation."

"Classified?" Laaksonen repeated in an icy tone. "The existence of this ship is classified. The survival of Dr. Shen is classified as well. She is now privy to any number of classified things. Is she from one of the cities? Did you at least have the sense to remove her chip?"

"It had already been removed," Thomas said, "by locals in the Greenville settlement."

"Dr. Shen—" Laaksonen began, but the older man cut him off.

"Young lady," Shen told Lena, "I'm going to have you escorted to the Rathskeller or, if you prefer, the showers, if you would like to tidy up. The rest of you will remain. Captain Dixon and his squad would have been privy to this conversation, and I think you should know what they died for and what you fought for."

A young woman with a sidearm stepped in from the hall and motioned for Lena to follow her.

"Thank you, Doctor," Lena said. "A shower would be nice."

When she was gone, Shen knitted his fingers and placed his elbows on the table.

"Sam?" he said.

Sam was trying to keep his expression neutral, but he couldn't keep from smiling.

"I found it, sir," he said.

Shen closed his eyes and expressed a deep sigh. "I had hoped," he said. "Sam, this is good news."

"Yes, sir."

"I feel I must still raise an objection—" Laaksonen began, but Shen shook his head.

"In the first few weeks of the war," he said, "we made some gains. It was clear that the alien technology was vastly superior to ours, and that to beat them we would have to understand it, come up to speed, and build our own version of it. We gathered scraps left from skirmishes fought with aliens as they abducted people. But we also managed to shoot down two of their aircraft. The first we found to be in excellent condition, but we were unable to maintain a position at its crash site long enough to study it. The second—and last—crashed during the final hours of the war, as our own systems were being compromised. The satellite data of its trajectory was destroyed at our command facility. I thought the information might have been backed up somewhere else. As it turns out, I was right. True, Sam?"

"Yes," Sam said. "I have the location. It's in a very remote spot, far from any of the New Cities. Chances are good that it's still there."

Shen swept his gaze around the table. "You understand what this would mean, I hope. I have managed to survive for this long because my base is mobile. But it isn't sufficient. If I had access to an alien ship, if we could get it flying again . . ."

"That's a lot of ifs," Thomas remarked.

"Indeed," the doctor replied. "Even if we can't repair it, we would still have access to their technology in a setting that will allow us the time to study and hopefully reproduce it. I once had my qualms about this; frankly, in some respects I still do. I was once afraid that if we used their means we would become too much like them. I still feel that way about their biotech, to some extent. But the past twenty years have convinced me that we cannot defeat them with minor raids here and there or by hacking their propaganda. It may further our cause, yes. But sooner or later, we must fight—go to war—to regain our world. This we simply cannot do with the weapons and materials available to us. Finding that ship is a huge step in achieving the capabilities we require."

"So that's where we're headed next?" Thomas asked. "The downed ship?"

"Not quite," Shen said, with a sparkle in his eye. "There is a stop we must make along the way."

***

Amar hit the showers after the meeting, his head more than slightly awhirl, but the hot water—*hot water!*—settled him back down. The blue shirt and ivory pants provided to him were soft and clean, and although part of him was dog-tired, he was also hungry enough to eat a live cobra head-first.

He hadn't any idea how the submarine had been laid out originally, but he was willing to bet this one had been significantly remodeled. The lighting was modern, and while there were no windows or portholes or whatever ships had, there were LED panels at intervals that were obviously tied to cameras outside. He stopped for a moment to wonder at the pale blue water through which they were moving, at the silvery clouds of fish fleeing their approach.

He reflected that the Elpis was indeed amazing, on its own terms, but it was like a stone knife in a world dominated by nuclear weapons.

But even a stone knife was deadly in the right hands.

The Rathskeller was on the upper of two decks and was very much like a pub. It was small—the ship was around ninety-five meters long, but it was only eight wide—and currently nearly fully occupied, largely by his squad. His choices of drink were beer, water, juice, hot tea, or coffee. He chose the beer and was happy to discover that, while it was bit skunky, it was actually beer, and it was cold. Dinner was a choice of salt cod, tofu, or lentils, pasta or rice, green beans or cabbage, all served from a buffet station by a bespectacled little bearded man who spoke very little English and none of Amar's other tongues.

The tofu looked best, and it was surprisingly good, covered in a red chili, lime, and fish sauce. He sat across from Lena, who was alone at a small table, picking at the lentils. She looked clean; her hair was combed and she had changed from the settlement clothing in which he'd last seen her into a green T-shirt and gray pants.

"Better than squirrel?" he asked.

She shrugged.

"The tofu is good," he said. "It's made from beans, not animals."

"I'll remember that," she said. Then she put down her fork and looked at him directly. He noticed her green eyes had flecks of gold in them.

"Thank you," she said. "I can honestly say no one has ever stood between me and a gun before. I was really quite . . . overwhelmed."

"Sam was never going to shoot you," he said. "I just had to make him understand that."

He was uncomfortable with her earnest gaze and turned his own to his food.

"You're a good man," she said.

It felt surprisingly good to hear her say that—perhaps in part because it was so unexpected—but probably more because he hadn't realized that he *cared* what her opinion of him was.

Yet he did, and he felt like he should respond to her.

"My father once told me he had only one goal in raising me," he said. "It wasn't for me to be rich or powerful or even brave, but to be good."

"He must be proud, then," she said.

"I think he would be disappointed," Amar said. "I don't know—can't know—because he went out one day to hunt, and he never came back. I was ten, and I swore then I would join the resistance as soon as they would take me."

Her expression shifted, became more melancholy and something else he couldn't pin down.

"I'm sorry to hear about your father," she said. "But your reaction, I can understand that."

"But the thing is I didn't join the Natives to fight for an ideal or to help people. I joined because I wanted to avenge him by killing aliens—to kill in the name of my father, the man who never hurt anyone and never would, except to protect his family. He lived a life of grace and peace, and I know in my heart he died that way."

He realized he had never said any of this out loud to anyone before. He wasn't sure why he was doing it now. Maybe it was because she was a noncom. If he brought this up with Nishimura or Dux, they would probably think he was whinging. Everyone who did what they did had issues, but you were expected not to bother other people with yours.

Now she looked puzzled.

"Then . . . you don't believe in this cause that you fight for?" she asked.

"That was then," he said. "Before I met these guys. Thomas, Rider . . ." he trailed off. "Now I've seen some of what ADVENT does with my own eyes. I know we're doing what we have to. But I've seen people die. And I've killed. The ADVENT soldiers—they aren't human. But they look like they might be part human, some kind of bioengineered hybrid. I don't know what's in those suits, if they're human or robots or something else. Do they feel anything? Do they miss their comrades when I kill them? I don't know these things."

She took a drink of her beer. "This is confusing for me. You know that."

"I understand," he said.

"I'm not sure you do," she said. "I had cancer. I was eighteen years old, and my life was over. Gene therapy saved me. How am I not supposed to be grateful for that? And all of the things you're saying—your father wanting you to be good, you with your moral dilemma—that's not how we . . . how people in the New Cities think of you. You're the barbarians pounding at the gate, hackers trying to ruin the good life. When people go missing, you're the ones they blame. And up until now, I didn't have any doubts about any of that. But if it's all a lie . . . Where are they all going? Upward of a thousand people went missing in Gulf City last year. If you guys aren't doing it, then who is?"

"I think the answer is obvious," he said. "I've seen some of the ADVENT facilities, spied on them, set up monitoring equipment to count the faces of those who arrive and those who leave. Only none of them ever leave. And we don't know what they do there. At least, I don't. Maybe Dr. Shen does."

She took a few more bites, looking thoughtful.

"Thomas told Shen ADVENT was holding me," she said. "You told me I was captured by smugglers."

"That's right," he said. "The guys in the bar probably drugged you. Then they took you up to their hideaway to remove your chip. That's what we think, anyway. But then an ADVENT patrol came across them. The black market guys were all dead when we got there. You were alive."

"So the troopers found me there," she mused. "Do you think they would have taken me off to one of those facilities you're talking about? To do what- ever they do?"

"What do you think?" he asked.

She sighed and put her hand to her brow. "Why didn't you tell me about this before?"

He shrugged. "At first I didn't want to frighten you. After that, well, you wouldn't have believed us, would you?"

"I guess not," she admitted.

"So what now? First all you wanted to do was get away from us. Then you were willing to risk death to tag along. What's your next act?"

She was silent for a moment.

"There is something I didn't tell you," she said. "My sister wasn't the first person I lost. My mother disappeared three years ago. She went to the Atlantic Seaboard, and I never saw her again. She was supposed to have been killed during a dissident attack. But in her case, I never saw the body." She looked at him frankly. "Maybe she's still out there. Maybe if I'm with you guys I can at least find out the truth."

"Maybe," he said. "Like Shen said, we can always hope. And if you're joining us, that's a better reason than revenge. But it's still not enough."

"It will have to do for now," she said.

CHAPTER 8

THE ELPIS HAD a crew of seventy-two, including Amar's squad, which made the ship feel rather small at times. Amar had never been much for small spaces, so he tried to quell his claustrophobia and fill his time learning more about XCOM, its history, the plans they were making.

Each Native cell had its own quirks, and these people were no different, except they had a deeper connection to the real thing. Sure, Thomas had been with XCOM, but her experience was almost exclusively military.

Their cell had coordinated with others in times past. They had sabotaged railways, looted food stockpiles, rescued more groups like the people in Oak-dale than he cared to think about, because that only reminded him of the ones they didn't manage to protect—the empty camps, the occasional mass graves they came across.

But there had only been the vaguest idea of a bigger plan. It was hard to organize.

They had their Morse code network and various ways of hiding information inside of what was ostensibly entertainment radio. Some cells had managed to hack into jabber propaganda and contradict it, but he wasn't sure how much good that did. Lena wasn't stupid, but she'd still been convinced the aliens were well intentioned, despite the occasional dissident broadcast claiming the contrary.

XCOM had been far more than a military organization. They had built infrastructure, done research and development, sought sources of funding and managed those funds to best advantage.

And in the end, they had failed. The governments that underwrote them lost faith in their ability to hold the aliens at bay—much less beat them— and folded. And that was very much how things still stood, with each region ruled by puppet regimes of collaborators.

But it didn't take a genius to understand that Shen had found funding somewhere, and that didn't just show in the ship itself. The Elpis carried a research lab in her bow.

Which is where he met the *other* Dr. Shen.

He guessed she was in early thirties. She had her father's onyx hair and a quiet intensity. She was never still, always tinkering with a widget, running computations, tuning the ship's engines. Not the sort of person who would drop everything to give you a tour. But she didn't mind talking as she went about her seemingly endless tasks. And she spoke Mandarin as well as English, which was nice to hear after all this time.

But most of the time it almost seemed like she was talking to herself, even when answering a question. As if he wasn't really quite there. She almost never stopped what she was doing to make eye contact.

He asked her about the ship's weapons once, and she made a dismissive little clicking sound.

"Yes, we have the deck guns," she said, "and we did retain minor torpedo capability, although what we bear is much smaller and deadlier than this ship originally carried. I'm standing where the forward torpedo batteries were. The fact is, the ship isn't at all about fighting. It's about hiding. If they ever really know where we are, they won't come within torpedo or gun range. They will torch us from the sky.

"So what have we been working on? Buffers to reduce engine sound. Filters to minimize the exhaust from burning diesel. The hull is wired with a stealth system that passes sixty percent of low-level energy emissions—like radar—around us rather than bouncing them back. We're not transparent, but we are translucent.

"But the number one thing that keeps us safe is that the enemy doesn't know we exist. So, weapons? We are already carrying more than we need."

The rest of the crew were standoffish at first, especially the soldiers, who consciously or unconsciously resented them for taking the places of their friends and comrades, and especially resented that Thomas was now the ranking officer.

But the fact was that despite having better armor and better weapons, what remained of Elpis's soldiers were on the green side, some having never seen any combat at all. Thomas dealt with that—and with the general boredom and restlessness that seemed inevitable on a voyage like this—by holding training sessions in close combat. When they surfaced, they went topside and took target practice and worked on basic tactics and communication.

Thomas had a style of command that got its results not from fear and intimidation, but rather from making you not want to let her down, and she was good at seeing the personalities of a squad and putting the right people together.

Usually. She had been right about Rider. Chitto, Amar still wasn't sure about. She had guts, and she had saved his life probably, back in the flood—but she couldn't hit the sub if she put the muzzle of her weapon against it, and she too often tended to act on her own, without consulting with anyone, including her partner.

Like the time she'd let Lena get the shotgun.

After the first week, Lena asked if she could participate in the drills, and Thomas put her in.

One day, after training, Thomas called Amar up to where she stood on the bow. Her fading blonde hair was in its usual long braid, but the strip above her forehead that she usually kept shaved was growing back in a bit.

"What's up, Chief?" he asked.

"Just checking in," she said.

"What do you mean?" he asked.

She fidgeted with her half-ear. "You know me," she said. "I'm not much on sharing and all that. But I know you took losing Rider hard."

"I'm fine, Chief," he said. "I'm doing my job okay, right?"

"Sure," she said. "Better than okay. But you used be . . . well, funny. Made jokes, told stories, poked fun at people. Now I rarely see you smile."

"You don't do any of that stuff, Chief," he said. "At least not much."

"True," she said. "But I never did. It's not in my nature." She sighed and looked out to sea. "We all have switches in us," she said. "To do what we do, sometimes we have to turn those switches off. But we also have to learn to turn them back on. You're not just a soldier to me, KB. You're *my* soldier."

"I appreciate that, Chief," he said.

He remembered his talk with Lena, his assumption that any complaint he made to his squad mates would be seen as a sign of weakness. Maybe he had undersold them—after all, they were the closest thing he had to a family.

"What I'm saying," Thomas went on, "is if you need to talk to someone, do it. I don't mean me. I'm terrible at this stuff."

"Okay, Chief," he said. "Is that all?"

"Not quite," she said. "I'd like you to start leading some exercises."

That came from a blind direction.

"Why me?" he asked.

"Because I see potential in you," she replied. "I think one day you'll make a fine squad leader. Why do you think I stuck you with Chitto? With any of the others, you would just follow their leads. With her, you have to learn to command."

So that was why. He knew there had to be something. But command?

"Begging your pardon, Chief," he said, "I don't think I'm the leader type."

"Exactly," she said. "If you thought so, you wouldn't be."

She clapped him on the shoulder and walked back toward the hatch, leaving him to wonder whether she was serious, kidding, or had just passed along a koan for him to contemplate.

***

The Elpis plowed along, on the sea and under it. They made much faster time on top of the water, averaging about eighteen or twenty kilometers an hour. Underwater, it was more like four.

As the trip wore on and they left inhabited lands farther behind, they spent more time on the surface, especially after dark.

One such night Amar lay on his back and watched the slow wheel of the stars, wondering at their beauty. The sea was calm, and the air was decidedly chilly.

He was remembering that some people believed the souls of the dead became stars. It seemed like a nice thought. If it were so, which would Rider be? The faint red one there, or the brash, actinic one near the horizon?

"May I join you?"

He saw Lena's silhouette against the night sky.

"Sure," he said.

She sat cross-legged beside him. "I never really saw the stars in Gulf City," she said, looking up. "There's always light. But this . . . this is gorgeous."

"You should see them from the high desert or the mountains," he said. "With air so thin and dry—it's almost like being in space."

"I would like to see that," she said. "Although it's hard to imagine them being brighter than this. Do you know the constellations?"

"Yes, some of them. I grew up just north of the equator. From there you can see all of the constellations in the Northern Hemisphere and most of the southern ones. We're starting to lose the northern stars."

"Do you mean we're in the Southern Hemisphere?" she asked.

"Yeah," he said. "We've been going south since we got clear of the gulf, and now it's starting to get cold."

"Where do you think we're going? Antarctica?"

"I don't know the specific destination any more than you do," he said. "But we're pretty far south, from what I can tell."

She looked back up at the stars. "I wonder which one they came from," she said. "The aliens."

Oddly, he hadn't thought about that since he was a kid. She was right; they had come from somewhere, and there was a chance at any given moment that he was looking at the homeland of their oppressors.

"Lena," he sighed, "you really know how to kill a mood."

She laughed, and he realized that it was the first time he'd heard her do so. He liked the sound of it. He remembered his conversation with Thomas, about how he never joked anymore.

Maybe his switch was resetting.

"Sorry," she said. "Not the first time I've been accused of that."

"It's okay," he said. "Before you showed up, my mood was about to take a bad turn anyway. I was thinking about a friend of mine."

"The woman who was killed rescuing Sam?"

"That's a good guess," he said. "Who told you about that?"

"DeLao. He said you were taking it pretty hard."

"I think I'm taking it just fine," he said.

First Thomas, now DeLao. Were they all talking about this?

"We were close," he admitted.

"Were you lovers?"

For a moment he was flat-out stunned.

"What kind of question is that?" he asked. "Why would you ask me that?"

"Auugggh," she said. "There I go again. I thought . . . I guess I thought you might want to talk about it." She paused. "And I guess I'm curious. About you."

What did that mean? he wondered. Her face was faint in the starlight, difficult to read. But she felt closer somehow. She was still sitting on the deck, and he was still lying down. Was she leaning over him?

"Curious about what?" he asked.

"Like, what's your real name? It can't be KB. That's just your pirate name."

"Amar," he said. "My mother named me Amar."

"I like it," she said. "What does it mean?"

He felt a faint smile on his face. "It can mean either tranquility or strife," he said.

"Kind of a conflicted name," she said.

"I suppose," he said. "What does 'Lena' mean?"

"I have no idea," she replied. "I'm named after my great-grandmother. But I like your name. It suits you."

She laid down beside him, and her hand fell so it was just touching his. Something akin to an electric jolt shocked through his entire body. For a moment he felt like he couldn't breathe.

She didn't move her hand, and after a moment her fingers moved to twine with his, and without really thinking, he gripped back.

They stayed like that, silently, for a long moment. Then she rolled onto her side so that she was facing him. Her face was very close, and he could feel the warmth of her breath.

"No," he said. "Rider and I weren't lovers. Maybe in another world, if we had met on a dance floor instead of downrange. But being that kind of involved with someone in your squad . . . it isn't a good idea. It can make you sloppy."

For a moment he saw her eyes clearly, bright stars shining in a nebula. Then she laid back down and returned her gaze to the stars.

"I see," she said. "Yes, I can see how it might."

She sounded disappointed, and he knew he was, and in that moment he wanted to go back to before he'd said anything.

Instead he just uncurled his fingers from hers.

***

Three days later, Thomas called them together.

"Tomorrow morning," she informed them. "O-four hundred, full gear. We're going ashore."

He noticed she had shaved her bangs again.

***

"I feel so pretty," DeLao said, examining himself in his new armor. Mostly new, anyway. They had all been measured for new stuff, but if they had, say, a chest plate still in decent shape, Shen just worked it in.

Their supplies weren't unlimited, but even more to the point, the three weeks they had spent at sea—as long as it had seemed—still wasn't that much time in which to fabricate full suits of armor, not with the scale of the engineering equipment and personnel present on the Elpis. Still, Amar had to agree they were at least 60 percent spiffier than before.

And a little safer.

***

The Elpis surfaced under an overcast sky. It was bitterly cold, and Amar was happy Shen had given them insulated body suits to go beneath their armor.

The ship lay off the lee side of an island that was the single most uninviting place he had ever seen. A truncated volcanic cone formed its core, and most of it was covered in snow and ice. What wasn't frozen over looked mostly like black gravel. The overall impression was that of a really filthy snowball, dropped from a height into a cold blue sea. From what he could see, the island was tiny, no more than a few kilometers in diameter.

A few elephant seals reclined on the stony beach, and maybe half a million birds, most of which were penguins of some kind. The smell of them was unbelievable, enough to bring tears to his eyes.

"What's she doing?" DeLao wondered. Amar saw Lena emerging from the hatch, just behind Sam. She had on a parka and flak jacket, but she didn't appear to be armed.

"Dr. Shen—the older one—asked if we could take her along," Thomas said. "So I don't want to hear anything else about it."

"Fine," DeLao grumbled. Their body suits had parka-style hoods. DeLao had his on but was wearing his Red Devils cap over it.

"Antarctica?" Toby wondered aloud, taking in the island through the scope on his rifle.

"Or pretty close," Amar said.

"There's nothing here," Toby muttered.

"That's the point," Sam said. He glanced around at the party, which included the usual squad minus Dux, who was a great deal better but not yet ready for combat. Carrying the rocket launcher in his place was a massive man named Aleki Palepoi. His face was soft, kind-looking, and didn't really seem to fit his size. One of his arms and half of his chest were covered in complex blackwork tattoos.

"We shouldn't see any action here," Sam told them. "But better safe than sorry."

"I don't know," Nishimura said. "Those penguins look pretty suspicious. If they start glowing, shoot to kill."

"And the smell," Amar said. "That can't be of this world."

"It's called *guano*," DeLao said. "You'd best get used to it."

"All the time I've spent with you," Amar said, "you'd think I *would* be used to it."

The nose of the Elpis was edged over a metal platform built up from the shore. They climbed down and in a few moments were standing on the desolate shingle.

Sam seemed to be looking for something, and Thomas didn't say anything about going anywhere, so they milled around a little. The birds and seals watched them, and some of the former even waddled over, near enough for him to kick one if he wanted to, but the birds didn't seem at all concerned that he would.

"Heads up," Nishimura said.

Across the beach, three vehicles were moving toward them, parting the sea of penguins. As they drew nearer, Amar saw two of them were jeeps and the third a large flatbed truck. The latter pulled up as near the sub as possible, and the crew of the Elpis began lowering crates onto the bed with one of the two cranes the ship sported.

The jeeps were for them. Once the truck was loaded, they piled in and started out along the beach.

The drivers seemed human enough and eager to talk. Amar's was named Eduardo and had a lot of questions about what was going on elsewhere in the world. The island was too far away from any place, he said, to receive the usual radio programs.

Amar filled him in when he could, but Eduardo mostly wanted to know about Argentina, and Amar had never been there. He remembered a few things from the radio—there had been a riot in one of the settlements, and they were doing okay in the underground football league.

Amar revised his estimate of the island to about five kilometers at its widest, and was just starting to wonder if they were going to circumnavigate it when the vehicles took a right turn toward the volcano.

At first, he could not imagine what their destination was: The mountain was far too steep to drive up.

But as they came nearer he saw that what he had initially taken to be part of the icy mountainside was actually a metal wall painted a matte white. As they approached, it began to rise, revealing the cavern behind it.

"Welcome to Wunderland," Eduardo said.

CHAPTER 9

WUNDERLAND WAS A series of manmade caverns and tunnels carved into the andesite rock of the volcano. Scatters of crystals winked from dark gray stone, reflecting the overhead lights. A petite blond woman named Marisol took the squad off Eduardo's hands and escorted them through the complex, which seemed to be mostly living quarters, laboratories, and little else.

"We get our power from the volcano," Marisol explained.

"It's active, you mean?" Thomas said.

"Yes, although we don't expect a major eruption anytime soon. It blew out a little ash back in the 1960s, I think. I like to hike in the caldera. It's warm enough you don't have to wear a coat, some days."

"That sounds great," Amar said. "Do you also enjoy surfing on tsunamis?"

"We'll have plenty of warning before it erupts," she assured them. "Ah, here we are."

They had entered a largish round room filled with banks of screens and controls. Most of them were dark, but about half of them seemed to be showing real-time images of the New Cities. Others had various projections of global maps depicting patterns, some constantly shifting, some relatively stable. They might have been network maps of some sort.

"So," someone said. "Dr. Shen has finally come up for air."

The speaker was a woman in perhaps her sixties, her auburn hair shot with silver.

"Dr. Vahlen," Sam said. "So nice to meet you in person."

"The pleasure is mine," she replied.

The name wouldn't have meant anything to Amar a month ago, but that was before he had spent three weeks reviewing XCOM history and tactics. Just as Shen had been the chief engineer of the organization, Vahlen had been the top scientist. Like the rest of the XCOM leadership, she had been presumed dead. But here she was, tunneled into a volcano in the South Atlantic. That, like the building of the Elpis, couldn't have been too cheap. This was starting to feel bigger and bigger.

"I suppose it was too much to ask the old man to come here himself," she said.

"He wanted to," Sam said. "I managed to talk him out of it."

She studied Sam with a slight air of distaste. "I see," she finally said. "Well, his communications were quite the tease. I have been quite agitated, not knowing what you have discovered, what brings you here to me. So sit down; tell me why you've come all this way and what I can do for you."

She ushered them to a round table. One of her assistants brought glasses and a pitcher of water as Sam explained about the downed spaceship. Amar noticed that Lena didn't seem all that surprised—although she had been left out of the initial conversation, after three weeks in a tin can it was hard for anything so big to remain secret.

Vahlen listened patiently, nodding now and then but otherwise not showing much of what was going on behind her gray eyes.

When Sam concluded speaking, she nodded again and tapped the table with her finger, then rose and began slowly strolling about the room.

"It's very odd," she said. "Dr. Shen was always quite . . . Well, I won't say timid . . . but rather *conservative* in his outlook. This plan of his is bold, perhaps even reckless. I wonder what has changed him so."

"I think the war shifted his perspective," Sam said. "And I think Lily—"

"His daughter is with him?" she interrupted, seeming surprised. "That would make a difference, I suppose. He's very lucky to have found her. But she must be an adult now."

"Yes," Sam said. "She is. And she's Dr. Shen's primary assistant."

Vahlen was silent for a moment before continuing, and when she did, it was on an entirely different subject.

"We have not been idle here," she said. "I've been studying their technology as best I can, from what scraps of it come to me, and by monitoring their communications, their movements, the locations of their power nexuses. I have a great deal of information about their aircraft, which has been languishing to no purpose. It was always our relationship, you know, that I would dream of things and he would build them. Usually these things were a little less than what I conceived of, but he was competent. I would be more than pleased to analyze the data you've brought, Sam, and to make copies of everything relevant I've collected over the years."

She leaned forward and became a little more intense. "But there is something I want in trade. Come with me, please."

She led them down through the maze of tunnels until they reached another room, which held a great deal of equipment that Amar did not recognize, and a few bits he did, such as the autopsy table. And as he turned his gaze around the room, he began to notice other things—like the large cylinders filled with some sort of liquid—and the body parts in them. Most were unrecognizable. Some looked alien, and a few human.

"My location has kept me secure," she said. "Most of what I have learned about their technology I've learned remotely. But it has been difficult to acquire specimens. Shen wants his ship, and yes, I will help with that. But you understand, this war will not be won with machines. It is their biotech we must master—and surpass."

She led them to a wall with a bank of large drawers, like those Amar had once seen in a morgue. She selected one and pulled it open.

"Here," she said.

Amar's first instinct was to reach for his sidearm—but then he saw the thing wasn't moving and was enclosed in what looked like glass, although it was glowing faintly green.

"Is it dead?" Thomas asked.

"Cryosleep," Vahlen said. "I prefer live specimens. So much more can be learned."

Her tone of voice was clinical, but there was something in her expression that suggested something more passionate.

Amar studied the thing. Like the ADVENT soldiers, it had a certain amount of humanity in its appearance—but less. The proportions weren't quite right: Its arms and legs were too long, its head a little too big, and its eyes even larger.

"Bloody hell," he breathed.

"Quite striking, isn't it?" Vahlen said. "All life on Earth is built from the same genetic code. Under such circumstances, genetic manipulation is relatively easy—genes from a tomato can easily be spliced, for instance, into a human genome. But the aliens have a radically different code—or codes, rather. Sectoids and Chryssalids, for instance, are from very different places, genetically—and probably cosmographically. And yet they've somehow made these incompatible systems work together to create something new. What you see here is a human-alien hybrid."

"Like the ADVENT soldiers," Thomas said.

"Precisely. But this specimen has been preserved here for ten years. From what I can make out from their propaganda, they now seem much more human. They're making progress. But toward what? For what reason? These are the questions we should be asking."

She slid the drawer shut. "Tell Shen I need more specimens, alive if possible. That is what I require if I render him my . . . machine knowledge." She studied their faces as if to make certain they understood.

"I'm sure we can work something out," Sam said.

"Of course," Vahlen replied. Her eyes narrowed a bit. "There is another thing," she said. "This so-called 'contagion.' What do you know of it?"

"Not much, I'm afraid," Sam said. "I've wondered if it's not just part of their propaganda."

"Have you?" Vahlen said. A faint smile appeared on her face, almost a smirk. "I see. Well, if you learn otherwise, I would be interested in what you find. In the meantime, please avail yourselves of my hospitality. Perhaps you would enjoy a hike in the caldera? It's lovely this time of year."

As they began to stand, she looked them over again.

"Which of you is Lena Bishop?" she asked.

"I am," Lena volunteered.

"A moment with you alone, please?"

***

Amar opted not to walk in the volcano. One of the staff members invited him to view their substantial library of preinvasion movies and television shows, and he decided that was probably a good use of his downtime. Chitto sat with him for a while but seemed to be mostly bored, and left after an hour or two.

Lena replaced her an hour later. "I've never seen this," she said after a moment, watching a situation comedy about people who worked together.

"You're not allowed to," he said. "They don't want anyone to be reminded of what things were like before they showed up."

She nodded but didn't say anything.

"What did the old lady want with you?" he asked.

"She offered me a job," Lena replied in an odd tone.

"Really?" he said, turning down the volume and facing her. "Doing what?"

"I'll be trained to do something," she said.

"Something? That's awfully vague."

He had been feeling pretty good, but suddenly things felt a little out of control again. He'd assumed that Lena would continue her training as a soldier. While he didn't feel terribly good about that, it meant she would be around. He wanted her around.

"I thought so, too," she said. "Apparently the main thing isn't what job I do but that I remain here."

His mouth felt suddenly a little dry.

"Why?" But he knew the answer. He should have guessed.

She smiled, but it didn't read as happy. Quite the opposite. "Sam warned me that if I came with you I would know too much for them to let me go. It seems he was right. They want me tucked away here, where there's no risk of me jumping ship whenever the Elpis comes to port."

"Vahlen said that?"

"Of course not," she replied, "but I can read between the lines."

"I can talk to Shen," he said. He should have already. How had he not seen this coming?

She shook her head. "It's okay. It's probably for the best. I don't think I could go back home anyway, knowing what I know. But I don't know that I belong on the Elpis—Thomas will never let me have a weapon, and even if she did, I don't know that I'm cut out to do what you do." She gave him a thin smile. "Who knows, maybe after a while I can build a little trust here. Do something useful. Find my mother, or at least the truth about what happened to her."

"Is that really how you feel?"

"I don't know," she said. "I'm trying to put the best face on things, since I don't really have a choice."

Amar nodded, but he wasn't sure what to say.

"There is one tiny little bright side," she said. "Maybe."

"What's that?"

"I'm not going to be in a squad with you."

It caught him off guard, although he knew it shouldn't have. He didn't know who started to lean in first, and he didn't care. Her lips were warm and soft, and in fact everything about her was abruptly completely amazing. And he knew that he shouldn't, that it was stupid, that when they sailed away and left her there it would leave a hole in his chest as sure as any mag rifle could drill. He didn't care. He'd spent years regretting the past and worrying about the future. To be in a moment, this moment, with her, was all he wanted.

He got the call from Thomas an hour later, and it had to end. That was difficult. He wasn't sure what to say to her, so he just touched his forehead to hers, and they stood that way for a few heartbeats.

"I wonder how long it will take Vahlen to analyze the data," Lena said.

"I don't know," he said. "A few more days. More. I hope."

"Me too," she said. "Find me later, okay?"

"Okay."

✦✦✦

Amar ended up getting his walk in the caldera after all. Thomas sent Toby and him up to patrol and check on some sensors for Vahlen. As promised, the mouth of the volcano was warmer than the rest of the island, so Toby eschewed his hood and instead wore his customary skullcap. He had several—this one was colorful—red, gold and green. It looked new, and Amar wondered if Toby had crocheted it on the Elpis. He usually wore black or brown.

The view down was better than the one from the beach. There was another island of about the same size as the one they were on three kilometers or so away, and beyond that nothing but marine horizon.

But they were fortunate enough to see the sun rise. Amar had always loved the anticipation as the sky grew brighter until the moment when the first fiery little slice of the sun appeared, spilling a golden river across the waves. He was still amazed by how suddenly the sphere appeared, how quickly it leapt from the horizon and then seemed to slow and settle into a statelier pace. It was like a magic trick, distorting one's sense of space and time.

Toby watched with him, looking thoughtful.

"You're a sunrise guy, aren't you?" Toby said.

"I like them, I guess," he said.

"That's not what I mean," Toby said. "I grew up by the water, like you, in Israel and later California. So I never saw the sun come out of the sea like that. I always saw it go into it, vanish, disappear."

"Okay," Amar said. "I've seen that, too."

"But you weren't formed by it," Toby said. "You grew up on the east coast of Malaysia, yes? How old were you before you saw the sun set into the sea?"

"I don't know. When I was seventeen, I guess," he said.

"Right!" Toby said. "I was older than that before I saw what we just watched. You're a sunrise guy. I'm a sunset guy."

"Is there really a difference?" Amar asked, wondering where the lean sniper was going with all of this.

"I don't know," Toby admitted. "I feel like there must be. To see birth every morning, instead of death. That must make a difference."

"Okay," Amar said, "now you're getting all metaphorical on me. What's gotten into you?"

Toby shook his head. "I don't know," he said. "Probably nothing. Too much time to think, I suppose."

He looked off into the far distance, leaving Amar feeling a little awkward. "You know," Amar said, "If you grew up on a little island like this, you would see both events every day. I wonder what that would make you."

Toby smiled. "Then you would get to choose," he said.

Amar's earpiece crackled. It was Thomas.

"You two need to get back here," she said. "Now."

***

They met with Vahlen in the same round room. She was clearly angry, reading data from one of her screens and ranting in what sounded like German. "The signal," she said to her assistant. "It's all wrong. Not at all typical."

She looked at them as they entered. "What have you done?" she demanded.

"I don't understand the question," Thomas replied.

Vahlen stabbed her finger toward one of the screens. It showed six small dots, moving in formation.

"ADVENT troop transports," she said. "Coming here. There can be no mistake."

"Are you saying we were followed?" Thomas said.

"I'm saying nothing of the kind," Vahlen snapped. "If they had followed the Elpis, they would have arrived here just after you did. And they would not be coming from South America. No, they were summoned. My instruments didn't pick up the signal. It was too subtle until I suspected it." She glanced down at the readings, then back at them.

"The signal originates here," she said, waving at her machines. "Something has hijacked my own system and is forcing it to transmit. I've shut it down, of course, but it's already too late."

She handed a small briefcase to Sam. "Get this to Shen," she said. "And hurry, you don't have much time before they arrive."

"What about you?" Sam asked. "We need you, Dr. Vahlen. Come with us."

"I am not without defenses," she said. "And I can't leave all of this for them to find. Go! Take the vehicles in the hangar."

As they started out, Amar noticed Lena stood as if rooted. Looking at him. Looking stricken. Vahlen had already turned away, poking furiously at a keyboard.

Between the space of one breath and another, he made his decision.

He grabbed her by the wrist.

"Come on," he whispered. "She's not thinking about you right now. In a minute she may remember."

***

"What the hell?" DeLao shouted, as Amar pushed Lena into the jeep and took the wheel. "We can't bring her. She's the one that signaled them; you know it was."

"We don't know any such thing," Amar replied. "Vahlen said it was her own equipment. Get in, and let's get out of here."

"If we take her back to ship, they'll track us there, too," Toby said. "DeLao's right. Nothing else makes sense."

"It wasn't me," Lena said. "I swear it."

The other jeep with Thomas, Sam, Nishimura, and Palepoi was starting to move out.

"We should go," Chitto said.

"Get in, DeLao," Amar said.

"You're a great actor," DeLao told Lena. "I remember when we first picked you up. Pretending you wanted to join us, then turning a gun on us. You're not going to fool us again. Or me, anyway."

Amar started the car and stepped on the gas. With a yelp, DeLao flung himself in.

"You damn fool!" Toby said.

"We've got no time for this," Amar said. "We'll figure it out at the ship."

They made it nearly halfway back before they saw the transports, flying in from the west. For one heart-stopping moment, Amar thought they were fine, that they hadn't been noticed. But then one of the fliers peeled off from the rest.

"You see?" DeLao bellowed.

"Just shut up," Amar said.

Thomas's voice crackled in his ear.

"Stop and get out," she said. "We can't lead them back to the Elpis. We'll fight them here."

The beach offered no cover whatsoever unless you counted the jeeps, which in Amar's experience never lasted long against alien weapons—and in fact tended to turn into bombs. So their only recourse was the mountain behind them. Where ice didn't cover the stone, Amar could see the shape of how the lava had come down in viscous, almost ropey flows with grooves between them that offered some cover. Amar found a likely place a few meters up the slope and took a position, with Chitto on his left flank and DeLao off to his right. Thomas was yet farther to the right, and Sam was with her. The new guy, Palepoi, was a little higher up, behind them. Toby was still spidering his way up the mountain to what looked like a deeper crack in the ice. Nishimura he did not see at all.

Lena was still with him.

"I swear," she said. "I had nothing to do with this."

"Just stay down," he said. "No matter what."

The slope was far too steep for the transport to land on, so the jabbers would have to land on the shingle where they had abandoned their vehicles. Amar watched the craft settle, trying to calm himself.

"This is going to be so much fun," Toby's voice crackled in his ear.

CHAPTER 10

THE HATCH OF the transport opened, and ADVENT soldiers poured out, twelve of them, most running toward their positions. One—a captain—hung back, taking cover behind one of the jeeps. Two shield bearers stood near him and began laying down suppressing fire. Ferromagnetic slugs spalled stone and hissed into the snow all around them.

High above, Amar heard the crack of Toby's high-powered rifle and saw one of the troopers stagger. Amar immediately lifted a bit and unloaded a few rounds on her. Enemy fire spattered against the lava flow in front of him. Everyone else was shooting now. He took aim and fired at the stun lancer trying to come around on his left, but the fellow ducked nimbly behind a burr of stone.

The air was alive with deadly hail, and the sharp scent of ozone nearly overpowered the stink of guano.

"Right there!" Chitto yelped and blasted away. Concentrating on the flanking trooper, Amar had missed the one coming straight toward them, arms flailing. He turned and fired almost point blank at the jabber as it lifted its lance to hit him. It poised over him for a moment, rocking on the balls of its feet as it tried to keep balanced. Amar shot it again, and it went jangling down the slope.

"Bloody hell," he muttered, turning back. Was the other jabber still behind the same rock, or . . . ?

No. It appeared farther upslope, coming almost from behind him. He lifted up to get a shot at it, but the cover fire from the shield bearers forced him back down.

Cursing silently, he waited.

Then, suddenly, the stun trooper was there, leaping forward . . .

No, falling.

"Nice shot, Toby," he said.

"Thanks," Toby said. "I . . . Oh, crap. Guys, they're coming from behind us. Must have landed another transport in the caldera. I can't hold this position."

"Come on down, Toby," Thomas said. "Everybody else get ready. We're going to do a Custer. Palepoi, open the front door. Amar, Chitto—mind the house. DeLao, you're with me."

Amar heard the rocket launcher fire, and then one of the shield bearers exploded in a billowing black cloud. To his right, Thomas bolted down the mountain, her assault rifle yammering.

Amar stood and began firing at the troopers as they emerged from the smoke. A rifle fired, just behind him, and heard Toby whoop.

"Got the captain," he said. Then he made a peculiar coughing sound. Amar couldn't turn around, but a few seconds later the sharpshooter came staggering by him, his eyes wide and glazed.

"Toby, get down!" he shouted.

Toby looked at him, puzzled, as if he didn't understand what he was saying. Then, a sleet of mag pellets fell on them from above. Toby's armor was shredded, and he tumbled down the slope.

Amar would be just as exposed in a few seconds.

"Lena," he said, trying to keep his voice steady, to not let the panic seep into it. "Get over there with Chitto. Do it now."

He raised and fired upslope as Lena tripped her way across the rough stone. Then he scrambled a little farther up, where a boulder offered some protection. He'd thought his knee was better, but it was aching again, and although his face was cold, inside of his bodysuit he was sweating.

He could only hope Thomas and DeLao were keeping the troopers behind him on the beach busy, because his back was now fully available to them.

They weren't, or at least not entirely. Slugs traced crimson trails up the slope less than a meter from him. There wasn't anything he could do about it, though, so he gritted his teeth and charged for the boulder, waiting for the burst he would never hear, maybe never even feel.

It didn't come. Instead, he heard a rifle fire. He reached the boulder and looked back down. Chitto had Toby's gun. As he watched, she calmly took aim at the remaining shield bearer and put a bullet right between its eyes. Then she shifted her aim to a trooper who had Thomas pinned down behind a jeep.

She squeezed the trigger, and it, too, dropped.

Then Lena stood up, lifting Chitto's shotgun, pointing it at him. He froze, unable to move, unable to believe what she was doing.

Then the muzzle lifted farther, and she fired.

A nightmare came tumbling over him.

His brain told him it was a spider, a spider that stood as high as a man, a spider with knives for legs and a centipede for a face. It hadn't been able to dodge Lena's blast, but it had tried, and it hit the rocks two meters from Lena and Chitto.

He knew he was screaming inarticulately, and he didn't care. He opened up on the monster and turned it into a twitching mass of horribleness.

He looked back up and saw three more of the things bounding toward them with unnatural speed.

Chryssalids. One of the nastier aliens, nearly mindless but incredibly dangerous.

"Let's go!" he hollered. "Now."

As they scrambled down, he saw Nishimura beheading a jabber with her sword. Thomas and DeLao were firing at the enemies coming down the hill, and they hauled ass toward the transports. He signaled for Chitto to go left, and he took right. A glance over his shoulder showed one of the monsters bounding toward him, and he knew he would never make it to cover.

Thomas stood from behind the jeep and fired a burst at the thing, jolting it so it lost its rhythm. But then it scrambled back up. Amar dove past the chief, hoping to get behind the transport. He rolled and turned, expecting the Chryssalid to be right on top of him. But it had changed targets.

As he watched it leap over the jeep, he had what seemed like a long moment to clearly see its four scythe-like legs and two spindly arms ending in four wicked claws, all coming down on Thomas.

Amar saw blood spray as Thomas fired a final burst, and the Chryssalid plunged its claws into her.

Thomas!

Then it turned its glowing yellow eyes toward him.

He emptied his clip into it. He reloaded, and would have shot it again, but it wasn't moving anymore, so he began looking for another target, his breath coming almost like hiccups, like his lungs had shrunk to the size of thumbs.

Troopers and aliens were swarming down the volcano. There were so many of them that he had trouble choosing which one to target. Worse, he saw another transport coming over the lip of the caldera.

He looked around at his companions. DeLao, grim-faced, changing his clip. Nishimura, her sword sheathed, pistol blazing. Lena, shotgun braced on her shoulder.

And Chitto taking shot after shot, as if she was on a firing range rather than in a battle for her life. Her face was a mask, devoid of emotion.

"KB!" Sam yelped from behind him. "Look!"

Where Thomas lay dead, something moved. He watched as the Chryssalid was pushed away, and Thomas staggered to her feet.

"Chief!" he said. "I thought . . ." Then he trailed off, remembering what he knew about the venom Chryssalids carried in their claws.

It should have been obvious, anyway: Thomas had gaping wounds, and her throat was torn out. There was nothing human about her eyes. Like Rider, there was no soul there anymore. No human soul, anyway.

Thomas took a step toward him.

He shot her, again and again, until he was sure she wouldn't get up again. Each bullet seemed to take something of him with it, hollowing him out.

"What are we going to do?" DeLao shouted. "We don't have a chance."

Amar glanced around, suddenly feeling weirdly calm. The penguins that had carpeted the beach earlier were all waddling to the ocean, which was only about two meters behind them.

"Sam," Amar said, "make a break for the water, now. Maybe they won't notice you amongst all the birds. It'll be cold, but you might make it back to the Elpis. It's a chance."

"I can't—"

"Go!" Amar barked. "You're no help to us here."

Sam stared at him, then nodded.

"I'll make it," he said.

"The rest of you, tighten up. Stay behind the transports. Target the Chryssalids first. If anyone has a grenade left, wait until they come in groups. That's going to be soon."

He watched the other transport come, wondering where it would land.

And then, without any warning, the mountain exploded.

In the first insane moment, he thought the volcano had chosen that moment to erupt, but—flash frozen in his mind—he saw a string of explosions too regular to be natural, hurling a thousand canisters skyward . . .

"Into the water, now!" he yelled.

As he turned to run, the canisters opened into blossoms of liquid flame. He saw the flying transport turning end over end, engulfed.

The concussion slammed him face first into the brine, which was only waist deep at that point, but the bottom fell off quickly. He struggled to stay under, let the armor drag him down, as the bitter chill of the water stung his face.

But then he felt blistering heat on his back and swam as best he could, trying to outrun the flame that was spreading on the surface.

He came up for air and saw fire curling all around him. He took one hot breath and sank down again, pulling himself along the rocks on the bottom.

The next time he surfaced, he was clear of the flames. The whole face of the mountain and most of the beach were burning like a torch.

Without their thermal suits, they would have all been dead within minutes. Once clear of the flames, they tried to keep their hands and heads above water to avoid frostbite, but Amar was shivering almost uncontrollably by the time they finally found a bit of beach that wasn't on fire.

They huddled there, warmed by burning propellant and choking on fumes until the flames finally subsided.

Aside from themselves, nothing on the island was moving.

Amar wearily counted heads. They had lost Thomas and Toby, DeLao's arm was half shot off, and Palepoi was wounded in the thigh. Statistically, not bad, but Thomas? Toby? To lose them was staggering.

It was like his past was being erased. Thomas had recruited him.

But he couldn't get bogged down in that now.

"We're still alive," Amar told the others. "We still have work to do. Drag yourselves up, and let's get back to the Elpis."

DeLao groaned but pulled himself to his feet, and they started toward the ship.

Amar glanced over at Chitto.

"Why the hell haven't you been using a rifle all along?" he asked.

She shrugged. "When I signed up, they gave me a shotgun."

***

When they reached the landing, they found Sam standing there. He looked up wearily.

"Thank god," he said. "I thought I was alone."

"What about the Elpis?" Amar asked.

Sam shook his head. "I think she left without us," he said.

But Amar was studying the platform, which was now perforated by magnetic rifle fire.

"I don't think they left," Lena said.

She pointed out to sea. A few hundred meters out a patch of flotsam floated, heaving up and down on the swells.

Amar stared at it, feeling numb. Behind him, the fire on the mountain had diminished to a few flickers amongst the rocks. In the sky above, a black cloud stretched southeast for as far as he could see.

"We've got an hour or two before sundown," Amar told them. "If we don't find someplace to camp, we're going to freeze to death."

"I may be okay with that," DeLao said gloomily.

***

The only plants on the island were moss and lichens, and most of that was now gone, courtesy of Vahlen's massive mining project. With nothing to make a shelter from, they had to sleep in a pile that night, sharing body heat. The next day they hiked back toward Wunderland.

Thomas and Toby were pretty much cremated, but since they could, they took time to gather their remains and bury them in the talus at the base of the mountain.

The doors to Wunderland had been blown open. The remains of the three ADVENT transports left were just outside, along with a lot of fried troopers and Chryssalids.

Inside, everything had been torched. The labs were still smoldering, and the power was down.

They found a handful of human bodies, but not enough to account for the population of the island. Hopefully, that was good news. Vahlen had avoided detection and capture for two decades. She must have had an escape plan.

They searched the ruins, looking for anything they could use and not finding very much.

"We can melt ice for water," Sam told them that afternoon. "Judging by the number of sea birds, there must be a lot of fish out there. I don't think survival will be a problem, although it won't be fun."

"Can you build a radio?" Amar asked.

Sam ran his fingers through his hair. "Vahlen did a pretty good job with the scorched earth bit," he replied. "I might manage to make something with very limited range, like I did back when you found me. That's not likely to do us much good."

"You're all missing the point," DeLao said. "The aliens sent out six transports full of goons that never came back. You think they'll let that go?"

"He's right," Amar said. "We need to find a hidey hole. If they don't find us, they'll assume we're dead or we left. Vahlen had some way out. Let's find it."

"What about her?" DeLao said, pointing at Lena.

"I didn't have anything to do with all of this," she said. Her face was smudged, and the hair on one side of her head was badly singed. She still had the shotgun in her hands.

Amar wanted to believe her, but even though he had shouted down DeLao earlier, he had his own doubts. She had been cozying up to him from the beginning, hadn't she? First to lull him into letting his guard down so she could make her escape. Had she kissed him to distract him from the obvious truth, that she was a spy in their midst?

But something about that didn't make sense. If she really was an ADVENT plant, why the whole New City girl act? Why actively make them distrust her if her job was to infiltrate them and lead the jabbers to one of their bases?

"Maybe it's not her," Sam said. "Or maybe it is, and she doesn't know it."

"Yeah, or maybe it's you," DeLao said. "What the hell do we know about you?"

"I know him," Palepoi said, sounding a little irritated, his normally placid face set in a frown. "He's been with Dr. Shen for a long time. He's no traitor."

"Or Chitto," DeLao went on. "She's new. Why exactly did you join up, Chitto?"

"To meet real winners like you," she said. "Gotta find a husband somewhere, right?"

"Stop this," Sam said. "DeLao, stop it. Vahlen said something about the signal being wrong, about something using her own instruments to send the homing signal. Wrong how? What was she talking about?"

Something suddenly clicked in Amar's mind.

"Lena's implant," he said.

Everyone turned to look at him.

"The smugglers took it out," Sam said.

"Maybe," Amar said. "But . . . didn't it feel like those guys gave up too easily?"

"Toby dropped two of them in two seconds," DeLao said.

"Right," Amar conceded. "Then they went a few rounds with us and took off. When has that ever happened?"

"We had the drop on them, and they knew it," DeLao countered. "It wasn't worth staying."

"That's how you or I might think," Amar said. "But jabbers usually call for backup and keep fighting. I thought it stank then, but it reeks now."

"Fine," Nishimura said. "You're saying they wanted us to find her."

"Sure," he said. "Maybe they used her as a stalking horse from the beginning. They must have known she was leaving Gulf City and heading out into the settlements. Right, Lena?"

"Of course I told them where I was going," Lena said. "You're supposed to register for travel." A look of horror was slowly spreading across her face.

"Right," Sam said. "So they followed you to Greenville, and when the smugglers drugged you, ADVENT followed them to their depot. Maybe they had already cut your implant out, maybe not. Either way, ADVENT killed them. Then they put in a new implant. A different kind of implant, maybe a more advanced one built for long-range tracking. We showed up, they made it look like a fight, and then they left."

"And they've been tracking us ever since," Lena said. "Oh my god."

"Hang on," DeLao said. "I examined her. Sure they sewed her up, but I checked. There was no implant."

"There's one way to find out," Nishimura said.

"Yes," Lena said. "Yes, do it."

DeLao got his medical kit. He gave Lena a local and then cut through her scar, pulling the wound open and dabbing at it with a cloth to stanch the bleeding.

"See?" he said. "No implant."

Instead of looking at her cut, Lena was staring at Amar.

"Dig a little deeper," he said.

Lena paled further as DeLao cut further into her muscle tissue. After a minute, his eyebrows lifted.

"*Mierda*," he said.

He changed out the scalpel for forceps and after a moment pulled something out. It was tiny, but as he pulled, long red strands as thin as hair came out behind it. Lena closed her eyes and began shaking, but she bore up until almost a half meter of the stuff emerged from her.

"What the hell is that?" Sam asked.

Amar studied the tiny bead from which the hairs protruded.

"If I had to guess, I would say it's biological. Maybe it amped up her nervous system so it could transmit a signal to Vahlen's equipment. It's really a question for Vahlen."

They debated trying to keep the thing for further study, but in the end the risk was too great. DeLao made some notes, and then they burned it and tossed the ashes into the ocean.

CHAPTER 11

NISHIMURA FOUND THE secret escape route, which was no longer quite so secret—the final blast that torched Vahlen's complex had shifted the hidden panel and revealed a corridor and stairs beyond. Locked and loaded, they followed them up and emerged in the gigantic bowl of the caldera.

But what they found was bad news—the hulks of five helicopters, as torched as anything on the beach. They could see a number of charred skeletons that must have been blown clear of the crash.

DeLao sat down, rested his bandaged arm on his knee, and put his head down.

"They didn't make it," Palepoi said, voicing the obvious.

"Yeah," DeLao said. "And now we have no way off of this island."

"Well," Palepoi said. "That's that, isn't it?"

It seemed so to Amar. He wasn't sure how far the nearest inhabited land was, but he was willing to bet it was a long, long way. With luck, they could avoid the next patrol ADVENT sent out, but then what? The base had just been resupplied by the Elpis. How long before another supply ship came?

Was there any other supply ship?

Sam turned slowly toward them, his face stern. His slight body seemed to grow taller.

"No," Sam said. "That is *not* that. We're alive, and we have information the resistance needs. So we do not give up. We hide. We survive. And we do the mission."

"How?" Amar asked.

"You lead your troops," Sam said. "Dig in someplace. Let me worry about the rest."

***

Chitto went up to the rim of the caldera with the scoped rifle to watch for fliers while the rest of them went to work on closing up the once-secret door, in hopes of using the upward passage as a hiding place; the crater end of the tunnel could be easily disguised with packed snow.

The problem was, they couldn't shift the thing back. The metal door had warped in the intense heat; it wouldn't slide or be shifted a centimeter in any direction.

"We're just going to have to blow it," Sam finally said. "Collapse the tunnel."

"With grenades?"

"I can make it work," Sam said "I just need to place them right and rig a way to detonate them from a distance. Nishimura, give me a hand."

About an hour later, Sam and Nishimura emerged from the tunnel. Then, a muffled explosion blew a cloud of black dust out of the tunnel mouth. They waited for it to clear and then went cautiously back down to see the results.

"Holy smokes," Sam said, when they arrived. "That is not what I was going for."

The ceiling had indeed collapsed—and so had the floor.

Amar's earphone crackled.

"I see something," Chitto said. "Coming from the west, like last time."

"Okay," Amar said. "This is it. Everyone in. Chitto, get down here, fast."

She did get there fast. She must have more or less skated down the crater wall.

Once she was in, they collapsed the pile of snow and ice they had hacked up. They couldn't make it smooth without leaving someone outside, but it was what it was. If anyone looked really close, they were screwed. They could only hope no one looked really close.

When they were all in the passage, Sam called him back down.

"I think I found something," he said.

***

The explosion had opened a second tunnel beneath the first, and in fact the first three meters had been a trap door laminated with stone to make it appear natural. It didn't lead up, but proceeded in a fairly level manner for maybe a hundred meters before widening into a large cavern. Most of it was filled with water, except for a walkway on their side and a floating dock. There was a small cabin cruiser tied up there, but there were six empty slips. The cavern wasn't large enough for the Elpis, but you could fit a couple of decent-sized vessels in there, or seven small ones.

"Son of a bitch," Sam said.

"But what about the helicopters?" Nishimura asked.

"A ruse, obviously," Sam said. "Misdirection."

"But the bodies . . ." DeLao protested.

"Maybe they were dead already," Amar said. "People killed in the attack. Or some of Vahlen's specimens."

"Maybe," Sam said. "It doesn't bear a lot of thinking about. It looks like she did escape, by boat. Like us, she probably figured the ADVENT would think she was dead and call off the search."

And now *they* had a boat. Things were looking up. If the jabbers up there right now didn't find them and kill them all, that is.

He was still thinking that a few minutes later when a series of tremors shook the island.

Sam laughed. "I guess it's a good thing we didn't search through the bodies," he said.

***

After twenty-four hours had passed, Nishimura went out to check and reported no sign of ADVENT troops or transports in the area—living ones, anyway. One ruined flier lay on its side in the blast radius that had earlier been wrecked helicopters, along with the bits and pieces of ADVENT soldiers.

That was the good news.

Sam told them the bad news. He had found some charts in the boat.

"We're about 13,000 kilometers from where we need to be," he told them. "That's as the crow flies. And we're not flying. What we have is a smallish boat."

"Where are we going again?" Amar asked.

Sam looked uncomfortable for a moment and then shrugged. "You might as well know. If something happens to me, the rest of you will have to carry on. Our target is in India, in the Western Ghats."

"Wait one moment," Nishimura said, her dark eyebrows crooked around a frown. "I've been looking at the charts, too. This boat has a range of a few hundred kilometers. You're talking about going east. Cape Town is more than 5,000 kilometers away."

"Sure," Sam agreed. "But there are islands between here and there, and some are marked as fuel depots."

"The nearest one I saw marked that way is around 2,500 kilometers," Nishimura said. "Still way too far."

"What do you suggest then?" Sam asked.

"South Georgia Island is a fuel depot, too. The Elpis stopped over there on the way down. It's just under 800 kilometers from here. From there we can hop to the Malvinas and on to South America."

"That's going the wrong direction, though," Sam pointed out.

"*Cojudo!*" Nishimura swore. "Don't you get it? This mission is *done*. That target is out of our reach—and even if we could get there, the Shens are dead. God knows where Vahlen is headed. From the looks of it, she had better ships with longer range than this one. Without them, what are we going to do with a crashed alien ship?"

"I know something about their technology," Sam said. "And I have Vahlen's data. Once we find the ship, we can attract others with the skills we need."

"But we won't make it," Nishimura said.

"There's plenty of fuel," Sam said. "We can drag extra tanks behind us to increase our range."

"And if we meet a storm, we'll go down like so many stones," Nishimura said. "I intend to be of use to this resistance. I don't intend to squander my life in a hopeless attempt to reach *India* from the South Atlantic in a glorified rowboat. When we had the Elpis, sure. Now we're just lucky to be alive. So let's take the information you have to someone who has the capability of using it."

"We can do it," Sam said. "I know we can. And sailing west, the distances are better, but we would still have to take on extra fuel to reach the Malvinas."

"Not nearly as much," Nishimura said. She lifted her chin and wagged a finger at him. "Wait a minute. You ran those numbers, too."

"Yeah," Sam said, "I did."

"But you didn't present going to South America as an option."

Sam sighed. "Is it just me?" he asked. "Is it just me who feels that when I close my eyes and try to sleep, I see Dixon, Sergei, all of those guys, Thomas, Toby, Dr. Shen—every night, more faces. Lily Shen, everyone on the Elpis. This was Shen's dream, Nishimura. People died for this, believing we would carry on, finish, seize the lightning. There's only one boat, and I know you guys can take it if you want to. But if you outvote me and retreat to South America, I won't be with you. I'll bloody swim to India if I have to."

For several long moments, no one spoke. Then Chitto cleared her throat.

"That's pretty dramatic," she said. "A little over the top. But if I can put in my two cents here—I'd kind of like to see India."

"The Ghats are supposed to be beautiful this time of year," Amar said. "And I have some contacts in the area."

Everyone looked at Nishimura, who threw up her hands. "The Andes are nice this time of year, too," she snapped. "But whatever. *Bacán.* India it is." She glared around at them. "So who knows how to sail?"

When no one said anything, Sam raised his hand.

"I found a manual," he said.

***

That evening, Amar went back up to the lip of the caldera alone and looked westward, out over the sea.

The sky was unusually clear, and the dark orange ball of the sun was just touching the horizon. He watched it disappear a little bit at a time, thinking about how much more slowly it seemed to happen than the sunrise. The last spark seemed to linger, a tiny ember drowning in the waters. Then, finally, it was gone, leaving the night to the stars.

"Goodbye, Toby," he said.

***

Amar dragged himself up to take his watch. It was midday, and the seas were rough. Sometimes the horizon was only a few meters away as they descended into a trough; when they reached the top of a swell he could see forever. But there was nothing to see except more water.

The temperature was still close to freezing, although they had been sailing northeast for five days. He—like everyone on board—was starving. They had managed to catch some fish before leaving, and they had some rations in their packs. But they had been a lot less successful at finding food out in the deep water.

What was more alarming was that they were running out of potable water—and, for that matter, fuel. The boat was not, of course, able to access any sort of global positioning system. Sam was sailing with charts, a compass, and an astrolabe. Given that this was his first attempt at such a thing, and that the island they were looking for was little more than a big rock, they might have even passed it a day ago.

South America was starting to sound pretty good, although they were way beyond the point of no return on that score.

He peered over at Lena, in her bunk, still asleep. Neither of them had mentioned what had happened back in Wunderland. At first, there had been too much going on, and now there was no chance for privacy. And although it had seemed like a good thing at the time—no, *had* been a good thing at the time, in that moment—now he wasn't so sure. Like Sam, he kept seeing Thomas and Toby in his dreams—not as he wanted to remember them, but as he had last seen them. He now believed Lena had not been an intentional spy, but it was hard to put aside the fact that if there had never been a Lena—if she had not left her life in Gulf City to pursue a naive, ill-advised adventure—his two friends would still be alive. They would all be on their way to India, not in a tiny ship designed for relatively short voyages, but in the Elpis. He wouldn't be freezing and feeling his gut growing tighter every day. He would have fewer nightmares.

Chitto had seen Thomas die as well, and early in the voyage she had some questions about that. Rather than having to explain it more than once, he'd called a meeting.

"Chitto was wondering why I shot Thomas after the Chryssalid attacked. Does anyone know?"

"I've heard about it," DeLao allowed. "I'm glad I didn't see it."

"I've seen it happen," Nishimura said. "In Tabasco."

"Yeah, me too," Amar said. "Two months in under Thomas, near Jakarta."

"That's real nice," Chitto said. "But I don't know what you're talking about."

Amar clasped his hands together. "There is a sort of wasp that injects its eggs into a species of orb spider. The pupae grow inside of the spider, eating away. Toward the end, the spider suddenly starts weaving webs of a kind it never has before, because the pupae have taken control of its nervous system and are forcing the spider to build a web to protect them when they've finally eaten their way out. There's another wasp that injects eggs into a ladybug, and when the larvae come out for cocoons, a virus that also came from the wasp forces the ladybug to stay there and stand guard over the babies. In effect, they turn their hosts into zombies.

"Chryssalids do something like this, but with humans, and they do it fast. The Captain Thomas who stood up wasn't Captain Thomas anymore. And in another few minutes, a brand new Chryssalid would have clawed its way out of her. So if you can, you don't let that happen. If one of those things takes your buddy down, the best thing you can do is shoot her."

Never mind that he still felt sick every time he thought of that moment, of seeing his rounds strike the Chief. It had felt like murder, and to part of him it still did.

But he didn't tell them that.

That had been on day one. Now, on day five, nobody wanted to talk about much at all. Chitto and DeLao were seasick a lot of the time. Amar usually felt okay on deck but not as well below if seas were high.

He had spent his share of time on the water—in the South China Sea, the Sulu Sea, a bit in the Indian Ocean. But that had mostly been going from mainland to island to island, never that far from land. They had crossed the Pacific stowed away on an automated container ship the size of a small city, and the weather had been tropical to fair. Not until now had he understood how bleak and utterly empty a place like the ocean could be.

CHAPTER 12

WHEN HE FIRST saw Gough Island on the horizon, it looked like a jewel. The sky was clear, unlike their last stop, and it wasn't covered in snow, but instead shone like an emerald beacon. As they drew nearer, he saw that it was equally treeless, however, its color the result of moss and lichen and maybe a few scrubby bushes. But it was land, and fuel, and hopefully food. They navigated toward where the map claimed the depot was.

As they drew near, Chitto spotted something rising from the shoreline. Amar's heart sank. It wasn't a transport. Transports weren't armed. This was one of the ADVENT's smaller gunships.

"Well, that was totally worth it," Nishimura said.

Chitto started firing at the edge of her range. Amar didn't pin a whole lot of hope on that. She might be a crack shot, but these things were thick-skinned. Maybe if Palepoi could hit it just right with his last rocket . . .

A red line appeared between their boat and the flier, and the impact hurled them all from their feet. Palepoi toppled overboard, and the boat listed as it started taking on water.

"They hulled us below the water line," Amar shouted. "They could have vaporized us with a missile. They may be trying to take us alive. Don't make it easy for them." He raised his weapon but waited. He only had one clip left and wanted to make it count.

He saw Lena looking at him, and he tried to smile. He wished that they had been able to talk, that he had been able to touch her face again.

Don't get sloppy, he told himself.

The flier suddenly jerked and spun half-around, a gout of black smoke curling up from it. An instant later, Amar heard the detonation. Then the craft erupted in green and yellow flame, spinning crazily as it sank seaward. It struck the water, stood up on its end, and then hit flat. The water around it began to boil, and just as it vanished from view, seawater rose in a half sphere ten meters high. A moment later, the shock hit them and lifted their little boat, but they were already so heavy from being half-sunken that they didn't capsize.

Beyond, nearer the island, Amar saw two puffs of smoke drifting off in the wind, revealing the Elpis.

***

Dr. Shen looked somehow frailer than when Amar had last seen him, although it had only been a matter of days. But for Amar those days had seemed more like months, and perhaps it had been the same for Shen. In fact, everyone seemed to be affected, so maybe it was because it had been laid bare how precarious their enterprise was, how slim their chances of success. There was the inevitable debriefing, and condolences for Thomas and Toby. And explanations from Captain Laaksonen. After greeting them, Lily Shen insisted her father retire. He'd apparently risen from his sick bed to see them come aboard.

"The first patrol dropped depth charges on us," Captain Laaksonen explained. "We released countermeasures—basically assorted junk, which is what you probably saw on the surface. We did sustain damage, however, and Dr. Shen was injured in a fall. That left me in charge, so the decision to leave was mine. It seemed impossible that anyone had survived the fire, and I felt I had to put the Shens and our mission before all else. When we got word that a second strike force was on the way, I believed we should be as far from that place as possible."

He looked a bit uncomfortable, which was out of character for Laaksonen. "I deeply underestimated your resourcefulness," he said. "Fortunate that you chose the same destination that we did."

"It was really the only choice if we were to carry out the mission," Amar said. "Sam saw that clearly. The rest of us had to be persuaded."

"You could have abandoned the mission," Laaksonen replied. "You did not, and for that I salute you." He quickly changed the subject, bringing a map up on the conference room screen. "The ADVENT put a relatively large amount of resources into trying to find us," he explained. "The craft we just shot down arrived here sometime before we did. We were submerged, but we couldn't leave because we needed to refuel—we had planned to do that on Vahlen's island. As you probably know, the next fuel depot is thousands of kilometers away. In another day, we would have been forced to surface. Fortunately you arrived in time to distract them."

He traced a rough circle around Vahlen's island.

"We believe they staked out every rock and atoll within about 2,500 kilometers of here. It is good news that Vahlen escaped, but I fear she may not be safe. Nor can we worry about that. Our task is to vanish again. We will depart as soon as we refuel and resupply, hopefully within the next ten hours. Then we will push on. If you need shore leave, take it now."

***

After nearly a week on a rickety craft, and not knowing when he would be able to set foot on land again, Amar decided a hike was worth doing. The fuel depot was near an old weather station on the southeast end of the island. Two rather dramatic peaks rose farther north, but they were too far away, so he settled on a nearby rise that would afford him a better view.

When he reached the summit, he was a little disappointed to find that Sam had had the same idea. It wasn't just the view Amar was after, but a little precious solitude.

"Reminds me a lot of Scotland," Sam told him. "Especially the Isle of Skye. Except for the penguins."

Amar had noticed a few penguins. These had funny little sprays of yellow feathers that looked almost like hair, and they weren't in anything like the same numbers as their less showy cousins back on Vahlen's island. Dozens of other bird species abounded, and what looked like seals sunned on the narrow beach below them.

"How long since you've been home?" Amar asked.

"If you mean the town I was from," Sam said, "it doesn't exist anymore. If you mean Scotland, I haven't been there since I was eleven. That's when Dr. Shen took me on the Elpis as a favor to my father. I've been there pretty much since then."

"Is Dr. Shen okay?"

Sam pursed his lips.

"The Elpis apparently took a pretty hard hit, and everyone inside got shaken up pretty good. He's got a concussion and a cracked fibula, all that on top of some more persistent health problems. But he's determined to find this ship. He really believes it will be the turning point for the resistance. For XCOM."

"Do you?" Amar asked.

Sam shrugged. "I don't know if will be a turning point so much as a start. We still have a long way to go and a lot to do, even after we find the ship." He glanced off to the sea. "I appreciate your support back there on Vahlen's island," he said. "Without you weighing in, I think it wouldn't have gone my way."

"I was trying to think what Thomas would have done," Amar said. "I think I got it right."

"Those are big shoes to fill," Sam said, "but I think you're up to it."

For a moment, he didn't even know what Sam was talking about. Then it sank in.

"What?" Amar said. "No. I'm not a squad leader."

"Who is, then?" Sam asked. "You stepped up when Thomas died. Anybody could have, but you were the one. DeLao is as experienced as you are, and Nishimura is more so. But you took command and nobody questioned it."

"All I remember is telling everybody to get in the water," Amar said.

"Maybe that's how it started," Sam pointed out. "But now you're in charge, trust me."

"I don't know that I want to be," Amar said. He remembered what Thomas had told him, back on the Elpis.

"If I know you like I think I do," Sam said, "you don't have a choice." He stood up. "I'll make a little room," he said, and began walking down the other side of the hill.

Amar wondered at first what he meant, but then he saw Lena approaching from the depot.

"Hey, no," Amar said. "It's not like that."

"Look," Sam said, "don't be a jackass." He continued on down the slope.

"Would you rather be alone?" Lena asked when she arrived, brushing a stray brown hair from her face. Her New City hairstyle was becoming not only longer, but more unruly. She looked entirely beautiful.

"No," he said.

She looked a little relieved. "We haven't . . ." she began, then stopped, looking embarrassed. "We haven't really had a chance to talk."

"Right," he said.

"Don't you think we should?"

He'd tried to get his thoughts on this together. He thought he had, but suddenly he didn't know what to say.

"I really wanted that," he finally managed. "To kiss you. I want to now."

"Why don't you then?"

"It distracted me," he told her.

She smiled. "I should hope so," she said.

"No. I mean that you put me off my game. I should have realized immediately that they found us through you. I should have left you with Vahlen. You would have been safe with her. Then I wouldn't have had to argue with DeLao, which slowed us down. I wouldn't have been worried about you during the firefight. Thomas might still be alive."

"You wish you had left me with Vahlen?" she asked.

"No," he said. "What I'm saying is that deep down I knew I should have left you there, for all kinds of reasons. But what I wanted was for you to be with me. And that's what I acted on."

"But that's what I wanted, too," she said. "And I know we're not exactly even, but I think I saved your life."

"Without doubt," he said. "That's part of the problem."

"That I distract you? Put you off your game?" she asked, her face beginning to flush. "Maybe in another life?" she went on, hurling his words back at him. "Is that what you're telling me? If we had met on a dance floor rather than downrange?"

"Yes," he said. "I guess it is."

"Let me clue you in about something," Lena said, stepping closer. "There *is* no other life. This is it. And do you really think that just because we're not actively making out it's going to change how you feel? That you'll be any less 'off your game'? Because I sure as hell know I don't feel that way."

A little tear began trickling down her face, but her expression was fiercer than anything. He reached to brush the tear, but she stopped him by grabbing his hand.

This is not happening, he thought.

But of course it was, and for a while on that hill overlooking the sea, nothing else seemed to matter but her, and time ceased to pass.

***

The Elpis set out in the early afternoon, and Amar watched the last land he would see for almost a month retreat into the distance and then memory. The prospect of being spotted by another ADVENT flier weighed heavily on them, but without the chip to track them, and presumably having no idea where they were going, the search zone would now spread in a circumference with Gough Island at its center. That made the first few days crucial, and they submerged at any slight indication of something passing nearby.

In a few days, however, with more than a thousand kilometers of open sea between them and the depot, they began to breathe easier. Still, they steered farther south of the tip of South Africa than was likely necessary, and when they put in to refuel at a secluded bay on the coast of Madagascar, Amar used it as a live ammo training session, even though every sensor they had—and the inhabitants of the depot—said there was nothing to worry about.

It turned out, mercifully, that there wasn't, but it gave the greener troops a chance to learn to maneuver on land rather than on the upper deck of a submersible.

Once everything was secure, it also gave him more time to be alone with Lena, which pretty much never happened on the ship. Even though everyone seemed to know something was going on with them, it still seemed like a bad idea to be obvious about it. She had backed out of the military training, which was a relief, because it reduced his qualms about their relationship. Sam, as it turned out, was right. Everyone seemed to think of him as Thomas's successor, and he was settling into the part. Being Lena's commanding officer would be very much a conflict of interest.

Lena began working with Lily Shen instead. She was apparently a quick study, even though her background in science and mathematics was pretty minimal. The ADVENT administration had very little interest in educating the populations of their cities beyond a minimum—and highly propagandized—curriculum.

"Or as Lily puts it," Lena told him, as they walked along the beach, hand in hand, "technology is something humans don't have to worry their pretty little heads about. ADVENT will take care of all of that technical stuff, don't you worry."

"That sounds like her," Amar said. "Does it jibe with your experience?"

"Yes, actually," she said. "But growing up that way, it doesn't seem like a bad thing. You don't have to understand biology to breathe, so why should you learn how a media screen does what it does?"

"No, I get it," he said. "I don't know much about the stuff either. I couldn't have built a radio, like Sam did."

"Well, you have other qualities," she said.

"Nice to hear. So what are you helping her with right now?" he asked.

"I'm learning a little about cybernetics," she said.

"Go on."

"It's all very hush-hush," she said. "You may have to torture it out of me."

"I've got training along those lines," he said. "Don't tempt me."

"I believe you do tempt me, sir," she said.

"I don't deny that," he said, leaning in for a kiss.

"Battle droid," she said a few minutes later, when they both got their breath back. "A sort of support robot for you guys."

He thought about that for a moment.

"What?" she asked.

"I just wonder how that will go over," he said.

"What do you mean?"

"Generally, when we run into a robot, it's trying to kill us," he said. "Having one on our side—that might be hard for some to trust."

"Well, it's only in preliminary stages," she said. "Lily is actually going to want to talk to you about the features it ought to have."

"Here's a better idea," he said. "Let's have a general round table on the subject with everybody, or at least the squad leaders. If they're included in the process, they'll more likely be on board with it."

"I'll mention that to her," Lena said. "We have to be back at the ship in an hour. Is there anything you want to do before we go back?"

"I'm doing it," he said.

CHAPTER 13

THE WESTERN GHATS were mountains in the southwest of the Indian subcontinent. The part of the range they were interested in lay in what had once been the state of Kerala. Civilization there was old, and it had formed the hub of the spice trade for millennia. Black pepper, nutmeg, cloves from the distant islands of Maluku all passed through the port at Cochin. Indeed, so important was Kerala that Prince Henry the Navigator of Portugal decided it ought to be conquered, so beginning an era of colonialism that wouldn't end until the twentieth century.

Now Kerala, like the rest of planet Earth, had new colonizers.

Much of the Ghats had always been thinly populated—the population of Kerala had lived mostly along the coast. This was now doubly the case— the Ghats were contagion zones, and strictly off limits. But whereas Kerala had once had an extensive backwater transportation system of inland waters, rivers, and canals, outside of New Kochi, these backwaters had not been maintained, and years of flooding and meandering had taken their toll, turning them into messy, brackish marshes.

Which made them an excellent place to hide the Elpis. The real challenge was finding a place deep enough that the ship would not be revealed at high tide. It took a little patience, but in the end they found such a place.

The plan was for Sam and Amar to lead an expedition to discover if the ship was still there after all these years and in sound enough shape to be worth their time. The elder Dr. Shen was better, but the way was going to be physically demanding, and Sam wanted to delay his journey there until it was deemed necessary. That meant that Lily was going instead, and she was taking Lena as an assistant.

Amar had deeply mixed feelings about this. In his time on board the Elpis, he had come to realize that Lily was not only healthier than her father but also that she was far brighter—and that was saying something. He didn't know what her IQ was, but it had to be off the charts. From their description, a handful of notes, and an examination of Lena, she had not only figured out how the bio-implant worked but also built a detector that would expose that sort of device. Of the two Shens, Lily was the least expendable.

But she was also stubborn, and she outranked him.

(Having Lena in harm's way didn't settle easily on his shoulders either.)

For his people, he chose Chitto, Nishimura, and Dux, who was by that time pretty well mended. DeLao's arm was still stiff. To round things out, he added Chakyar, a young man originally from Dubai. He had some medical training and spoke Malayalam, the predominant language of the area. He was only twenty-three, but he already had a streak of gray in his otherwise black hair and eyes like a summer sky.

They made their way over the crumbling infrastructure to Piravom, a settlement on the outskirts of New Kochi that was supposed to have a resistance cell tucked away in it. When they reached it, they found an ADVENT patrol checking the place, but they soon left.

Pivarom was bigger and more crowded than most of the settlements Amar had experience with. It appeared to go on forever and seemed more convoluted than a human brain. Among the huts and stalls and family-sized tents, a few old architectural gems stood out: Syrian Christian churches that didn't look quite like anything he'd ever seen, a Hindu temple of Shiva. A river separated the settlement into two parts, which had once been connected by a bridge. It bustled with attractive houseboats called *kettuvallam*, adorned with elaborate wicker roofs and walls.

He very soon had cause to celebrate bringing Chakyar along. English had lost much of its currency here. But even with the advantage of a translator, Amar began to think they were getting the runaround. This man said to go see that man, that man to see such-and-such woman. They seemed to be going in circles.

Then they turned a corner and found themselves surrounded by men with knives. One of them, a sharp-featured, clean-shaven fellow in his late forties or early fifties, stepped forward.

"You've been looking for us," he said in English. "Tell me why."

"Don't you want the current passcodes?" Amar asked.

The man gave him a long, searching look. It felt as if the others were drawing nearer.

"We aren't current," the fellow finally said. "Our radio is down."

"If you have the parts," Sam said, "I might be able to fix that."

The man studied them again and then nodded. "We are vulnerable here," he said, "so I must be cautious. You will wear hoods and be conducted to our base. Is that acceptable?"

"It is," Amar said. He had more or less expected it.

***

"My name is Valodi," the man said, when they reached their destination and their stifling black hoods were removed. "Welcome to my command."

It appeared to have once been some sort office building, although it had decidedly seen better days. Valodi offered them a seat and had some food brought, some spiced lentils and rice with a little fish.

"I'm sorry if we seem rude," Valodi said. "But we've had to relocate several times this year, and raids have become near constant."

"I understand your caution," Amar said.

"Tell me why you are here," Valodi said.

"We need a guide," Sam said, "into the Ghats. I can show you the place on a map. It would be good, too, if we had some sort of ground transportation."

"That's a lot to ask," Valodi said. "What do you have to offer in return?"

"Well, for starters," Sam said, "I can fix that radio. We also have medicine, ammunition, and so forth. You tell us what you need, and I'll tell you if we have it."

The man nodded. "Medicine we can use, certainly."

"But the most important thing I can offer you is hope," Sam said.

"That is also in short supply," Valodi said. "Can you explain more plainly what you mean?"

"Not yet," Sam said. "Not here. But I promise you, it will be worth it." He smiled. "One more thing I can offer you is of immediate practicality."

He took a small, baton-shaped device from his bag.

"One of our scientists just developed this. We haven't tested it, but it should be able to tell you if someone has been chipped without having to find the scar. Test it, and you can have it. And several more like it."

Valodi took the device and examined it curiously.

"That's easily tested," he said. "Fix our radio, and we can discuss the rest."

***

After Sam got the radio working, the Pivaromis warmed to them quickly. The chip detector also worked and was a big hit with them, as they had apparently also once been Trojan-horsed by someone who appeared to have had their chip removed. Valodi assured them that he would guide them into the mountains himself, but the vehicles would take a couple of days to procure. As a sign of good faith, he let them wander the settlement, which of course meant they now knew their way to and from his hideout.

It was toward the end of the southern monsoon season and stifling hot. The rain pounded outside as it had for most of the day and all of the night before. Amar and Sam sat playing cards with three of Valodi's men in a dirty white room with no electric lighting. All of the illumination came through a bank of broken windows and the liquid curtain beyond. A few mosquitos had taken refuge in the room and were doing their best to suck him dry. A tokay gecko the size of a squirrel clung to one corner of the room, croaking now and then.

Amar had been playing for about an hour and was still a little uncertain of the rules, although Sam seemed to be doing fine.

Lena walked into the room.

"What's up?" he asked.

"Lily is getting restless," she said. "There's a power node just outside of town. She wants to get some readings from it. She says it could help her synthesize their energy source."

"That sounds like a very bad idea," he said. "Please ask her to consider not going."

"I second that," Sam said.

"And if she insists?"

He sighed. "Then come back here and get us. We'll assign her a detail."

"I'll tell her," Lena said, "for a kiss."

"Oh, whatever," Sam said. "If that's what it takes."

Lena's look of outrage was probably not entirely affected.

"You threatened to kill me once," she said, "if you don't remember."

"Well, that was, what, a couple of months ago?" Sam said. "Cut me a little slack."

"If you try and kiss me, I'll cut *something*," she said. She said it lightly, but beneath her tone, Amar felt there was still some resentment there. Lena did not forget, and she did not easily forgive.

"I'll take one for the team," Amar said. He stood up and walked her out of the room.

They stood in the darkened hall for a moment. Her gaze searched his, as if trying to find something. Then she stood on her tiptoes and kissed him. It was soft and sweet and seemed to linger well after their lips parted.

"I'll tell her the Chief said to sit tight," she said.

He returned to the game, but his mind was no longer on it. Instead he stared out the window at the rain, the misty encampment, at some children rolling around in the mud, just as he had once. It rained almost every day during monsoon season, and kids got bored.

***

An hour later, Lena burst back into the room, soaked, out of breath, and ashen. Her face and arms were covered in small, blood-bright scratches, as if from thorns.

"Lena!" Amar blurted, running over to her. "What happened? What's wrong?"

"I tried," she said. "I tried to talk her out of it, but she insisted."

"Lena," Sam said, "slow down, ease back. What's going on?"

But Amar already knew. Back in the kampung, when he was a kid, families would get together and watch bootleg movies from back before the conquest. Some of them ended badly, and every time he watched them he hoped that this time everything would turn out okay. Of course, it never did. This felt like that to him. As Lena gasped out her story, he let his hands drop from her shoulders and stepped back. He hoped it wouldn't turn out the way he feared, but he knew better.

Lily Shen couldn't be convinced. Lena had tried to talk her out of it at first and then begged her to let her find some soldiers to bring along. Lily had been impatient, arguing that soldiers would only attract attention that a woman alone would not.

Lena didn't know exactly where the power node was, and was afraid if she came looking for help they might lose Lily entirely, so she'd instead chosen to go along with her.

"I thought she was just going to take some readings," Lena said. "But then she opened up a panel and starting fiddling with it. The next thing I knew, an ADVENT patrol showed up. They took Lily."

"Alive?" Sam asked.

"She was alive when they took her," Lena said.

"What about you?" Amar asked. "How did you get away?"

"I ran," she answered. "I was unarmed, and there were four of them. Lily ran, too, but she tripped and fell into a canal. I was already on the other side."

He remembered a joke his uncle used to tell. Two men were running from a bear. One of them said, "It's too fast—we'll never outrun it."

"I don't have to outrun it," the other man said. "I just have to outrun you."

It didn't seem all that funny at the moment.

"You left her there," Amar said.

She stared at him, a look of stark betrayal on her face. "What else was I supposed to do?" she asked. "Would you rather I was taken, too?"

He realized that he had spoken aloud what he had meant to be a private thought, almost never a good thing.

"No," he said. "No, of course not. You're right. Now at least we know what happened. You did the right thing. I'm just trying to wrap my head around this."

But what he was thinking was that Lena should have found a way to stop her.

"I've got mine wrapped," Sam said. "This is a disaster."

"You can say that again, brother," Amar sighed.

Everything had been going great. They were a few days from finding the ship. They had the beginnings of a supply route and the support of the local resistance. And now this.

Lena still looked stricken, but now she also looked a little angry.

"I'm sorry," Lena said. "I wish I could have stopped her."

If wishes were horses, Amar thought.

"It's fine," he lied. "It's going to be okay. This just makes things a little more complicated."

He looked northeast, to where the night sky was tinged with blue city light. The rain began to come down harder.

"We're going to have to go get her, that's all." He stood up. "I need to talk to Valodi."

***

"They didn't kill her outright," Valodi said. They were in his command room, an unassuming space with a small desk and a map drawer. A faded portrait of Mahatma Gandhi was fixed on the wall, slightly crooked. "That's a good sign. Next they'll take her to processing."

"Do you know where that is?"

He nodded. "We've surveilled it but never made any attempt to rescue anyone. If that's what you're planning, it won't be easy."

Valodi had a tendency, Amar found, to understate things. His expression suggested that what he really meant was that it would be nearly impossible.

"That's what I'm planning," Amar said. "Lily is vital to this mission."

"What's so special about her?" Valodi asked.

Amar was weighing whether he should tell him when Sam made the decision for him. "Have you ever heard of Dr. Raymond Shen?" he asked.

"Of course," Valodi responded. "I was with XCOM. Only for a short while, near the end, but we'd all heard of him."

"Lily is his daughter."

The leader's eyes widened. "And her father?"

"Still alive," Sam said. "But losing his daughter will be a terrible blow—maybe even a fatal one. But to be frank, she's a genius. I don't know that we can pull things off without her, even if he lives."

"You still won't tell me of the mission?"

Sam sighed. "I would rather not," he said. "Not here, in a settlement, where a thousand electronic ears might be listening. But you have the power in this situation. If I have to tell you to get your help, I will."

Valodi considered that. "When we first met, you said you were up to something big," he said. "I think maybe I've nevertheless been thinking too small."

"Game changer," Sam said.

Valodi nodded. "Okay," he said, "I can wait. Right now, we'll concentrate on freeing Shen. We can discuss the other matter when it's appropriate. What's the plan?"

Sam's relief was evident on his face.

"This is your city, so to speak," Sam said. "What would you suggest?"

***

Lena showed up while they were prepping the mission. She had a shotgun and was wearing a flak jacket, along with a highly determined expression.

"No," Amar said.

"I lost her," Lena said. "I'll get her back."

"You're not fully trained," he said.

"I'm trained enough," she said. "Put me out front, use me as a diversion. But let me come."

"Lena—"

"KB."

It stopped him cold. She had never called him that before.

"I heard the tone in your voice when I told you what happened," she said. "The doubt. There's some little part of you that thinks I might have turned her in. That I knew about my implant, and that this is all some elaborate plan. Can you tell me that thought didn't go through your head?"

He didn't want to hurt her, so much so that he was tempted to lie. But that wouldn't help anyone, least of all Lily Shen.

"No," he said, "I can't. Do I really believe you would betray us? No. But I have to consider the possibility. If I didn't, I wouldn't be doing my job. I wouldn't be faithful to the mission. When it comes to you, my judgment is suspect, because I'm so . . ."

He stopped himself there.

"So what?" she asked softly.

"You know," he murmured.

"I'm not sure I do," she said. "Maybe I don't know anything. But I need you to have faith in me. Please."

It hung there between them, and everything seemed to turn on that pause. But he knew what he had to do.

"Lena, you can't go," he said. "That's my final word."

He saw the hurt in her eyes, and he wanted to take her in his arms. But this wasn't the time for that. He had to focus.

He tried not to watch her walk away.

CHAPTER 14

AS MESSY, PERSONAL, and idiosyncratic as the settlements were, the New Cities were all the same. The ADVENT administration liked to claim that their carefully planned communities had sprung from the ashes of the old—that their foundations were New York, Mexico City, Mumbai, Beijing, but there were a couple of things wrong with this assertion. The first was that only a fraction of Earth's cities had been reduced to rubble in the conquest—most of the world's governments had capitulated after the first few were trashed. Instead, Earth's urban centers had been meticulously deconstructed and replaced after hostilities ceased. So in most cases, there had been no ashes to spring from.

The second fact of the New Cities was that they preserved nothing of the old within them. One could stand where Paris or München or New Orleans had once stood and not know the difference between one and the other. No Notre-Dame Cathedral, no Hofbräuhaus or Jackson Square. ADVENT propaganda maintained that in this sameness was equality—that it dissipated the sort of national, regional, and ethnic pride that had once led to bigotry, war, and pogroms. This was another way of saying that the human race was being cut off from its history and what it had accomplished—good and bad—in the millennia of civilization before the aliens came. The cities were not built by humans, but for them, like the habitats in a zoo, but on a far grander scale.

During the day, New Kochi was a city of glass and steel, air and light. There was no mixture of architectural styles; instead, the same modular elements repeated themselves in different combinations and at varying scales. Green space and water features like fountains were evenly distributed throughout the city, but none of those fountains featured tritons or swans or little boys peeing. They were simply jets of water that went up and came down. There were statues, however, portraying humanlike aliens and alienlike humans while avoiding the nasty reality of, say, the Chryssalid that had killed Thomas. The most striking sculpture was that of a tall, lean alien with a bulbous head and huge eyes. It held hands with a reclining human, and it was supposed to look like the alien was helping the human back on his feet. Amar always thought it looked more like the alien was leaving a pleading human behind. In every New City Amar had ever entered, some variant of that statue could be found in the public squares.

The cars that wandered the wide street grids were as difficult to tell apart as the buildings, and they moved at highly controlled speeds. ADVENT claimed to have reduced traffic fatalities to nearly zero, which was probably true, since they didn't consider or even gather any statistics beyond the city limits.

Billboards like the ones in the settlements recounted the "news," but were much, much larger.

They made their way into New Kochi at night, using the remains of an old sewer system the resistance had tied into the shiny, highly efficient new one.

At night, New Kochi appeared more sinister. There was plenty of light, but light like one might find in a prison camp—high beams shone down from tall buildings, the dull red glow of scanners that citizens were required to submit to now and then. But the presence of troopers was slight, and they interacted with people in an almost friendly sort of way. It accounted for the very different ways in which Lena and Amar saw them, at least initially. Growing up, he had been afraid whenever ADVENT troopers came into Kuantan. They did rough searches, beat people, took them away. Lena had grown up thinking of them as protectors, and even felt relieved when she saw them. They indicated that she was safe from the dangerous dissidents.

That was another reason she shouldn't come along, he told himself. But the look on her face when he had last seen her haunted him.

They split into two groups immediately upon arrival. One was led by Abraham, one of Valodi's lieutenants. He had a motley squad of six, armored head-to-toe and bristling with weapons. Then there was Amar's group. They were dressed in New City street clothing purloined over the years by the local Natives. They each had a handgun concealed beneath light rain jackets. Dux and Amar had colorful duffel bags thrown over their shoulders, as if they were possibly off to play a cricket match.

Valodi had charted them a path to Processing that avoided scanners, and they didn't have much trouble staying clear of troopers. As they had hoped, they blended in on the crowded streets—no one gave them a second glance.

There were certain inevitabilities about how a police station was organized, but the ADVENT administration had neatly dissected the task of dealing with those who broke a law of some sort from that of "processing" anyone they thought might be a security threat. There were therefore no police desks where statements could be taken, or anything of the sort. Instead there was a series of holding and interrogation rooms around a central hub.

The building itself was round—a clean, modern structure of a single story surrounded by an immaculate lawn. The one thing that set it apart was its lack of windows. Instead it had glowing panels that suggested the interior was aquamarine, then pastel pink, then ecru, viridian, and so on.

"Okay," Amar said. "Now we just have to wait."

He watched the stream of humanity around him, wondering which ones had been born here and which lured in. Most of what he knew about their lives came from Lena, but it was still hard for him to imagine. He knew some of them worked for the ADVENT, and knew also that didn't make them evil any more than Lena was. Misguided and misinformed, perhaps, but not evil.

He desperately hoped they had the good sense to clear when things started. The last thing he wanted was any sort of collateral damage.

The wait ended with a muffled explosion in the distance as Abraham and his group began their diversion—an attack on a gene therapy lab. Amar heard a few screams, and the people around them picked up their pace, moving away from the area until they were almost alone on the street—just what he had hoped for. Perfect.

"Let's go," Amar said.

They opened the duffel bags, where their weapons were waiting. Full armor was a luxury they could not afford for this mission.

"Dux," Amar said.

"Yep," he replied, settling the rocket launcher on his shoulder.

The few remaining people on the street cleared off, fast.

The rocket blew the door in, and they all quick-timed it across the street. Although humans worked for the ADVENT, intelligence suggested that they were never employed in processing centers. Amar prayed that was true. Of course there would be prisoners inside, but they should be well away from the blast. He knew all of this, but his breath drew cleaner when they came through the door to find only the ADVENT troops picking themselves up from the rubble.

One of them was a captain. Nishimura went at him with her sword. Amar and the rest turned their attention—and their weapons—to the others.

The surprise and the explosion turned out to be a huge advantage, and they shortly had the room cleared. Amar put Chitto at the front door to deal with reinforcements coming from outside. Then they began searching for Lily, one corridor at a time.

Most of the cells were empty, but a few were occupied, and they released the prisoners they found, who either fled without a word or babbled thanks before doing so.

They didn't encounter any resistance until they tried the third corridor, where they were greeted by magnetic rifle fire.

"No grenades or rockets," Amar said. "Shen may be in there."

He leaned in and took a shot. He missed, but he saw there was a pair of troopers on either side of a door that led into the next room. They were about six meters away.

They answered him with by shooting through the wall. If he'd been standing an inch nearer the door, he would have been hit.

"Okay," he said. "High-low. Nishimura, you stay low."

"Got it, Chief," she said.

Chief? It took him a moment to realize that she was talking to him. But Lena had called him that, too, hadn't she? In a joking way, yes, but . . .

"Go," he said.

He and Chakyar leaned around their respective walls and began firing at the troopers, head-high. Nishimura dropped to all fours and scrambled up the corridor.

When they stopped shooting, one of the jabbers stepped out to return fire. Nishimura cut his arm off. Then she dropped to the floor as the second trooper began shooting at her, stepping from cover as he did so.

Amar and Chakyar opened up again, riddling the armored figure with bullets.

Out in the central room, Chitto's rifle spoke out.

"Okay," she said. "Any time you guys are ready. Things are getting a little interesting out here."

Nishimura stood back up and took a quick look into the room. She jerked back, raising her weapon, but then stood strangely still.

"Nishimura?" Amar said. What was wrong with her?

She turned, and he saw. Her eyes were blank, dead-looking, and faintly phosphorescent. She raised her sword and charged.

Chakyar shrieked in terror and opened fire. Nishimura ignored the bullets and cut toward his head. He got his arm up, and his scream turned to one of pain as the sharp blade bit through his armor.

Amar dropped his weapon and grabbed Nishimura's blade arm, twisting it so that she dropped the weapon. He punched her in the chin and sent her sprawling.

"Dux!" he yelled. "Sit on her."

Then he picked up his assault rifle, took a deep breath, and ran down the hall. Before he reached the end of it, something was trying to get into his brain.

It started like pins and needles at the base of his skull, and then began quickly creeping around toward his face, like a foot falling asleep. His thoughts went soft and strange, like words in a foreign language he almost understood and, if he paid attention for a moment, probably would understand. . . .

He blinked. He'd missed some time. How much?

He was in the room. He saw someone he thought he recognized, and there was something else, tall and lean and gray, with huge eyes . . .

A Sectoid . . .

What was he supposed to be doing? He needed to know what to do.

And the voice began to tell him—was telling him—when something hard and cold rose up from deep inside of him, clotting behind his eyes, forming an image. A picture, a snapshot. Rider, lying on the ground, her lifeless eyes staring up at him. Her cold lips twitching.

"Shoot it, dumbass," she said.

It was like a rubber band snapping inside of his head. He pulled the trigger and felt the recoil of the weapon, saw green tracks walk up the alien's body, felt it pull out of his mind like a snail from a shell.

He vomited, and the colors behind his eyes faded to black and gray. The muscles of his ribs and chest knotted into spasms, and he fell to the floor.

Then someone was standing over him.

"You'll be okay," she said. "It will pass. I know."

It was Lily Shen.

"It was a Sectoid," she said. "Modified. Bigger and stronger."

She helped him stand.

***

Nishimura was propped against the wall, her hand over a hole in her armor, red leaking from between her fingers. Her pupils were huge and her breathing ragged.

"Chief," she said. "Don't know what happened. Jesus. What happened? "

"Never mind that now," he said. "Don't worry about it. Let's just get you out of here."

"I think I can walk," she said.

"Just stay here," he said. "Keep pressure on your wound."

Chakyar had been cut to the bone, but fortunately Nishimura missed the joint of his arm, or else the whole thing would probably be off. Still, he'd bled enough to fill a bucket.

Amar moved up to where Chitto was taking aim.

"Four of 'em out there," she said. "Probably be a lot more, soon."

"Yeah," Amar said. "Dux, get those two on the right, then we'll run for it. Chitto, you cover our backs. I'll carry Nishimura."

He heaved her up over his shoulder and couched his weapon under his arm. Chakyar couldn't hold his rifle up, so he slung it and took out his pistol.

"Go!" Amar said.

Dux fired, and a car went up in a fireball, taking out the two jabbers hiding behind it. Then everybody ran but Chitto. Mag rounds screamed by him, tearing into the street, spattering against buildings. Then, he heard the bark of Chitto's rifle—once, twice, three times. He risked a quick look back and saw she was now following them.

After that it was all blurry, a nightmare dash through the city streets, civilians screaming, the whine of aerial patrols and floodlights searching through the night. He knew they were being followed when red streaks smacked into the building ahead of them, but there was nothing for it now but to try to stay ahead of them, reach the sewer, and get out.

They came around a corner and found themselves face-to-face with Abraham and his men.

"Keep going," Abraham said. "It's just down that way. We'll be along soon."

"Thanks," was all he could manage.

***

What seemed like an hour later, they emerged outside of the city, where Valodi and more of his men were waiting for them. Someone took Nishimura from him, and in a daze, he followed Valodi back to the settlement. Nishimura and Chakyar were carted off to the infirmary, or what passed for one.

Amar sat outside, breathing, trying to forget what had just happened, the thing in his head. He felt like a tunnel spider had walked into his mouth and built a nest there, like it was still in him and always would be. He had heard plenty from old-timers like Thomas about the aliens with psi-powers, but somehow he hadn't quite believed it and had thought that, even if it was true, only the weak-minded would succumb to such an intangible weapon.

If so, then he now knew he was weak-minded. If it hadn't been for Rider . . .

But Rider was dead. He didn't believe in ghosts. And yet *something* had broken the contact, if only for an instant. Something had stepped up, if not from outside, then from within him.

"Hey," Valodi said. He'd been in a hushed conference with some of his men. "You look like you could use some of this." He proffered a bottle of clear liquid, which he knew from experience contained hooch fermented from palm sugar.

Amar did very much want a drink, but he feared it would make things worse, not better. He didn't want anything else messing with his brain.

"No thanks," he said. His mind was sluggishly starting to piece together the last awful moments of their flight from New Kochi. "Abraham. Did he make it back?"

Valodi shook his head. "I fear not," he said grimly.

"What about the others?"

Valodi squatted down and put a hand on his shoulder. "Their orders were to make certain you got back. That they did. I am proud of them."

Amar took that in. He wanted to cry, but he was too tired.

CHAPTER 15

WHEN VALODI WAS gone, Lily Shen joined him. She had never seemed very emotional, but now she had a sort of constant frown. He wanted to rail at her, tell her how stupid she'd been, how her actions had led to good people being killed. But she wasn't really stupid. She knew all of that already and didn't need him to sort it out for her.

"I'm so sorry," she said, her voice flat. "Lena tried to tell me—"

"Listen," he said wearily. "Forget all of that for now. What I need you to tell me is what they did. Did they implant a chip in you?"

"No," she said. "I don't think so. And Valodi's men tested me just now. Unless they've developed something new, no."

"Okay, good," he said. "Here's the main thing: Did you tell them anything? Is the mission compromised?"

Her face contorted a bit.

"You felt it," she said. "You had it in your head, too."

"That's exactly why I'm asking."

She put her head in her hands. "I told it everything," she whispered. "The mission, the Avenger, the Elpis, my father. I gave it all up. Everything."

Of course she had. How could she not?

"When?" he asked, as gently as he could.

She shook her head. "I don't know. It was in my head, and then there was gunfire, and you were there . . ."

He felt a faint glimmer of hope.

"So maybe we got there in time," he said. "Maybe we killed it before it could fill out a report or send a brain fax or whatever it is they do."

"Maybe," she said. "I hope so."

"Well," he said, "we'll find out, won't we? I'll send word to your father and Captain Laaksonen that we might be compromised. And hope."

She sat down and gathered her knees to her chest with her arms, rocking back and forth.

"Yes," she said. "Hope."

"Listen," he said, "it's been a rough couple of days. I can have you escorted back to the Elpis if you want."

She shook her head. "No. You'll need me to assess the target."

"If you're sure."

She nodded.

"If I've screwed this all up," she said, "I want to be there if it falls apart. To see the consequences of what I've done and deal with them."

He accepted that with a nod. He wondered where Lena was and wished that she were with him. But he stopped short of trying to find her and went to bed instead.

Chances were very good that she didn't want to see him anyway.

***

Amar had been asleep for about two hours when one of Valodi's people—Miriam, he thought her name was—shook him awake.

"There's an ADVENT patrol coming," she said. "A big one. Valodi thinks they may be heading toward the infirmary."

Amar rubbed the sleep from his eyes and reached for his weapon; he'd fallen asleep in his armor.

The infirmary? It made sense. ADVENT had to know that some of them had escaped, despite the sacrifice of Abraham and his squad. It wouldn't be all that hard to figure out that some of them were injured; Nishimura and Chakyar had left plenty of blood in the processing center and probably a trail of it on the street. Any sort of medical facility in the settlement would naturally be the starting place for a search.

"Can you lead me there?" he asked Miriam.

"Yes," she said. "Quickly. The rest of your people are being gathered."

"Infirmary" was probably too fancy a word for the place, just a few beds and an operating table. Nishimura was still on the table, and a man in an off-white apron was fussing over her. Valodi was there, shouting orders to his men and women. Amar didn't see Chakyar anywhere.

"How is she?" he asked the doctor.

He shook his head. "She shouldn't be moved," he said.

Amar examined her. She had been stripped of her armor, and bandages were wrapped around her belly, where some blood was leaking through. Her face was still, but he could see that her eyeballs were darting about beneath her lids. He shuddered to think what she might be dreaming about.

"Gut shot," the doctor said. "She's lucky it was a bullet rather than a mag round, but the damage was pretty extensive. I think I sewed everything up, but I can't be sure. If there's even a nick in anything, she'll get peritonitis or worse."

"We don't have a choice," Amar said. "I won't let the jabbers have her. Have you got a stretcher?"

"There's the one she came on," he said.

The stretcher was bloody but serviceable. They loaded her on it, and Valodi ushered them out the back door. Amar could already hear the approaching troopers, prattling in their outlandish language.

Nishimura groaned as he and Dux carried her through the winding alleys of the settlement. Behind him he heard shouts of outrage and screams of pain, but thankfully the jabbers' magnetic rifles remained silent. That would probably change if they caught sight of Amar and his companions.

Valodi led them to an old canal where three small boats awaited them. Amar and Dux laid Nishimura flat in one of them, but with her stretched out in it, there was no way to use the oars. He motioned Dux into one of the other boats and then eased himself into the water, hoping it wasn't too deep.

It came up to his shoulders, so he took the mooring line and began to tow the small craft in the direction Valodi indicated. Everyone else piled into the other boats and began to row.

There was no current. The water was warm, often thick with weeds, and smelled distinctly of sewage. He didn't even try to imagine what might be living in it, instead just concentrating on putting one foot ahead of the other. Behind him, Nishimura cried out. Not loudly, but it wasn't a whisper, either. A few minutes passed, and he thought everything was fine.

Then she screamed.

The jabber must have already been following the canal, maybe having heard her first cry. Amar hadn't seen her, but he did now as she stepped through a beam of moonlight striking the bank. He froze, hoping against hope the trooper wouldn't see them in the darkness, wouldn't think to look down into the canal.

She almost didn't, but then Nishimura whimpered. The shadowy figure stopped and raised its gun. Amar let go the line and sloshed toward the berm. He didn't have a chance, but he wasn't just going to stand there and take it.

Then a second shadow appeared behind the jabber. He heard a sort of choking gasp before the ADVENT soldier toppled into the canal. Amar saw moonlight flash on steel. Then whoever it was blended back into the shadows.

It could almost have been Nishimura herself, but she was still in the boat, breathing hard.

A little after midnight they made it to the river, which proved too deep for him to walk in, so he had to go around to the back and push the boat by swimming. Dux joined him, and together they made enough of an outboard motor to keep up with those rowing.

After about another hour, Valodi led them to one of the *kettuvallam*, the big houseboats, where his men helped him and his people aboard, Nishimura included. The doctor from the settlement checked her vital signs.

"Hard to tell," he said.

***

Amar dozed again and woke to Nishimura screaming something in Spanish. He groped his way to where she lay and took her hand.

"Nishimura," he said, "it's okay."

She gripped him back with her calloused fingers and gasped.

"KB?" she said weakly. Her hair was free of her bandana and looked like an oil slick on the white pillow. The hollows of her eyes were dark.

"Yeah, Alejandra," he said. "It's me."

"*Mi bróder,*" she gasped. "*Estamos in el infierno?*"

"I don't understand you," he said softly. "You're speaking Spanish."

"Are we in hell?" she asked.

"Not yet," he told her. "Although I don't blame you for thinking so."

She grunted.

"It feels like we're in hell," she said. "I thought I saw Toby. He was . . ." She stopped.

"Something happened," she wailed. "What happened?"

"You were shot," he said. "You've got a nice wound in your belly, so don't move around too much. You'll start it bleeding again."

"I don't remember," she murmured. "*Asu, no me acuerdo . . .*"

"It's okay," he said.

She fell silent, and he thought she had drifted off to sleep. But then she stirred again. "It's not true," she said. "I do remember. I just wish I didn't."

"It got in my brain, too," he said. "I understand how you feel. There was nothing you could do."

"Did I kill anyone? Chakyar . . ."

"No. Chakyar will have sore arms for a while, that's all."

"Did anyone get killed?"

"No. None of ours, anyway." He could tell her about Abraham and the others later.

She took a long breath and winced. "I'm in pretty bad shape, huh?"

"You'll live," he said.

"Yes," she said. "I'll live. So I can cut the throats of every last one of those sons of bitches."

The next day, he sent Nishimura to the Elpis for medical attention. There, she had a chance. Where they were going, she had little to none, despite her attitude.

***

The first leg of their trip was in the *kettuvallam*, following the course of the Muvattupuzha River north and east, then further along on the smaller flow of the Killiyar. The boat was a comfortable fourteen meters long, with bedrooms, toilets, and a small galley. Although the wood-and-wicker houseboats had once served as cargo vessels moving spices through the backwaters, in the last few decades before the invasion they had been redesigned as tourist craft, affording a quiet, comfortable exploration of the area. Now they had been repurposed once more into movable living space and smuggling vessels.

Like the Mississippi Delta where they'd found Lena, much of inland Kerala was returning to an untamed state. What had once been rice paddies were now full-on swamps, complete with mugger crocodiles sunning on muddy banks, pythons, hornbills, and a bewildering variety of plants and animals. It reminded Amar very much of the country of his birth.

Lena had been avoiding him since Lily's capture and rescue, and he was inclined to give her the space she wanted. Something had gone wrong in Piravom, and it was because both of them had lost focus—because they had been too busy making goo-goo eyes at one another. More rested upon his shoulders now, and he felt it, knew how close he had come to letting it all fall apart.

And she had asked him to have faith in her, and he had shown her that he didn't. She probably didn't know how much that had hurt him to do, and he wasn't going to tell her. If she didn't want to talk to him, it was better he leave it that way, at least for now, if not forever.

Their boat ride ended in what had once been a small village, but which now served as a hiding place for munitions, fuel, and two all-terrain vehicles. Valodi and two of his men debarked with them. The rest began their voyage back south.

They traveled dirt roads for several kilometers before reaching a narrow blacktop road in surprisingly good condition. From there the country got hillier and drier, but as their elevation increased, the vegetation grew lusher. They returned to dirt roads, and at times Valodi's man Mitchum had to clear the trail with his sword. Mitchum was a compact, dark-sinned American in his fifties, a bit on the brash side. It was he who had killed the jabber at the canal.

Amar felt safe under the rainforest canopy, safer than he'd felt in a long time, even on the Elpis. He knew it was an illusion but decided to take what little comfort he could get.

On the morning of the third day, as he went down to a nearby spring to wash his face, he saw a lithe form moving through the shadows. He stood very still, watching the tiger pass, with a sense of wonder and no small measure of terror. Even though he knew intellectually it wasn't likely to attack him, its very shape and the way it moved sent alarms through his primate brain, which had evolved largely to avoid tigers.

He suddenly felt a profound awareness of the world, a connection to it that all of the hiding and fighting and death had pushed deep into his marrow. In that moment, he remembered that the world was beautiful, and that he was a part of it, would always be a part of it. As Rider and Thomas and Toby were still a part of it.

He had grown up with a large menu of things to believe about the afterlife, and he had never subscribed to any of them, not specifically or with any conviction. But it was good to be reminded of the wonder of it all, the dread and ecstasy of existing.

The tiger turned and stopped, its eyes fixed on him, and for what seemed an eon they locked gazes. Then the great cat faded into the jungle. As it went, Amar felt as if the ghosts that he had been carrying were now following the great beast, and he didn't know whether he felt sadder or more relieved. But he felt he was a little bit lighter.

When he returned to camp, Chitto looked at him strangely.

"What?" he asked.

"You look different, Chief," she said.

He smiled.

"I saw a tiger," he told her.

***

The ship had flattened a swath of forest when it crashed, but the jungle was doing its best to take it in, as jungles tended to do. It was huge, so huge that at first he wasn't sure what he was looking at. It could have been an odd upthrust of stone. But when they were closer, and he could see beyond the climbing vines and dense young growth around it, it became obvious that it was nothing the natural world had produced.

From what little he knew about the aliens, he had been expecting something disc-shaped. He'd been wrong. It was somewhat boxy, longer than it was wide, thickest in the middle and tapering off at either end. Two winglike struts did support large saucer-shaped structures that were almost certainly its engines.

"It seems to be remarkably intact," Lily said, running her fingers along the metal of the hull. "The force of its crash must have been terrific, and yet there's hardly a scratch."

"Everything could be jelly inside," Sam said. "The fact that it's been here so long, undiscovered, speaks to the probability that the crew must not have survived."

"Yes," Mitchum said. "But they didn't all die in the ship. Look."

Amar hurried over to where he stood, near the perimeter of the crash site. The empty eyes of a skull looked up at him, but it wasn't human. It had a smallish hole in its forehead and a much larger one in the back.

"Looks like a Sectoid," Sam said. "The old kind."

Amar felt a tremor at the name, remembering the monster that had turned Nishimura against them.

They did a careful sweep around the area and found dismembered bones from both humans and aliens, but no intact bodies. Tigers and other beasts were probably responsible for that. But from their wounds, they all seemed to have been killed in a firefight.

"We're sure these guys were XCOM?" Amar asked.

"There are no records that a squad ever made it here," Sam said. "The location came from satellite data, not reconnaissance."

"People lived in this area back then," Valodi pointed out. "I believe there was a military outpost not terribly far from here. I can imagine it wasn't hard to miss this thing coming down."

"Secure a perimeter," Amar told his squad. "Doc, what next?"

"Well, we'll want to get inside," she said.

That didn't prove terribly difficult; whosever bones now lay scattered about the ship had left a hatch open in the back of the craft. Mitchum cleared back the vines and saplings, and then Amar peeked inside.

Something jumped. He had a brief impression of a figure that was somewhat humanoid, but which wasn't human—it was too small, its limbs were too long, it had a tiny head . . .

His finger eased off the trigger as the frightened macaque leapt from the interior of the craft and vanished into the trees.

Amar had seen any number of ADVENT transports and even the occasional gunship like the one they had encountered in the Atlantic. It was possible he'd seen some of their long-range craft in the distance. But this was something new to him.

ADVENT technology had been designed to set humans at their ease, to seem at least a little familiar, even if what lay under the hood wasn't recognizable at all. Here, that layer of familiarity wasn't present at all. He could stare at some of this stuff for years and never be able to guess what it was.

In other words, it was alien.

And dead. No lights flickered on consoles; no panels glowed with pale light. Aside from the cones cast by their torches, the ship was dark. And a tomb. Things had died here, too, and the tigers hadn't fooled with them. He didn't blame them. The whole place gave him the shivers.

Lily didn't say much, but she took a lot of notes. Amar stayed with her; the fact that the first thing to jump out at them had been harmless (well, close to it—macaques could give you a pretty nasty bite) didn't set him at all at ease. Not all of the aliens had been flesh and blood. He remembered they had robots and drones as well.

But after several hours, nothing had coming whirring to life to try and end him.

Lily didn't stop when the sun went down but instead worked long into the night. Amar split up the squad into thirds so they could watch her, keep watch outside, and get some rest.

He awoke the next morning with someone prodding his ribs. It was cool, and misty, and for a moment he was disoriented. Then he saw it was Lily.

"It's time to go get my father," she said.

Part III
The Avenger

*"We have paid a heavy price,
but our efforts have not been in vain."*

—DR. VAHLEN, XCOM CHIEF RESEARCH SCIENTIST

CHAPTER 16

AMAR WATCHED THE trucks arrive with more than a little trepidation. Valodi didn't like these guys, and Valodi dealt with some pretty horrifying people. He supposed they couldn't be picky, not at this stage of the game. Anyway, it was Sam's call.

They were several kilometers from the location of the alien ship, just off the main road in a field surrounded by forested hills. It had rained in the night, and the cool lingered, although by midday it would probably feel like a steam bath.

Amar didn't glance around to make sure everyone was in place. He didn't want to give anyone away.

The doors opened, and a rough-looking crew stepped out. The leader was a short, thick man wearing an old flak jacket that was too big for him and a helmet that wouldn't have looked out of place in World War II. He also had a knife the size of a cutlass and a submachine gun.

"So," he said, "we're here to talk."

"We appreciate you coming," Sam said. "And so promptly on time."

He was being sarcastic, although he didn't show it in his tone. They were four hours late.

The man shrugged. "We encountered ADVENT patrol."

"Where?" Amar asked.

"No worry, they did not see us," he replied.

He sounded pretty sure of himself, but that meant exactly nothing in Amar's book.

"Are you Kasparov?" Sam asked.

"Call me Caspar," he replied. "You know, Caspar?"

Sam looked at him blankly for a moment, then shrugged. "Caspar," he said. "I'm told you're good at getting things."

"Sure. What you want? Liquor? Chocolate? Woman, maybe?"

"No," Sam replied. "For starters, I need cuprate-perovskite ceramic. I need a cryogenic still, a variety of rare earths, diamond lasers . . . Well, here, why don't you just take the list."

Caspar took the paper and looked at it incredulously. "This is all very difficult," he said. "Dangerous things to get."

"Sure," Sam said. "And we'll pay you for that. And for your discretion."

"Some will have to be 'liberated' from ADVENT Administration."

"I'm aware of that also," Sam said. "The price will be fair."

Unless he was lying, Sam didn't know who their financial benefactors were any more than Amar did; only the Shens had that knowledge, and they were guarding it, at least for now. When Sam was being candid—which usu-ally involved a glass or two of the stuff they were distilling from coconuts—he speculated that there was a network of donors, some of them possibly even inside of the collaborationist governments.

There were rumors that some of those who had sided with the aliens in the beginning only did so to be on the inside, to bide their time until the moment was ripe to take action. To Amar, this had always seemed like wish-ful thinking. Now he was starting to believe it was possible.

But all he really knew was that currency arrived, usually in the form of valuable trade goods.

"Let's see what you have to trade," Caspar said.

Sam motioned him behind their truck and threw open the flap.

"Antibiotics," he said. "Electronics. Whiskey—real whiskey; I have no idea where they got it, but it's good Scotch. Power rations. Have some hacks, too, for detecting implants, and also some counterfeit implants. You can really only use them once or twice, but you understand the possible bene-fits."

The latter were things the Shens were now producing themselves.

"So this is my upfront, then?" Caspar said.

"Oh, no, no, no," Sam told him. "This is just so you see we're bargaining in good faith."

"Well, that's very interesting," Caspar said. "But I think we'll take it up front."

"Well," Sam replied, "then I suppose we'll have to find another bunch of feckless hyenas to do business with. Too bad. This is going to be big, and you could have been part of it."

"Sure," Caspar said, lifting his hand and drawing it across his throat.

Then, he looked a little surprised. He repeated the motion.

"Oh," Amar said. "We took the precaution of disarming the snipers you sent in here yesterday. They're perfectly fine. And their positions have been filled with our own sharpshooters."

One of the men reached for his gun and then spat out a groan as a bullet smashed through his shoulder. A few seconds later, they heard the report.

"This is awkward," Sam said as the man swore and sank to his knees. "We were really hoping to avoid any bloodshed, and now look. Do you think you could help us keep things at this point, Caspar? Help end the violence?"

The man glared at him but nodded grudgingly.

"Here," Sam said. "Take the list. I have copies. If you're the first to bring me what I need, you'll get paid. And if you ever try to screw us again, we'll put the lot of you in the dirt. Is that good?"

"It's good," Caspar grated, after a moment. He and his men climbed back into their trucks and left.

"What if they turn us in?" Amar asked.

"That lot?" Sam said. "ADVENT would shoot them on sight. Caspar might die knowing he got his revenge, but I don't take him for that sort. For one thing, he hates the aliens. Us, he's merely put out by. He may even come around one day. We might be buddies."

"I don't know about that," Amar said, "but if he can get us the stuff, I'll put up with a lot."

***

Back at the ship, a village was growing. But it wasn't huge, and its inhabitants were a pretty select bunch. Captain Laaksonen—now entirely in charge of the Elpis—was quietly bringing on board scientists, engineers, machinists, and chemists from around the globe, where they were carefully moved by the Valodi's people along the route Amar and the rest had followed to the crash site.

A number of huts had been constructed, and solar panels provided most of their energy. The population was now thirty, enough to make Amar start to feel edgy. The more people, the more likely they were to be noticed by the ADVENT, especially when people and materials were moving into and out of what was supposed to be a restricted area.

He spent a lot of his time trying to fortify the area as well as he could. Components for a few larger guns found their way to him, which couldn't hurt—but what he was most interested in was early detection. He established lookouts up to two kilometers away and set up motion-activated cameras along every trail big enough for a bicycle.

A few days after their meeting with Caspar and his men, one of the lookouts broke radio silence, transmitting a short, encoded message:

Inbound transports. Five. Search spread.

Amar had been taking a much-needed rest in his hammock when the message came. He rolled out and picked up his assault rifle.

"Incoming," he shouted. "You know your positions. Get to them. All noncoms—into the ship."

They had run this drill a few times, so it went relatively smoothly, despite the panic that overcame a few. Amar's own gut was tight.

In all of his earlier encounters with the ADVENT, there had been an objective, or they had been in the wrong place at the wrong time. In either case, after winning the fight, they were free to hightail it out of there.

But here the objective was to resurrect the Avenger, which was what Dr. Shen had begun calling the alien ship. At this point, the Avenger wasn't something they could carry with them. Whether the transports represented a random patrol—or worse, a targeted one, triggered by, say, Caspar turning them in—they were screwed. Even if they killed every trooper in all five transports, the ADVENT could just keep sending soldiers until they were overwhelmed.

If they were spotted now, it would be over before it had even really begun.

Moments later they heard the purr of alien engines. Amar searched what little he could see of the sky. He thought he saw a metallic flicker. Then it was gone.

He was just starting to breathe again when a shadow fell on him. He looked up through the trees and saw the aircraft moving over. Heart hammering, he checked his rifle for the third time.

The shadow continued on. Half an hour later, the lookouts gave the all-clear. It had been a routine patrol, and to all appearances, they hadn't been noticed.

It could be months before another such patrol came by. It could be hours. Either way, they were far, far from safe.

***

"We were wrong to assume the power was completely out," the elder Dr. Shen said, at the next day's briefing. Amar was invited to these meetings, although he often didn't understand much of what they were talking about. "There are certain key areas where there is a small amount of energy still manifesting itself, a kind of low-level maintenance, or perhaps even a long-term healing process."

"Are you saying the ship is alive?" Sam asked.

"Not in any biological sense," Lily picked up. "But the aliens' technology has a very complex set of feedback loops at every level, so you might compare it with, say, the human body. If a cell in your body is damaged, it either repairs itself or is replaced by neighboring cells. This happens without reference to the higher systems of the body, which govern health and healing at larger scales. If, for instance, you receive a bigger insult—a cut or gash—blood must clot, leucocytes must arrive to combat infection. Heart rate and blood pressure may adjust, and your cognitive system will modify behavior. On an entirely different level, intelligent beings will employ first aid—washing or disinfecting the wound, closing it up in some manner, and so forth. This ship is currently functioning, so to speak, mostly at a cellular level. The higher systems seem to be detached or at least in deep hibernation. For the most part, this is probably a good thing for us. Like their transports and other equipment, this ship was probably originally equipped with any number of safeguards against being taken over by anyone other than its creators. These are all shut down at the moment. We need to identify these systems and make sure that they remain dysfunctional when we turn the power back on."

The elder Dr. Shen tapped up a display of the ship they had mapped it thus far.

"Parts of the ship remain inaccessible to us," he added. "We don't even have a guess as to what they do. Some we have been able to open up using our own power sources. But this large section near the nose of the ship is a true enigma. It may be that only the computer can open this area, and there are a couple of problems there. The first is that we need power, and a lot of it. That is the next really crucial step in this project. It became clear to us in the early days of the war that the aliens had a power source far superior to anything we possessed. Other than a few confusing readings and a bit of research on fragments of their technology, we were never even certain what it was. Our research came to an untimely end.

"Of course the New Cities and everything the ADVENT Administration has built runs on this power source of theirs. In the twenty years since the conquest, Dr. Vahlen gathered a great deal of data concerning this matter, and as a result I can say that we now have a fairly firm grasp on it. The key is an element that does not seem to be naturally present on Earth—Elerium. When this ship crashed, it lost much of its Elerium. Indeed, it might have ejected it or neutralized it in some way. Of what remains, I have prioritized repurposing some of it for a more immediate use, since we don't have enough of it to bring the ship into a more responsive state."

"So we need more of this Elerium," Sam said.

"That is correct," Dr. Shen said.

"That shouldn't be a problem," Sam said. "It must be everywhere. All I need to do is alert our black market assets. Just give me the specs—how they can recognize it, how to handle it, all of that."

"Speaking of assets," Dr. Shen said, "There is another matter, one I do not believe we should involve the black market in—or, in fact, anyone outside the core of this group."

***

After so much time in open country, Amar had forgotten how confining the Elpis could be, especially for two people doing their best to avoid one another. And although he thought about approaching her every day, it was Lena who very typically broke their mutual silence first. He was in the Rathskeller at lunchtime, picking at his calamari when she walked in and saw that the seat across from him was the only empty one. She paused and turned as if to leave, but then, with her usual determination, proceeded to his table.

"Do you mind?" she asked.

"No, please," he replied.

Once she was seated, he nodded at her plate. "The cod?" he asked. "Really?"

"It's growing on me," she said. "We all have to adapt, right?"

"I guess so," he said.

"Good," she replied. She began eating. He tried to think of something to say, something to begin with, but he couldn't imagine where to start. So instead he just picked at his food.

"I saw Nishimura," Lena said. "Looks like she's doing well."

"Yeah," Amar said. "I ran her through her paces the other day. She'll be going along on this."

"Great," Lena replied. Then she returned her attention to the food. When she was done, she picked up her plate and looked as though she were about to leave. Instead, she turned back.

"It's a little crowded here," she said. "Could you meet me above when you're done?"

"Sure," he said.

***

Amar remembered talking to Lena by starlight and later—on the voyage from Gough Island to India—slow-dancing across the gently rolling deck, holding her in his arms. They were in those same seas now, but headed south.

Twenty years ago, they would have sailed east across the Arabian Sea to the Gulf of Aden and the Red Sea, through the Suez Canal and thence to the Mediterranean. But the aliens had trashed the canal, and so they had to go the long way, the way the Portuguese had in the fifteenth century, around the Cape of Good Hope.

The same seas, but a very different season, he thought.

She was waiting for him, arms crossed. He waited for her to say something.

"So," she began. "You and I, we're stuck together for a while. Not just on this ship, not just on this mission, but maybe for the rest of our lives, however long or short that may be. So let's adapt."

"I'm sorry," he said. "I know I hurt you . . ."

"You don't want to talk about that," she said. "To say I was hurt doesn't begin to cover it. Don't tell me you understand, because you don't. And that's not the point of this conversation."

"Is this where you say we should just be friends?" he asked.

She actually laughed at that. "We are not and have never been friends," she said. "I've been your captive; I've been the tagalong you were trying to get rid of; I've been your makeout buddy; and I've been the girl you've been avoiding like poison. But I have never been your friend."

"Wait," he said. "Back up one second. You were avoiding me, too."

"Yes," she said, "because you were a jackass. You owed me the apology you started in the Rathskeller immediately, not a month later. And you owed it to me to tell me how you felt. But that would the hard thing for you, wouldn't it? You're very good at what you do, Amar. Good at being a soldier. You're one of the bravest people I've ever known when it comes to that sort of thing. But you're one of the most cowardly people I've ever known when it comes to your personal relationships. You have all of these justifications for what you do and don't do, but what it all boils down to is that the easier thing for you to do is back away from anything like real investment. What you don't have can't be taken from you, right? For you, quitting is always easier than trying."

She stopped and took a step back.

"Wow," she said. "I promised myself I wasn't going to rant like that."

"Pretty good rant," he said.

"I don't know if it's occurred to you, KB, but I've been having a pretty awful time these past few months. My sister died, and I'm faced with the fact that pretty much everything I've ever believed was a lie. I'm not used to death and shooting and explosions or being lost in the ocean. Not really my thing, except that now it is, inevitably, unavoidably. This has all been very hard on me. Maybe I used you as a crutch, I don't know. So maybe I bear some of the responsibility for this state of whatever-it-is. That doesn't really matter now. We are going to adapt. We have to work together, so we have to be able to communicate, especially when we get to the site. Maybe we can be friends. Maybe we can't. But we can work together."

Amar felt like saying a number of things. Like how hard it had been to lose Rider and Thomas and Toby. How hard it would be to lose Lena. That she was probably right about him, and that he would like to learn to be braver.

Instead, he just nodded and said okay.

"You know I'm going this time, right?" she asked.

"Of course," he replied. Not as if he had a say in the matter this time. This whole project was Lily's. He was just in charge of the muscle.

CHAPTER 17

THEY BYPASSED GOUGH Island for fear that it was being watched because of the incident with the gunboat.

They refueled instead at St. Helena, another speck in the Atlantic that had once been the final prison of Napoleon Bonaparte. Unlike chilly Gough, St. Helena was mildly tropical, but it was every bit as rocky and isolated.

They stayed for a day, and then proceeded north, stopping once more at Madeira Island before going on to their final destination.

The Elpis surfaced along a barren strip of beach on the coast of Brittany. The sky was gray with a few blue lenses here and there, and the wind tousled the treetops almost playfully.

Chitto stood watch on top of the ship as Amar went with Nishimura and Dux to secure the beach, after which Lily and Lena came down, followed by Chitto.

Lily had two bags, one of which felt as if it were full of lead. They took turns carrying it.

That night they saw the lights of New Nantes in the distance and the next morning a settlement. They avoided both and moved deep into a contagion zone.

It was chilly but not quite cold, and the leaves on the trees were gold and crimson and brown, something Amar had heard of but never seen before. He found it really quite beautiful and slightly depressing. He remembered Toby's meditation on sunrise and sunset people, and wondered if one could make a similar speculation about people who were conditioned by temperate, northern, or tropical climates. In France, one was faced with a yearlong cycle of death and rebirth, of graduated change. Around the equator, death and rebirth happened, too, of course, but not written on the landscape and installed on the calendar in the same fashion. Trees did not shed, appear to die, and then return to bloom. When something died in Malaysia, it was usually actually dead.

You could even say there were two seasons, wet and dry—but the psychological impact might be different.

He soon wearied of this. Toby had been overthinking things, and now so was he.

Sometimes they were able to follow a road, but more often it was easier to go cross-country. They passed overgrown petrol stations, an ancient abbey of crumbling gray stone, and a cemetery with hundreds of headstones. They cut their way through hedges and waded across creeks and slept beneath the stars—but more frequently under clouds.

One clear morning, under a rare cerulean sky, Amar called a halt because he wasn't quite sure what he was seeing. Across a field, something was moving at the forest's edge.

"What is it, Chitto?" he asked.

She raised her rifle to look, but after long moment, she didn't say anything. Instead she handed the weapon to him.

Peering through the scope, he saw what appeared to be a wild boar—no, three. One was closer and more obvious, but now he could make out the others a little deeper in. They looked as if they were confronting something; their legs were set and splayed, heads down, swaying from side to side in unison. The nearest looked very thin, almost emaciated, and most of its fur was gone, replaced by something that glinted in the sunlight, like glass or crystals.

"What am I seeing?" he wondered aloud.

"It's like they're guarding something," Nishimura said. "Or watching out for something."

"I'd like to have a closer look," Lily said.

"Not until I do," Amar said. "The rest of you stay here."

"Chief," Nishimura said. "You don't always need to be the one stirring up the hornets. Let me have a look."

He knew she was probably right, and certainly she was better suited for the job. But it was hard, putting someone else in harm's way. Easier on his conscience to go himself . . .

Lena didn't say anything, but he remembered her little diatribe about easy and hard.

So he did the harder thing and sent Nishimura.

He watched her move stealthily through the tall grass.

"Chitto, put that thing in your sights. The one in front."

He took out his field glasses and watched.

Nishimura stopped about ten meters from the animals, which did not appear to see her. Their eyes looked glassy and dead, but they were nonetheless swaying, occasionally stamping their hooves.

She took another few steps, and the nearest one charged her. He noticed its gait was odd, as if it were running on three legs.

Nishimura bounced back, bringing her weapon up. Then she abruptly fell backward, vanishing in the grass.

"*Asu!*" he heard her yelp. "*Miercoles!*"

Chitto shot it. The boar exploded like a puffball mushroom, except that instead of a cloud of brown spores, the pig seemed to sublimate into a sparkling, rainbow cloud.

"Oh, man," he said. "Nishimura, get out of there."

"It's okay, Chief," she said. "I just tripped."

He suddenly smelled something very strange, something he had smelled only once before, the night when they had seen the ADVENT soldiers using flamethrowers.

"Get back here, *now!*" he shouted.

He saw her reappear and start running.

"Contagion, do you think?" Lily asked.

After all of their trekking in so-called contagion zones, Amar had seriously begun to doubt the existence of any real contagion. It seemed more likely that ADVENT just wanted people roped off into areas where they were more easily controlled, and that the "contagion" was just another fabrication, a tactic to suck more people into the New Cities. He figured the guys they had seen that night were probably burning a pile of corpses or something, covering up their crimes.

It wasn't the first time he'd been wrong.

"Yeah," he said, "I think."

The other animals hadn't moved, but now one did, limping up to stand where the one that Chitto had shot had been.

"We should try to get a sample," Lily said.

"With all due respect, I don't think that's a good idea," Amar replied. "We've no idea how contagious it is. For all we know, we're already infected. But if we're not, I want to keep it that way. This mission has to come first."

"But if what we're seeing is really the contagion—it's the one thing we know the invaders really fear. It could be an important weapon to use against them."

"I will grant you that," Amar said, "but still believe we should try to get very far from here as fast as possible."

"I am in charge of this mission," she reminded him.

"Sure," he said. "Of *this* mission, not that one. Let someone else come study this some other time. Someone with the equipment to do so. We have nothing. No test tubes or petri dishes or whatever you need—we don't have it."

Lily sighed and looked at the remaining animals with what he could only describe as longing.

"Very well," she said.

***

Lily walked up beside him later that day.

"Thank you," she said.

"For what?" Amar asked, equally startled and confused.

"You were right," she said. "I am ... impatient. I don't like to have time on my hands. When I see a problem or a puzzle, I want to solve it, right then, and I don't always think through what the costs might be. My father says I'm like a rabbit, always dashing ahead. In New Kochi I dashed ahead, and people died. So, thank you for asking me to take a step back."

Amar nodded. "You're welcome."

"You will probably be forced to do so again," she admitted.

"I know."

She laughed and swept her arm at the countryside. "How are you enjoying France?" she asked.

"I was expecting cheese," he replied. "So far, no cheese."

***

Two more days brought them to their destination, an old airfield deep in the countryside. The strip was cracked and grown up around the edges, but the control tower still stood, along with several large hangars. From the tower, Amar could see the ruins of a city and the river they had been paralleling for most of the trip.

They hadn't seen any more signs of the contagion—if that was in fact what they had seen—but Amar urged vigilance. He checked his own skin every few hours at first, looking for anything that was remotely sparkly, but now he was down to once a day.

In the overgrown hangar, they found what they had come for—a thick, stubby, powerful-looking aircraft. It had wings, but they were short, and from the look of it, the craft relied more on jet or rocket propulsion for its motivation.

"I almost don't believe it," Lily said. "After all of these years. Once again, luck is with us."

"Some luck," Amar said. "A squad from Le Mans confirmed it was here last year, and the word got back to Vahlen."

"Is that a Skyranger?" Nishimura asked, a bit of awe in her voice.

"You've seen one before?" Lily asked.

"My father carved a wooden one for me when I was a little girl," Nishimura said. "He worked on it, you know."

"I didn't," Lily said.

"On the design, anyway," she said. "He was the propulsion engineer." She cocked her head. "It looks a little different than my toy."

"Bigger, probably," Chitto commented.

Lily ignored Chitto's quiet sarcasm. "The original Skyranger was shot down during the war," she said. "This one was a prototype for the next model. Several were being built at different locations, but this is the only one we know survived. It was never finished. It has never been flown."

"What use is it then?" Dux asked. "Spare parts?"

"No," Lily said. "We're going to finish it."

Amar walked around the flier, admiring it.

"It can land and take off vertically," Lily went on, "and in quite tight circumstances. And it will fit very nicely into the Avenger. The Avenger will serve as a mobile base, much as the Elpis does now. But we can't very well fly something that size into a New City to extract a squad. We need something smaller."

"No more walking," Chitto said. "Or pickup trucks."

"Exactly," Lily said. "As handy as the Elpis has been for keeping the resistance going, it's very slow. Our response time to global events is tallied in days, weeks, months, as you all know. We can now cut that down to hours." She was almost twitching with anticipation. "Now if you don't mind," she said, "I'm eager to get busy working on this thing."

After setting up a perimeter and watch schedule, Amar began inspecting what was left of the airbase in hopes of finding something useful—weapons, food, and so forth—but it appeared the place had been looted long ago, probably by the same resistance fighters who had informed Vahlen about the Skyranger. After that, he organized forays into the empty suburbs of the nearby town, which didn't turn up much either but did a little to ease the boredom. Lena and Lily were doing most of the work on the ship, which left the soldiers very little to do.

A week passed, and heavy clouds brought cold rain and mist. By then they had set up a barracks in the building beneath the tower and managed to get an old radio working, so they had a little entertainment and news from the outside world. Most of the music was from before the invasion, but there was also radio theater, which mostly adapted movies and books from the old days, but lately new, original content was coming into favor.

And most of what went out over the radio waves was more than it appeared to be. To get the news, you had to know what you were listening for. Anything important was couched in apparent nonsense, but if you knew the code it was decipherable. When the announcer said, for instance, that he would like to dedicate the next song to his dear old mother in New Paris—and then the song itself mentioned Marseille—it meant that it was time for the resistance cell near Marseille to carry out whatever they had been planning. "Sister" on the other hand, currently referred to a settlement, so "To my ailing sister in Berlin" was a warning that New Berlin ADVENT was making a big push in the surrounding settlements—or a specific one, again indicated by something in the song.

It was not a good system for conveying detailed information—that tended to happen in Morse code—but it helped to minimize radio traffic that the jabbers might be able to track. The broadcast network had been growing somewhat organically over the last decade or so, or at least so it was generally said. However, Amar was beginning to wonder if there wasn't a more centralized, guiding hand behind that, just as the Elpis and Wunderland must have been receiving their funding from someone or some group of people.

He was half-listening to the radio when Nishimura came in, wearing a rain poncho.

"Chief," she said, "there's something you need to see."

***

There were four of them: two boars, a dog, and a deer in a little cluster on the other side of the river. Under the overcast sky, they looked like they were covered in gray patches, but he was sure that if the sun had been out they would be scintillating like the ones they had come across earlier. Like those animals, these weren't doing much, just sort of bobbing, facing in their direction.

Amar felt cold in the pit of his belly.

"Do you think they followed us?" he asked.

"Maybe," Nishimura said. "Looks like they came from that direction, anyway."

"How can you say?" he asked. "They don't seem to move."

"Well, they weren't here yesterday," she said. "Maybe they only move at night. Or early in the morning. Or midday. But unless they grew there, they came from someplace else."

"For all we know, they did grow there," Amar said. "Or maybe it's something in the soil. Step on it and you become infected or whatever."

"Should I shoot them?" she asked.

"No," he said. "Set up a tree stand back there and watch them. I want to know what they do."

The next morning the animals were all still right where they had been—except for one of the dogs, which now stood on their side of the river. In addition, a hedgehog and another dog had joined the balance on the farther side.

A hedgehog, he thought. How could something be so ridiculous and so horrifying at the same time?

Amar hurried back to base to find Lily Shen. He found her hard at work, digging around in the engine panels. They had brought a few tools with them, but fortunately the base had a machine shop that was still pretty well stocked with tools, so she had everything she needed—except maybe time.

"How much longer before it's ready?" he asked.

"It's coming along," she replied. "Why, are we in a hurry? You think we've been spotted?"

"Not by ADVENT," he said. He explained about the animals while she continued tinkering.

"That's pretty curious," she said.

"I find *terrifying* a more apt word," he replied.

She shrugged. "Figure out what to do about it," she said. "That's your job. I'm busy doing mine."

After their conversation on the road, he was a little taken aback by her tone. But she was deep in this now, all of her resources focused on what she was doing. When she got like that, she didn't take the time to be considerate or kind. That required mental energy she didn't have to spare.

"You told me that you saw ADVENT burning something in the contagion zone back home," Lena said. "They probably know more about it than you do."

She made a good point. The one thing the old base had plenty of was fuel, stored in tanks underground. He wasn't sure he could build a flamethrower that wouldn't explode in his hands, and after a round table with the other soldiers, they decided it was probably better to make something like Molotov cocktails using detonators and cans filled with fuel.

By the time they had a few of them rigged, three of the animals were on their side of the river.

Dux pitched one of the cans. It hit the ground, bounced, and wobbled to a stop about a meter from the middle dog.

"Nice throw," Amar said.

"Bocce champion of Rosedale, Ohio, two years in a row," he said, grinning, running his thick fingers through his copper hair.

The animals didn't react to the presence of the can at all. Dux tossed another one, which almost bumped the first one. He took out the remote.

"Let's see about this," he said.

The can detonated very satisfactorily, spraying burning fuel in all directions. Amar flinched involuntarily and took a step back, remembering the immolation of Vahlen's island.

The animals continued to stand there, burning, until they collapsed into fuming piles. He didn't see anything sparkly in the air.

"Well," Dux said, "that works."

"I guess," Amar said. "What about the ones across the river?"

"I dunno. Maybe we could build a catapult or something. I could use a rocket, but I hate to waste ordnance on something like this."

"No," Amar agreed. "We're a long way from an armory."

"Hey, Chief," Chitto said, peering through her scope.

"Yes?"

"That stuff that's on the animals? The crystals or whatever? It's on a few of the trees, too. See? On the leaves?"

Now that he was looking, he realized he didn't need the rifle; he could see the shimmer when the wind blew.

He glanced down at the ground around his feet, where dandelions were beginning to put out their seed heads. If the contagion could get into plants, could it hitchhike on their seeds? Or their pollen? Because if so, in a few days it would be everywhere.

He watched the flames subside on the corpses. He hadn't worried much about a little smoke being noticed; they hadn't seen aircraft of any sort flying over since their arrival. But if he had to set *everything* on fire? That would bring the ADVENT, fast.

"Build your catapult," he told Dux. "But don't burn anything else unless you have to."

But they had to. The animals kept crossing the river, and they kept burning them. On the other side, the infection seemed to be spreading. It was like everything had a light layer of frost on it, and more and more animals joined the party.

And here, as well as across the river, the dandelions were starting to open. He found some old filter masks in the machine shop and insisted everyone wear them. He doubted it would do any good, but it seemed better than nothing.

***

Two days later, at the two-week mark of their arrival at the airfield, Lily decided to put the Skyranger through a few tests. Amar felt unexpectedly excited when the running lights blinked on and the wheels on the landing gear began to turn. He found himself smiling broadly as the craft rolled out of the hangar. Like the elder Dr. Shen and Dr. Vahlen, it was a blast from the past, a reminder that humans had once been resourceful creators and inventors. And a promise that they could be again.

Lena and Lily hadn't just "fixed" the Skyranger—they had altered the design. The craft had two engines in the back—like a jet—but the wings were really just struts now, supporting two massive engines that could rotate. He watched as Lily tested the hydraulics, pointing the engines down—the position they would be in for touching down or taking off vertically—and back, where they would augment the rear jets once they were in full flight. A fifth under jet beneath the craft completed the Skyranger's propulsion system.

"There's only so much I can do here," Lily said. "I have other modifications in mind once we get back to the Avenger. Let's fuel her up and run a few more diagnostics. Then I'll take her up for a test flight."

"That's it, then?" Nishimura asked. "We just get in and fly back?"

"No," Lily said. "We have one stop on the way."

"*Miércoles*," Nishimura grunted. "I've heard that before."

"I'll tell you about it while we're fueling," Lily said.

Amar had been present when the trip was planned, so none of what Lily said was a surprise to him or Lena, but the others, it had been determined, hadn't needed to know. If Amar and Lily were both killed, captured, or badly wounded, the whole thing was to be scratched anyway. But now it was time for everyone to know the next step.

"We've figured out why we can't turn the power back on in the Avenger," Lily said. "The heart of the whole system is the computer. If we go back to the organic analogy, it's the central nervous system, limbic system, and circulatory system all in one. While it's not put together like one of our computers—in fact, we're not sure how some of the pieces work—we have been able to parse out some of the functions. In doing so, we discovered severe damage to what for reasons of simplicity I'll call its central processor, even though in some ways it's more of an adapter. The memory and programs are all still there, intact, but there's nothing to coordinate them. We have no hope of learning to build one of these things anytime soon. So we're going to steal one."

"Where?"

"New Singapore, probably," Lily said.

"One little stop," Nishimura said, "halfway around the world."

By that time, the Skyranger was fueled. Lily and Lena began working through another checklist as Amar trudged down to the river with Dux to see what the latest in their contagion situation was. He was only about halfway there when Nishimura called him from the tower.

"Incoming," she said. "Two ADVENT transports bearing in from the northeast. From Paris, probably."

Perfect. Bloody hell.

"Get everyone to the hangar and in position," he shouted. "We may be taking that test flight all together."

"Chief, you better watch it," Nishimura advised. "One of them is circling around your way."

Even better. They might have satellite intel. It was possible the ADVENT had been watching them for days.

Amar saw the shadow overhead and realized the transport had already arrived and was landing between Dux and him and the base. He motioned to Dux to move off to the west. The vegetation was thicker there and the terrain rougher, which would slow them down considerably, but at least they would be in cover. Behind him, he heard the jabbers debarking. He slowed and got behind a big tree, determined that he wasn't going to die from being shot in the back. Maybe the troopers still didn't know about the Skyranger—after all, it had been in the hangar until a few hours ago. He and Dux might be able to divert them here long enough for the others to escape with the ship.

Then he saw the other transport. It had settled beyond the river, which seemed like sort of an odd move. But he didn't have much time to think about it—the patrol was only a few meters from them.

He turned back to look toward the trail, searching for a target but knowing he wouldn't find one until they came in after him. He could see movement through the autumn leaves, but nothing substantial.

He heard a sort of low whooshing sound, and suddenly a dragon's breath billowed into the trees, setting them instantly ablaze. With sudden horror, Amar realized that they didn't intend to fight him at all; they were going to burn him out.

He backed away from the flames as more of the liquid fire sprayed through the undergrowth. It was completely unreal, and he felt like he was missing something. He had never seen jabbers carry flamethrowers before. Only that once, back in the Delta . . .

Oh, he thought. Of course.

He broke radio silence.

"No one shoot," he said. "They're not here for us. Stay hidden."

The troopers weren't out to get him, but the fire seemed to harbor a real grudge of some kind. The wind gusted up, pushing the flame downwind, toward them, and actually encircling them in the north, which was exactly where they needed to go in order to return to the Skyranger. If they weren't fast enough to get around it, the fire would push them into the river, which would mean they couldn't help but be seen by the troopers.

Why couldn't it be raining today? Amar wondered. But, of course, ADVENT wouldn't be here with flamethrowers if it were raining. Panting, he forced himself to reach a greater speed, willow branches whipping him in the face and the muddy ground sucking at his boots. The red wall in the north continued to lengthen, and flames behind them were catching up.

"We've got no choice," Dux said. "It's outstripped us. We have to go to the river."

Grimly, Amar agreed.

By the time they got to the water, Amar was so dizzy from all the smoke that he blacked out momentarily, coming to a minute later with Dux dragging him along the river's edge. The water was colder than seemed possible, and in moments his feet and legs were numb. He looked back upstream but all he saw was fire and smoke, so the worry that the jabbers would see them lessened.

How had they known that the contagion was here? Did they have some way of detecting it remotely? Or was there just a lot of it in this area, and they were following the leading edge to keep it in check?

They came to a tributary creek that was for the moment acting as a firebreak. It allowed them to get out of the water and start pushing back northward, where they would hopefully find the road and make their way back to the base. He was fairly sure they would be able to see the base from the next high hill.

He was right. The hilltop had an old, industrial-looking structure on it, made of brick with a flat tile roof that was dangerously dilapidated. With the aid of the sapling at the base of it, they were able to climb atop the aging structure and get a commanding view of the landscape.

The fire had consumed a huge swath of forest on the other side of the river, and he could see smoke boiling up from much farther to the southeast. He didn't see any ADVENT transports, which seemed like good news until he spotted the control tower of the airfield, burning like a torch.

The whole place had been overrun.

"Chitto?" he sent over the radio. "Nishimura? Anybody?"

His only reply was static. His heart sank.

"Let's go see," he told Dux wearily.

They hiked down to the road and were starting up it when his earphone crackled. He wasn't sure whether it was words or just a burst of static.

"Come again?" he said.

"*Chief . . .*" someone said, but then static swallowed the rest.

"You hear that?" Dux said.

Amar did, and he knew the big man wasn't talking about the radio. Over the low grumble of the flames rose a profound roar. He saw the transport dropping toward them and crouched, feeling like a mouse under a sky full of hawks.

But then he saw it wasn't a transport. It was the Skyranger, her jets blazing.

Nishimura was leaning out of the open hatch.

"Come on, Chief," she shouted. "Let's get the hell out of here."

CHAPTER 18

"**WELCOME TO NEW** Singapore," the young man said. He was pleasant-faced, with a wide smile and dark brown eyes. "My name is Jonathan," he went on as his fingers flickered over the glowing icons on the board in front of him. "I think you'll like it a lot here. New Singapore is the very best of the New Cities, lah? You're from which settlement?"

"Kuantan," Amar said. It felt funny to say because it was the truth—a single lonely truth in this place built of lies—and in contrast to everything else he was telling Jonathan. About why they had come here, how they wanted to finally feel safe and be part of something bigger than themselves, and on and on.

"Okay," Jonathan said, tapping his screen. "Great. You have some excellent choices when it comes to housing." He looked them over. "Not to be presumptuous," he said, "but may I assume you two are a couple?"

Amar glanced at Lena. "Yes," he said, taking her hand. Another lie.

"Wonderful," Jonathan gushed. "Do you have a preference of which district you live in?"

Lena studied the prospects. "What about this one?" she asked, pointing to one.

"Well, that's fine," Jonathan said. "Not as nice as some others, though. You can't just take the apartment itself into account; you have to consider what's in the neighborhood. And see, this one has a terrace." His voice grew more confidential. "If you're planning to start a family, I can get you something even nicer. Here in New Singapore, we encourage family life—the bigger the better. There are lots of perks for young parents."

"That's kind of private—"Amar began, but Lena cut him off.

"This other one has a balcony," Lena said. "That's the one I want. Don't you agree, dear?"

"Whatever you say, sun bear," he said.

"As you wish," Jonathan said, his tone making it clear that he thought they were making a mistake. "Now, will either of you be signing up for gene therapy today?"

"Not today, no," Amar replied. "This is all really new to me. I need a little time to adjust."

"I know it must be overwhelming, coming from a settlement," Jonathan said. "You can change your mind at any time, however—just visit your nearest therapy center. You may think you're perfectly healthy, but you might be surprised. The settlements are just repositories of filth, and—well, I guess you know, don't you?"

"Yes," Amar said. "Farewell, filth. Good riddance."

"Now, let's see about setting you up with a meal plan," Jonathan continued. "Nobody goes hungry in New Singapore!"

He ticked off a few things and then handed them each a small slip of plastic.

"Are either of you planning to work right away?"

"Actually," Lena said, "I was told there might be a job in Cybernetics Eight. An old friend of mine works there and has recommended me. I have an interview tomorrow."

"Well," Jonathan said, taking back her plastic. "Let me put a work visa on that, then. Sir, what about you?"

"I've got nothing lined up," Amar said. "But I would like a visa, if possible."

"Of course," Jonathan said. He finished up Lena's card. "Cybernetics, eh? But with a face like that, you really ought to be in hospitality. It's where all the real fun is."

"I'll bear that in mind," Lena said. "If the other thing doesn't work out."

***

"Why the high-rise and not the terrace?" Amar asked, as he examined their apartment on the eighty-fifth floor. Jonathan had called it small, but it was the biggest—and certainly the cleanest—place Amar had ever lived.

And it gave him the absolute willies. It was like being in the belly of a monster.

"Well, we want our privacy, don't we, dear?" Lena said. "If you live down in the community developments, everyone wants to be friends, and have you over for drinks, and hang out at the community pools and tennis courts and so on. The people in high-rises, not so much. They keep to themselves. A lot of them are shut-ins."

Amar, nodding, acknowledging that was something he wouldn't have known. He didn't like Lena being involved in this, but she was the only one who knew much of anything about living in a New City.

"Did you grow up in a high-rise?" he asked.

"Nope," she said. "I was a terrace girl, all the way. That's why I know we shouldn't be down there. It will be distracting, and well . . . you know."

The apartment had quiet pastel blue walls with recessed lighting that somehow did not cast shadows. It had three rooms—a general purpose area that contained a media screen, a couch, a small kitchen with a fridge, one burner, a microwave, and a few drawers that functioned as a pantry. The utensils and dinnerware were made of some lightweight filament that was disposable and recyclable. A balcony opened on one side, with room enough for two people to sit comfortably, and it looked out over the tidy city of New Singapore. The view was mostly of other high-rises, but a few slivers of ocean were visible in the distance.

The balance of the apartment included a bathroom with a shower, and a bedroom.

"One bed," Amar said.

"Well, honey," Lena said, "we *are* a couple. Otherwise we would be living in different places, right?"

He smiled and nodded, a little irritated at himself. This had all been talked about in the planning stages. No one knew to what extent New City residents were surveilled—whether or not the walls had eyes, so to speak. Sam hypothesized that apartments were probably wired, but that not every apartment was watched—with so many millions of people, that would be a staggering task. Instead, there were probably algorithms running, searching for particular turns of phrase and behaviors that would attract heavier scrutiny. So they had to be careful what they said, and to some extent what they did, but how careful? If he built an explosive device, it would likely be noticed. But would it attract attention if he slept on the couch? It was going to be hard, always imagining an audience that could be watching but never being sure what those watchers would consider suspicious. Since they were new arrivals, would surveillance be more heavily weighted toward them?

Or maybe no one was watching them at all. Most New City citizens had implants, which certainly monitored their behavior. Wiring apartments would be costly and redundant.

But why take the chance? They knew what they were supposed to do. They didn't have to talk about it, at least not much.

Lena cooked dinner for them, which consisted of a lump of CORE in a reddish sauce, green beans that were almost a meter long before she cut them down to size, and brown rice.

"The beans are really good," he said.

"Thanks," she replied.

"Really big."

She nodded. "I hear they're using this new fertilizer that makes vegetables grow to a humongous size. It's also supposed to make them more nutritious." She smiled in a slightly devilish fashion. "You should try the CORE. It's good with this sauce."

He stared at the vaguely ivory-colored stuff. Maybe he could pretend it was tofu. But just the thought of it almost made him gag.

"I'm really stuffed," he told her.

"I thought so," she said. "It's a good thing I'm not the sort to make fun of somebody for what they will and won't eat."

He took the jab. He deserved it.

He decided to risk sleeping on the couch. He was already too distracted by Lena's presence. Lying next to her would only worsen matters.

She watched him arrange his pillow. "We can switch tomorrow night, if you want," she told him.

"It's okay," he said. "Have a good night."

"You too," she said, closing the door.

He lay awake in the too-clean apartment, staring at the ceiling, feeling very alone and stupid.

We're going to adapt, she'd said.

And she had.

***

The next morning, they had coffee and sweet pastries, both rare luxuries outside of the cities. Lena smiled at his reaction.

"I wondered why you were all making such a big deal about that coffee Captain Simmons gave you," she said. "Now I get it. Coffee, tea, chocolate, all the stuff I took for granted growing up . . ." Her face lit up with excitement. "We should get drinks tonight. That horrible stuff you guys drink, and the way you feel the next day—*ugh*. They have the good stuff here. You're not going to believe how good it is. And ice cream. Have you ever even *had* ice cream?"

Amar didn't know if the room was wired, but his own algorithm gave him a sort of mental twitch when she said "you guys." He'd thought she had moved firmly into the XCOM camp, but maybe being back in a city— surrounded by the stuff of her old life, a life that comprised all but a few months of her existence—was making her think twice. She was certainly excited about being here. She wasn't acting.

"Drinks," he said. "That sounds good."

"Okay. So. I have my 'interview' this morning, and hopefully by the end of the day, we'll have something to celebrate." She finished up her coffee and roll. "Probably best if you stay here," she said. "It would seem strange to have a tagalong at the interview."

"That suits me," he said.

When she left, he dithered for just a moment, knowing that there was really no right way to deal with the situation. He was ashamed of his suspicions, but at the same time, at this point in the game, could he really allow himself to be blinded by his feelings?

He left the apartment and followed her.

***

He knew almost instantly something was wrong. They had both memorized the city plan. They had chosen New Singapore because it was one of the few places that manufactured the component they needed. The plant was located at the edge of town. Lena was headed toward the City Center.

Maybe she was just trying to kill a little time sightseeing. The interview was at no particular hour—the objective was just to get her name in, to announce "I'm here" to their contact on the inside. The contact would then arrange for her to get clearance to enter the factory. When she'd said they would have cause to celebrate, she didn't mean because she would have a job, but because the next hurdle of their mission was cleared.

It didn't have to happen right away. But the quicker, the better, right? So it made sense for her to go in the morning. But she wasn't going there, and she wasn't wandering either. She knew where she was headed, and a few minutes later so did he, when she allowed herself to be scanned by an ADVENT trooper before entering a gene therapy clinic.

***

Amar returned to the apartment, trying to sort things out, but he was never able to come to a good conclusion.

He watched propaganda and a supposedly unscripted show about living in the settlements. It was meant to be funny, and if you had never lived in one, it probably was. He turned the media screen off. He took a shower. He waited.

Lena walked in toward the end of the day. She gave him a smile that seemed obviously false.

"I got the job!" she said. "I start tomorrow. Now, how about those drinks?"

His own smile probably seemed no more sincere than hers, but he tried anyway.

***

Like everything else in the city, the bar was clean and orderly, a far cry from some of the filthy ratholes he had frequented in his time. And Lena was right—the drinks were very, very good. Amar had drunk things called "whiskey," "vodka," and "tequila," but they had all pretty much tasted the same, like jet fuel. Here they were subtle, distinct, and didn't hurt his throat and sinuses on the way down.

"Well?" Lena asked. She had changed into a crinkled yellow sleeveless dress and looked like a flower planted in the place it was supposed to grow. He realized he enjoyed seeing her like this, which made him feel a little sick. He nursed his drinks carefully, trying not to get drunk. Because if he got drunk and started talking . . .

"You like it here, don't you?" he said.

Crap, he realized. Too late. The drinks were a lot stronger than they tasted.

"You mean this bar?" Lena asked. She wasn't exactly sober either and had in fact been drinking with more abandon than he had ever seen her do. Now that he understood how bad the outland hooch was, he sort of understood. Or maybe it was just because she felt comfortable here.

"The bar is nice," he said. "But that's not what I meant."

She pointed the index finger of the hand she was holding her martini with. "You mean New Singapore," she said. It sounded like an accusation, albeit a lighthearted one.

"Right," he replied.

She leaned back and crossed her legs. The dress was short, and he realized he was seeing her knees for the first time. She gazed at him with an unread-able expression.

"Sure," she admitted. "It's familiar. It's not infested by bugs, snakes, or lizards. And this tastes good." She finished her drink and set it down for the bartender to replace. "I like air conditioning. Hot showers are wonderful—for that matter, so is not having to boil water before you drink it. And the not being shot at all the time. Huge bonus."

She leaned back toward him, uncomfortably close. "What about you?" she asked. "What do you think?"

"I guess I see the attraction. But—"

She put her hand on his thigh and squeezed hard, digging in her nails.

"First of all," she said, "don't go there. I know what you're about to start on about, and you know you shouldn't, not here. And even if you could, I wouldn't want to hear it. Just one night, okay? With no moralizing or guilt—just let me enjoy my damn drink, okay?"

A couple of people were looking at them now. Lena turned on her stool. "Are you all enjoying the show?" she asked.

They quickly turned away.

"I'm tired of this place," she said. "Let's find a different bar."

The next place looked pretty much exactly like the last. They ordered a light meal and later had neon-colored ice cream, which he had to admit was very tasty. Then more drinks, and finally they walked around to the waterfront, which was as manicured as the rest of the city. A half-moon looked as if it was sailing in the harbor, and a few couples were rowing in iridescent flatboats.

They sat on a bench, and after a moment, he leaned over and embraced her. He felt her stiffen.

"What are you doing?" she demanded, pulling back.

"Settle down," he whispered. "Just pretend like we're kissing. I need to say something, and I don't want to be overheard."

She looked at him doubtfully, then leaned over so their cheeks were touching.

"Did you get a chip put in you?" he asked.

He felt her tense and then sort of sag.

"You followed me?" He wasn't sure how to read her tone. Was it despair, disappointment, or both?

"Yes," he said. "I'm sorry."

She began to quiver, and he realized she was crying.

"No," she said. "I brought a chip with me, a counterfeit one. So I could get in. So they can't hear you or see you, if that's what you're worried about. Not through me, anyway."

"Then why? Why go in there and not tell me about it?"

She drew back a little, so he could see her eyes, glistening in the city light.

"One last time," she whispered. "Once more, and I'll never ask this again. Amar—I need you to have faith in me."

He had been thinking about those words—and the last time she said them—for a long time.

"Okay," he said. "Okay." He stood up. "You should get some rest. You start the job tomorrow."

***

The next day Lena returned from work and flashed him the pass. She suggested they take a walk before dinner, so they took the lift down and were soon exploring one of the more bucolic areas of the city. Here the housing was grouped into little compounds with raised, shared green spaces, many of which were on the roofs of the houses.

"Terraces?" he asked.

"Yep," she said. "I grew up in that one." She pointed at one of three houses that shared both a terrace around them and a sort of courtyard between them.

"I thought you grew up in Gulf City," he said.

"Right," she allowed. "But in that model house. You could put a blindfold on me and I would be able to navigate the inside of it without much trouble."

"So this is the old home place," he said.

"As close as I'll ever get," she said. "So. Ask me how things went today."

"I saw the pass," he said. "I guess things went well."

"Yep. I'm now officially the quality control monitor for augmented processing units."

"Which means you do what?" he asked.

"Well, the units are inspected by automated assessors. The modules either pass or fail. If they pass, I send them to packing. If they fail, I direct them back to production."

"Couldn't the automated assessors do that?" he asked.

"Says the man whose job is to sit on a couch all day," she said with mock disdain.

"Don't get touchy," he said. "I'm not knocking your career."

"Just remember, I'm the one putting CORE on the table."

"How could I forget?" he sighed. Then he grew a little more serious. "How, um, *safe* do you feel there?"

"Very," she said. "The security system is top-notch. I was warned there are a few glitches in it, but those will be gone soon enough."

"And your boss? How is he?"

"I didn't meet the boss," she replied. "At least I don't think so. And my orientation was mercifully brief."

"So you think things are going to work out?"

She nodded. "I think it'll work out just fine," she said. Then she noticed he had stopped to stare at something. It was a little park, but unlike the others they had passed, it had some odd structures in it—tubes, narrow inclined smooth surfaces. Children were climbing and sliding on them. Others were swinging back and forth in flexible strips of plastic suspended from a metal frame by cables.

"Amar?"

"What is that?" he asked.

She laughed. "You're kidding, right?" She put her hand up to her mouth. "Oh god, you aren't kidding. It's a playground."

He knew each word individually, but the two together sounded weird.

"You didn't have playgrounds?" she asked in a disbelieving tone. "You didn't play?"

"Sure, we played," Amar said. "We just didn't have a particular place for it. Or . . . things."

"You mean slides and swings and monkey bars?"

"We had monkeys," he said. "But they weren't drinkers."

"Funny," she said.

"My uncle made us this sort of thing to jump on once, from a tarp and some springs—"

"Like a trampoline."

"That was what he called it," Amar said. "ADVENT troopers trashed it the next time they came through."

"I guess that explains why you didn't have playgrounds," she said.

"There you go," he said as he continued to watch the children. "It doesn't seem like such a bad idea, a playground. Maybe one day . . ." He didn't finish the thought. He had been and was involved in the creation of several things—the Avenger and the Skyranger, for example. If he lived long enough, he would likely be involved in the building of any number of weapons, facilities, and defensive capabilities. But the odds that he would ever be in the place or have the time to build a playground seemed pretty close to nil. That would be for someone else to do, when it was all over. If it was ever going to be over.

"Yes," Lena said. "One day."

They began walking again, back toward the apartment.

"We were both drunk last night," she said. "Is there anything you want to say now that we're sober?"

"No," he said, "I think I covered it."

"Okay," she said. "Tomorrow."

"Tomorrow," he echoed.

CHAPTER 19

IT WAS THE sitting on his thumbs that was the most difficult part for Amar. Lena had been trained to recognize the particular "augmented processor" they needed for the Avenger, so it made perfect sense that she was the one tasked to work in the factory. But it left him too much alone with his thoughts. He could not stomach watching the media screen for more than a few minutes at a time—even the games available were so clogged with nonsense and outright lies that he couldn't bring himself to play them.

So he was left with his own thoughts, and right in the middle of that was his decision to trust Lena, a decision he second-guessed on a nearly hourly basis. But he also kept returning to the reason he was able to keep his resolution: He would be able to cancel the mission almost until the last second. If he did, he would probably die and would certainly never escape New Singapore. But no one else would be involved. Shen could try again with someone else, possibly in New Seattle, one of the other targets they had considered.

But he didn't believe Lena would lead him into a trap. He couldn't.

He continued to explore the city, thinking he could at least come to understand it better. The playground had been an eye-opener, a sign that he had his own prejudices and blind spots when it came to places like this. He still did not at all approve of New Singapore, but he felt he needed to understand it. The battle they were fighting against the ADVENT was not and could not be merely military. They needed the help of the people in the New Cities to win; they needed those people to *want* to be free. And right now, the ADVENT were winning the propaganda war.

As in New Kochi, the billboards here were much larger than those forced on the settlers, and they were constantly filled with images and stories of how the dissident few were making life harder for everyone, how twenty years of mutual cooperation for the common good of humanity and their benefactors were threatened by malcontent thugs who thought only of their own selfish needs. Even the contagion was being blamed on the resistance: The story was that it was a biochemical weapon developed by unscrupulous scientists to blackmail population centers, and that it had somehow gotten out of control.

And people bought it. He watched and listened to them in coffee shops, bars, and public squares.

On the other side of it, images of ADVENT peacekeepers were everywhere, posed heroically. Children wore ADVENT T-shirts and played Peacekeepers and Bad Guys, and no kid he saw ever wanted to be the Bad Guy.

He wondered, if he hadn't grown up where he had, if he didn't know the things he knew—would he be happy here? Would he watch his screen and eat CORE burgers and never wonder too much about what was really going on, why the aliens would try so hard to make people feel secure and happy, to draw them into the cities until there was no one left outside?

Maybe. Probably. But he didn't have the choice of accepting all of this without qualms, without wondering about the price.

***

The factory hummed along a constant twenty-four hours, so they went in at night. With Lena's pass and the "glitches" in security she had learned about, it wasn't difficult to get into the place.

Nothing manufactured here had any direct military use—most of the components, in fact, went into building entertainment systems and the autopilots for cars, trains, and transports. The only real exception seemed to be the processors themselves. This had seemed odd to Amar, so he had remarked on it during their last walk.

"Oh," Lena said. "No, the part we're talking about isn't used in ships of any kind. It's mostly used in traffic grid guidance systems and to replace the processors in older satellites. We wouldn't have had any chance at all to get our hands on anything meant for a modern military or deep-space ship. Those places are incredibly well guarded."

"But that's exactly what you're trying to repair—a ship."

"Yes. A twenty-year-old ship. The aliens have made serious upgrades in the past couple of decades. From what we can tell, their computer technology has changed substantially. But the APs they build here are old technology, perfectly adequate for our purposes. It will probably take some tweaking, but the Shens are quite sure they can make it work."

"So the security is minimal," he said.

"Yes."

"Do you think you could just walk in, take it, and walk out?"

"Walk in, yes. Take it, yes. Walking out will be a problem. The security is low, not nonexistent."

Now they had done the walking in part and were on to the taking.

The human staff was negligible, and only a few of them looked up as Amar and Lena passed through the corridors and open fabrication rooms. None took any notice of the empty backpack on Amar's shoulder.

In truth, almost everything in the factory was done through automation, with alien overseers and a few human collaborators at the top to give them a public face when they needed one. Most of the jobs that didn't involve public relations were like Lena's—humans watching machines that could already watch themselves. After all, the aliens didn't have any particular interest in educating humans in their technology.

Amar had the impression that most jobs in the city barely met the criteria to be called that. His time in New Singapore had sharpened his sense of what the New Cities were *for*.

The cities of the past had for the most part evolved from crossroads or ports or defensible places. They had economic and social reasons for existing, and if they grew larger than a village, there were a number of demographic forces that caused that to happen. The old cities had been places of production, of commerce, of innovation in the social, technological, and artistic senses.

The function of New Singapore wasn't anything of the sort. It was about control, pure and simple. It had the outward form of a city but nothing of the essence.

Lena had sorted through the various configurations available to select the augmented processor with the best possible fit for the Avenger's computer. She had marked it, packed it, and sent it down to the loading dock, which was what they were entering now. Dimly lit with dull red lights, it was about half empty. Bundles of parts sat on small trams. Across the room was a pair of massive doors.

"What's through there?" he asked.

"A hangar," she said. "And a junction with a rail line. Some things get loaded onto rail, some are flown out—a few things go by truck."

"Well, let's find it first," he said.

"I have my handy inventory stick," she said, taking out a slim rod. It glowed and scrolled a few glowing characters.

"Right over here," she said.

The cylindrical container wasn't quite half a meter in length and half again that in diameter.

"That's the one?" he asked.

She examined it again and nodded.

"So exactly when does the alarm go off?"

"Everything that comes in here gets counted and has a match code to whatever is supposed to pick it up. If this leaves any other way than through the loading doors, there are alarms. If it goes out the loading doors but gets put anywhere other than its appointed destination, alarms again."

He examined the doors. They were thick and heavy, and would reel up into the ceiling when opened.

"Can we open these?" he asked.

"I don't have the codes or even access to the controls," she said.

He didn't think a rocket launcher would punch through them, either.

That was too bad. It would make things much easier. The front door, however, could probably easily be compromised.

"I guess the plan is we take it and run for the front door," he said, stuffing the processor into the backpack.

"I was really hoping the brilliant chief could come up with a better plan," she said.

He shrugged. "We could hang out here until they open the doors and start loading," he suggested.

"There will be ADVENT security for that," she pointed out.

"Then I like my first plan," he said. "Give me a moment."

He paused only a moment before flipping on the radio.

***

As predicted, the alarm started braying as soon as they exited the dock. Amar had debated whether they should just walk and try not to draw attention, but he decided instead on running like hell. Lena hadn't reported any jabbers in the building in the four days she had been there, so the real danger was from the troops that would show up from the outside. The longer it took them to get to the front door, the greater the odds that they would meet with resistance.

This time they were noticed. Most of the workers were sort of milling in confusion, wondering why the alarm was sounding—until they saw Lena and Amar. Then they started ducking into rooms or under things. Whether they thought Lena and Amar *were* the danger or were running from the danger wasn't clear, but the billboards taught that where there were alarms and people running, there would soon be explosions and bullets.

One guy had a different reaction. He was a big man, tall and broad-shouldered, and he moved to intercept them, yelling for them to stop. Since he was blocking the corridor, there was no avoiding him.

Amar jabbed a fist at him, without slowing down.

"Do not!" he shouted. "You do not want to do that."

But the guy stood his ground.

Amar stopped just long enough to hand the backpack with the part to Lena.

"I don't know what you've stolen," the man said. "And I don't care. Just wait here until the police arrive."

"What's your name?" Amar demanded.

"Brian," the fellow said, looking mildly surprised.

"Brian, I'm in a hurry," Amar said. "You have exactly two seconds to move out of the way."

"Now, look—"

Amar decided two seconds was too long. He feinted a punch to Brian's face; Brian threw up his hands to protect himself—also effectively blinding himself as Amar drove his hand into his solar plexus. Brian made a sucking sound; Amar swept his front foot and pushed him over while he was off-balance.

Big men could get away with a lot in a fight just by being big, which meant that a lot of them, especially civilians, thought it was *enough* to be big. Being big usually just stopped fights from happening to them, leaving them relatively . . . uneducated. If it had been Dux or Palepoi standing there, it would be Amar on the ground gasping for air, perhaps with a broken limb or two.

He let Lena keep the pack in case it happened again, and they continued on.

When they reached the front door, it was locked, naturally—the entire building was sealed. Odds were there were already ADVENT police closing in on the building, so they didn't have long.

"Now," he heard Lena say. She took him by the arm and pulled him back, away from the door.

He was surprised. He hadn't realized she also had a radio.

Suddenly one of the workers appeared from nowhere, dashing toward the exit, a look of pure terror on his face.

"Hey, no!" Amar shouted, but the young man showed no signs of slowing down. So he did the only thing he could. He sprinted forward, tackling the guy below the waist, trying to roll aside before . . .

The door exploded, along with a significant fraction of the wall. The shock knocked him another four meters and hammered the breath out of him. Black spots threatened to blot out his vision entirely.

He crawled off the young man.

"Are you okay?" he gasped, hardy able to hear his own voice.

The man looked around, bewildered. "I think?" he said.

"Run the other way," Amar said. "Farther into the building. You tell anybody you see, stay away from here."

That was all he had time for, he knew. Lena was tugging at his arm, and together they ran out the door, where the Skyranger was waiting. Dux was firing his rocket launcher again at some target down the street. Nishimura and Chitto were laying down cover fire.

A mag round skipped off the pavement, and another screamed by near his head. Across the street he saw something immense coming out of the shadows. It was like something from a nightmare, a nightmare inspired by the folktales his Malaysian grandfather had told of him. He only had a glimpse of it, but it looked like a cobra the size of a man.

It couldn't be real. . . .

Then it was out of sight, behind the Skyranger, and he and Lena were climbing into the ship. ADVENT troops were closing in from every direction, and it was definitely time to go. Chitto and Nishimura fired once more each and jumped in as well. Dux was right behind them, but as Lily kicked in the under jets, something wrapped around Dux's ankle and yanked him back. He yelped and grabbed at the door, dropping his weapon. Amar threw himself on the floor and grabbed his wrists, trying desperately to pull him back.

Dux wasn't looking at him, but at whatever had a hold of him. His eyes were wide with terror and disbelief, but as he turned to look back at Amar, his face hardened and became grim, angry.

Then something yanked him so hard that all of Amar's strength and determination amounted to nothing. An infant could have done as well.

And Dux was gone. The Skyranger lifted free.

"Wait," Nishimura shouted at Lily. "Dux! We have to go back for him."

As she started forward, mag rounds sang through the open door and punched through the hull.

Amar realized everyone was looking at him, including Lily. His throat almost seized up. Nishimura started toward the door again, but he stopped her with his hand.

"Close it," he told Lily. "Get us out of here."

The Skyranger turned and accelerated toward the sky. The rattle of the weapons' fire was like popcorn popping, and like popcorn it diminished, the seconds between each concussion drawing further apart, until the only noise was the roar of the engines.

Amar regarded Nishimura. "Alejandra—" he began.

"No, Chief," she said. Her eyes were red. She had her helmet in her hands, resting on her lap. "You were right. I just lost it."

"That wasn't 'losing it,'" he said. "I would rather be in a squad that cared too much about me than too little. But it was just too late."

He thought he was saying the words just to comfort her, but the minute they came out of this mouth he realized he meant it. He couldn't have said that a few months ago.

Nishimura put her head down. "I just hope he went in style. Took another couple with him. He would have wanted that."

"He bought us a working Avenger," Lily said. "That's not nothing."

New Singapore dropped away behind them. Somewhere, ADVENT was probably scrambling gunboats to come after them. They still might not make it home.

He turned his attention to Lena, whose gaze was fastened on the receding city.

"Are you all right?" he asked her.

She turned to him and nodded. "Thank you," she said.

"For what?"

"You know what," she said, and took his hand. After a few seconds, he gripped it back.

CHAPTER 20

AMAR WAS A little amazed at how much the Avenger had changed in the month or so since he had seen her. Not so much on the outside as on the inside. The first big surprise was that a hangar had already been cleared to house the Skyranger. It also contained the armory. Crew quarters fit for human beings had been constructed, and the tent city outside was vanishing as people moved into the ship.

A bar and restaurant similar to the Rathskeller on the Elpis was up and functioning. A workshop and an engineering department had been built. Most of this had been done using decades-old technology, although some of it was powered using Elerium. The result was something that felt a lot more like home—a human environment in an alien skin.

The "Enigma" chamber remained inaccessible, although it was unclear why. The elder Dr. Shen believed that once the power and computer systems were functioning, it would cease to be an issue.

Some individual systems were already online, including life support, which circulated breathable, climate-controlled atmosphere throughout the vessel. Others had been added; a jamming field had been erected around the ship—if a patrol did find them, the field should be capable of preventing communications from the immediate area, giving them a chance to deal with the enemy and keep their location secret for at least a little longer.

"We're a long way from flying, however," Dr. Shen told them. "Even after the computer is online, there are a number of parts we will have to either steal or fabricate."

He studied the item Amar and Lena had taken from New Singapore. It was a cylinder, flared slightly on both ends. Its metallic surface had a rainbow sheen, like titanium—except that the rainbow was always gradually shifting, like oil on water that something stirred now and then.

"This, however," Shen went on, "should work. I commend you all. I'm very sorry for the man you lost."

"Thank you, sir," Amar said.

"Well," Dr. Shen said, "let's see what we can do with this."

***

The rains of the northeast monsoon were tailing off, and the weather was growing drier and cooler, making patrols and hikes to the watchtowers much more pleasant. Amar held a briefing on the contagion and instructed patrols on how to identify it.

And things moved on. Lena was furiously busy the first few days after their return, but they both rose each morning before sunlight and shared a cup of coffee together. It wasn't as good as the stuff in New Singapore or even the pot Captain Simmons had brewed, but it didn't matter. The coffee wasn't really the point.

"When will you guys install the processor?" Amar asked on one such morning.

"We already have," she said. "We're taking baby steps in terms of connecting it to the rest of the systems, in case we find something ugly. Or something else ugly, I should say. We've already disabled several internal defense systems. We want to be pretty sure what we're turning on before we do it."

"That makes sense," he said. But it made him itchy. There was only so long that they could sit here, grounded, using energy, bringing in supplies, before being noticed. Caution was all well and good, but there were mounting risk factors in moving too slowly as well.

But there was no point in saying that. She knew it as well as he did.

They listened as the cloud forest changed its score from night to day, and the sky brightened.

"This is my favorite time of day," she said softly.

"Mine, too," he replied.

"I wish it lasted longer."

He took a little breath and let it out. "I'd like for it to last a lot longer," he said.

She peered at him over the brim of her coffee cup, sitting with her legs drawn up under her, looking beautiful in her ragged green fatigues and brown T-shirt.

"What?" she said. "Like all day?"

"Like from now on," he replied.

She pursed her lips and seemed about to say something, so he knew he had to get ahead of her.

"I love you," he said. "I was an idiot not to tell you before. I know I screwed things up. I know there aren't always second chances. But—"

"Hush," she said. "Just . . ." A brittle little smile appeared on her face. She couldn't quite meet his eyes.

She set the coffee cup down. "The reason . . ." she began, "the reason I went to the gene therapy center was because I suspected something, and I had to know if I was right."

"You don't have to tell me anything," he said. "I think we've been through this."

"I believe I do need to tell you," she replied. "You deserve to know."

He suddenly really didn't want to know, but he didn't say so. He just nodded and waited for her to gather herself and find whatever words she was looking for.

"My cancer is back," she said.

He heard the words, but he couldn't quite sort them out.

"You said gene therapy had cured it," he finally managed.

"It had," she sighed. "It did. I don't know what went wrong. For all I know, it's designed that way—if you stop the treatments it comes back, so you never want to leave the city." She shrugged. "I was starting to feel sick, like before. So when we were in New Singapore, I went in for a diagnostic."

"Okay," Amar breathed. "And you had it treated."

"No," she said. "No, I didn't."

"Why?" he asked. "We were *there*, you were in, and you had the fake chip. It would have been easy."

Her smile was a little more genuine this time. "Would you have, if it had been you?"

"I don't know!" he exploded. "I'm not sick. I haven't been sick. I've never thought about it."

"Let's just skip all of that soul-searching," she said. "You, Amar Tan, would not go into a gene therapy center to save your life. And neither will I. It was dangerous enough to get the checkup, but if they had done the therapy, they might have discovered my genome is already in the system. But even if that weren't a problem . . ." She ran her fingers through her hair.

"So that night, at the bar . . ." he said.

"Yeah," she said. "I knew I was sick, and I didn't want to think about it. I wanted to enjoy myself. Yes, I miss a lot of things about living in the city. But I know I can never really go back there."

Amar felt himself becoming increasingly more desperate, but he tried to keep his tone level, to not show it.

"Look," he said. "We can go anywhere—New Madrid, New Providence, any city—and act like we're coming in from the cold, just like we did before. You get cured; we leave. It's that simple."

"No," she said, "it isn't. We're lucky we got out last time, and someone died so we could do it. And that was for something important."

"Your life is important," he said.

"Amar, please understand. I'm not dead. I still have my life," she said. "For the first time, I really have my life. I don't know for how much longer, but however long it is, I want to spend it doing something important. Something my sister would have been proud of." She looked at him directly. "Something you would be proud of."

He was having a hard time forming words.

"Of course I'm proud of you," he finally got out.

"I was avoiding this conversation," she said. "I was hoping you wouldn't . . ." His throat caught. "Ah, wouldn't tell me what you just did. But now that you have . . ."

"Wait. You knew I was in love with you?"

"Of course, dumbass," she said.

He stared at her for a moment, stunned.

"Oh," he said at last. "But you don't—"

"Of course I do," she said. "God, you really are a numbskull."

"I'm starting to get that," he said.

"Yeah. *Starting* to." She wiped the corners of her eyes with her palms and picked her coffee back up. He watched her, tried to see every detail, the golden stars in her green eyes, the small spray of freckles on her forehead.

"What are you thinking?" she asked.

"I'm thinking . . ." he said. "I'm thinking you say you don't know how much longer you'll live. I don't know how long I've got either. Rider, Thomas, Toby, Dux—and a bunch before them—all gone in the blink of an eye. DeLao and Nishimura are the only people around who I've known for longer than a year. Odds are, next mission it'll be me. So I wish . . . whatever time we have left . . . I wish we could spend it together."

She reached for his hand.

"I can deal with that if you can," she said.

They were married the next day. They honeymooned farther up in the Ghats, where the air was cooler and thinner, and the Milky Way blazed like a white river in the sky.

***

The bridge of the Avenger was still a work in progress, but it was coming together. The ship's original sensors and some new ones engineering had built channeled and displayed information from the small—the temperature and humidity outside, for instance—to the grand, such as a relay that sorted thousands of coded radio transmissions by subject and priority.

By the way Sam was grinning, Amar figured there must be something else he'd been called up to see. He watched the analyst fiddle with some controls, and then took an involuntary step back as a column of blue light suddenly appeared in the middle of the room. Floating in the light was an image of Earth.

"Wow," he said.

"This is the hologlobe," Sam said. "Since we got the computer up and running, we've been able to do all sorts of cool things. This is one of them. We've wired in Vahlen's old network and started adding our own tracking information. We've now officially got a command center for our operations."

"That's pretty cool," Amar had to admit.

"I finally feel like I'm home," Sam gushed on. "Exactly where I need to be. It's all coming together, KB. You had a lot to do with that. You and . . . the others."

Amar didn't have to ask who he meant by "the others." The list was long, and growing longer.

"When we first met," Amar said, "you told us that you had found something worthy of their sacrifice. Do you still believe that?"

"Even I had my doubts at times," Sam admitted. "There were some pretty low moments, weren't there? But I promise you, it's going to pay off. We'll be able to organize on a scale we could only dream of before. The computer is working now. We've got a way to strategize at the global level. Once we figure out how to get this thing off the ground—"

"Yeah," Amar said. "That tiny detail."

"We've been trying to find Vahlen," Sam said. "We desperately need someone of her caliber in research. But no luck so far. She's like a ghost."

Amar thought it was likely she was quite literally a ghost, at least if you believed in such things. So many miles of open ocean, with days of sailing to reach anywhere. ADVENT patrols had managed to find his tiny boat. Vahlen would have been in either a relatively large ship or a fleet of little ones. Unless. . .

Unless the Elpis had a sister.

The thought made him smile, but he dismissed the speculation as pointless. Vahlen either couldn't be found, wasn't around to be found—or didn't want to be found. In any case, she wasn't going to be on the team.

Sam was still talking. "Anyway," he said, "there are other candidates for a chief research scientist, good ones. We should have one soon."

"When you pick one out, we'll go get them," Amar said. "But thanks for showing me this. I'd like to catch up on the defensive systems later, but right now I've got a lunch date with my wife."

On his way to the bar he passed Dr. Shen in the hallway. He was fiddling with a computer pad and looked perturbed.

"I just saw the hologlobe," Amar told him. "Congratulations."

"Thank you," the old man said distractedly. "I'm sorry, Amar, no time to talk."

"I understand," Amar said.

Lena wasn't in the bar, when he got there. He thought about going down to engineering to collect her, but if she was late, she usually had good reason to be.

So he sat alone. A few tables over, Nishimura was having an animated conversation with a new recruit. DeLao was at the bar, flirting with the bartender, a young woman from France whose other job was assistant mechanic on the Skyranger.

Chitto walked in, saw him, and came over.

"Got a minute, Chief?" she asked.

"Sure," he said. "Have a seat."

She looked around the bar. "Lot of new faces, huh?" she said.

"I was just noticing that," he said. There were now more people in the Avenger whose names he didn't know than ones he did.

"They look so damn young," she said.

He laughed. "I was thinking that, too," he told her. "How old are you, Chitto?"

"Twenty-four," she said.

"Yeah," he said. "Nishimura, she's thirty. DeLao is around twenty-eight. I'm a year older than you. But we look like old-timers compared to some of these kids."

"It's all in the clean living, I guess," she said.

"It wasn't all that long ago that you were the rookie," he said. "I thought you looked like a baby."

"I know I was pretty green," she said. "I know you hated being stuck with me. But you hung in there for me, Chief. I appreciate that."

"So what's on your mind?" he asked.

She eyed him as if he was a little slow. "I just told you, Chief," she said.

"That's it?"

"It was big deal to me," she said. "I just never felt like it was the right time to thank you. We were always in the middle of something, or you were busy with other things."

"Oh," he said. "I was worried you were working up to quitting or something."

"Nah," she said. "I don't really have any other skills."

"Good," he said, "because I've been thinking. DeLao already has his own squad. I offered Nishimura a command, but she turned it down. I've been thinking you could head up a recon unit. What do you think?"

Her eyebrows lifted fractionally. He remembered when Thomas had had this same conversation with him, what seemed like years ago.

"I think I'm not the leader type, Chief," she said. "It was hard enough to learn to be in a unit. You may remember I kind of tended to do things my own way."

"Believe it or not," he said, "that's a leadership quality. You might surprise yourself."

Oddly, she did look surprised. Very surprised, so much so that he thought she was having him on.

"Okay," Amar said. "You don't have to be sarcastic."

"No, Chief," Chitto said. "Listen."

He heard it then, close to inaudible at first, but growing steadily in volume.

CHAPTER 21

AT FIRST HE thought it was just some strange music someone had slipped into the intercom, some form of electronica.

But then he realized it sounded more like talking, a stream-of consciousness soliloquy without breaks to draw breath. The words were unfamiliar and the articulation was very weird. Some of the sounds he was pretty sure the human voice couldn't reproduce. And it got louder and louder.

He didn't know what it was, but it sounded *wrong*—yet somehow familiar.

Now conversation had tailed off completely—everyone in the bar was listening. Most had puzzled expressions on their faces, but Nishimura looked horrified. She covered her ears and starting muttering in Spanish, and with creeping dread he began to understand why. Something about the cadence of the language, the tonal inflection, reminded him of the thing back in New Kochi, the monster that had reached into his brain.

And also of the jabbers—the language they spoke.

Trying not to lose it, he tapped on his radio. "Sam?" he said. "Sam? Dr. Shen?"

He got back only static.

"What the hell is it?" DeLao shouted. "Whoever is doing that—"

Amar had a bad feeling, and it was quickly getting worse.

"Chitto, Nishimura," he said, "find Palepoi and gear up. DeLao, get your squad together."

"What's happening, Chief?" Chitto asked.

"I have no idea," he said, "but it can't be good. Call everyone in. I want a squad guarding the bridge, one in engineering, one in the workshop, and one in the armory guarding the Skyranger. Nishimura, check in with the perimeter; make sure nothing is coming in. I'm headed down to engineering. My squad, come as soon as you're armed and armored, and someone drag my stuff down, please."

***

Engineering was a madhouse. Lily Shen was barking orders, and her half-panicked staff was scurrying around like confused ants.

"What's happening?" Amar demanded.

Lily looked up. Her expression was somewhere between irritated and panicked.

"The computer," she said. "Something's taking control of it."

"Something?"

"Lena, explain to him," she snapped. "I don't have time."

Lena looked at him apologetically. "She's freaking out," she said. "I don't blame her. The bridge has been sealed off, and her father is in there. Our internal communications have been shut down."

"What do you mean, 'sealed off'?" he asked.

"It's a security feature," she said. "In case the ship is invaded."

"I've already sent a squad there," he said, trying to sound calm. "I should hear from them soon. Lily said something had taken control of the computer. What exactly did she mean by that?"

"At first we thought it was a bug in the system," she said. "A virus or something. But now it looks like it's some kind of artificial intelligence."

"I don't understand," he said. "The computer has been on for weeks."

"But not fully operational," she said. "We tested it a bit at a time, remember?"

"Well, what happened?" he demanded.

"Obviously we missed something," she said. "As careful as we were, we weren't careful enough. The system is too alien. It must have been slightly aware the whole time, hiding, playing along with us, waiting for this moment."

"Bloody hell," he murmured.

"Yeah," she said. He could tell she was worried, but she shot him a little smile.

"You're really cute when you say that, you know," she said.

"You mean sexy," he said.

"That's exactly what I meant." She kissed him. "Go do your job," she said. "I have to get back to mine."

***

Nishimura, Chitto, and Palepoi showed up a few minutes later. Amar took his gear from Chitto and began putting it on.

"DeLao," he called. "What about the bridge?"

"Locked down, Chief," he replied. "Can't get it open. There's a kid here from engineering working on it, but so far, no luck."

It was getting hard to hear, as the ghastly chatter rose to a nearly deafening level.

And then, very suddenly, it stopped. Dead silence followed for the space of a few heartbeats.

"*Zao gao!*" Lily swore into the stillness.

Amar stood frozen, waiting—for what he wasn't sure.

Then the lights went out, and they were in utter darkness. Lily uttered a few more colorful Mandarin phrases, and several people screamed. Amar flipped on his helmet light.

"Everyone keep calm," he bellowed.

Then the diesel generator kicked in, and the auxiliary lights came on. He made his way to Lily.

"What's happening?" he asked.

"I'm frozen out," Lily whispered. "It's completely taken over the ship. And it has turned off the air."

"And sealed all of the hatches, I would assume," Amar said.

"Of course," she replied. He saw that she was trembling.

"You've got this," he told her. "You can do it."

She looked at him. "The noises," she said. "Did you hear?"

"Yes," he said. "I get it. But you have to shake it off and save us, right?"

She took a deep breath. "Of course," she said.

"Okay," he said. "So how long have we got? Before we suffocate?"

"That's difficult to calculate," she said. "We have at least a few hours before carbon dioxide levels start to become toxic." She thought for a moment. "If I can devise some way of scrubbing the CO_2, we could last a little longer."

"How about this?" he asked. "Is there some way to manually open any of the outer hatches?"

"No. Not without explosives, and maybe not even then," she said.

"Chief?" That was DeLao, over the radio.

"Yes, go ahead."

"The bridge just opened up," he said.

"Is Dr. Shen okay?" he asked.

"Yes, he and Sam are fine," DeLao said.

Amar turned to Lily. "Why would the AI lock the bridge and then unlock it?"

"I don't know," she said. "It doesn't make any sense." Her brows beetled up. "Unless—"

"Guys," Lena interrupted. "Lily, Amar—look at this."

He stepped over to see what she was studying so intently. It turned out to be a screen divided up between security cameras they had installed early in the refit process. At first he didn't see what had attracted Lena's attention.

"Here," she said, pointing. "That's the Enigma chamber."

"Oh," Amar said.

Slowly, as he watched, the hatch began to open.

"Unless the computer didn't lock the bridge," Lily continued. "Maybe the security system locked it before the AI got control of it."

"Oh, no," Lena said.

Amar keyed the radio. "Everyone, watch for hostiles, originating in the lower fore of the ship. Repeat, we may have hostiles."

His earpiece crackled.

"ADVENT?" DeLao asked.

"I don't think so," Amar said. "But it could be just about anything else. Watch the lifts and the access stairs and squeal if you need help. If they get through you, they can come at us from any number of directions. Akira, same for you guys in the workroom. We have to keep these things on the lower deck."

"Right, Chief," Akira said.

"Mak, are you there?" Amar asked.

"Mak" was Mukharymova, a fresh recruit from the New Moscow area, but she was anything but green, having fought with an isolated cell since the age of fifteen. She had dark eyes and honey-touched hair that was driving half of the men crazy, but if she noticed the attention, she ignored it. Her squad was still in the armory.

"Yes sir," she replied.

"Get down here and guard engineering. We're headed to the Enigma chamber."

He signed off. "Come on," he said.

The Avenger, he thought, suddenly didn't feel like home at all.

The armory was on the top deck of the ship, in the rear. The Enigma chamber was in the front of the craft and three decks down, on the same level as engineering, which was in the back, underneath the bar and the armory. Between engineering and the Enigma chamber were three interconnected compartments that currently didn't have any use.

Through these they now advanced, cautiously opening each hatch until they came to the third, from which they could see the now-open Enigma chamber. Amar couldn't make out anything inside other than darkness and something in the distance radiating a pale green light.

He was about to give the order to move up when something came hurling through the hatch and bounced off the wall.

"Grenade!" he shouted, ducking back behind the bulkhead. Thunder boomed, and a blast of heat and fury came through the hatch.

Amar leaned around. He saw movement and fired without waiting to see what it was. His bullets rang like they were hitting a steel wall.

"Robots!" he yelped.

This particular robot was flying, and another came out just behind it. It looked a little like a human torso with no head and nothing from the waist down. It had one arm with a mechanical claw and the other was just a long tube.

Which suddenly spat green fire. Not a mag rifle, some kind of energy, and *hot*. He felt the scorch of it in the air, even though it missed.

Nishimura shot the same one he had, and it went rattling back against the wall. Amar tossed in a grenade, seeing as he did so more robots streaming through the opening. And they had nowhere to go except through Amar and his squad. If he got pushed back, though, they could potentially go anywhere using the lifts or stairs connecting the decks.

For a while, they managed to hold them. A few made it through the door but were gunned down as soon as they did. A pile of robotic debris was beginning to build up in the chamber.

But finally, there were too many. One shot Palepoi, sending him stumbling back. Nishimura came up and sliced its weapon off, but another was right there. Amar shot it, threw another grenade, and gave the order to fall back to the next room just before it went off. He slammed the hatch, but it wouldn't lock.

Palepoi, still on his feet, fired another rocket as the hatch popped back open. Then they set up and waited for the assault to continue. They had now been pushed back almost to Mak's position.

"DeLao," Amar said, "report."

"Nothing yet, but we can hear you guys catching hell. What is it?"

"Mechanicals," Amar said. "Figures. What else could last twenty years in a sealed chamber?"

It was starting to feel hot and stuffy. The scent of propellant and ozone clogged the air. Was he imagining it, or was it already getting hard to breathe?

Nishimura leaned out and fired.

Amar glanced over at Palepoi and nodded at him.

"I'm okay, Chief," he said. "Just a little scorched. If that had been a mag, I'd be done."

"Okay, Chitto, go back and set up a supply line. We need people to walk ammo down from the armory. Tell Mak to move someone up to take your place."

"Rather stay here, Chief," she said.

"Not much use for a sniper in this situation," he pointed out.

"Fair," she said. He and Nishimura covered her retreat.

"KB," the radio said, "this is Sam."

"What's up?" Amar asked.

"I think I can take control of the ship," he said. "Dr. Shen says there's a kill switch—"

"Hell yes," Amar said. "Do it."

"I'm on my way," Sam replied. "I just wanted to keep you in the loop."

"Thanks," Amar said. "Do it."

Things were looking up. The robots kept coming, but with two squads working together and a steady supply of ammunition, they weren't making any advances. They seemed to have them contained and were even starting to push them back.

He realized he hadn't heard from Sam in a while, so he tried the radio. The analyst didn't answer.

"DeLao?"

But he didn't answer, either.

"Has anyone heard from DeLao?"

"Haven't heard anything, Chief," Akira said. He was in the workroom, a compartment below the bridge. "It's real quiet up here. Should I send someone up?"

"No," he said. "Keep your position. Engineering?"

"This is Lily Shen," his earpiece informed him. "What has happened to my father?"

"I don't know," he said. "I'm going to find out. Could just be a problem with the radio." He didn't believe that, but he needed to give her something to hang on to.

"Sam said something about a kill switch," he said. "Where is that?"

"There's an access tube that runs between the hull and the bridge," she said. "There are a series of kill switches Dad placed there in case something like this happened. They should literally cut the computer off from the rest of the ship, at which point we can open the hatches using the generator. I should have been able to detonate them from here, but something has severed the connection—perhaps the computer itself, using some sort of remote. Sam went to try and execute manually."

But Sam wasn't answering the radio.

"I'm coming back," he said. "Show me."

Gunfire rattled behind him as he came back into engineering. Lily had pulled up a detailed plan of ship. He studied it for a few minutes.

"What do we do when we get there?" he asked.

"Don't worry," Lena said. "I'm going along. I know the procedure, and there's no time to teach it to you."

CHAPTER 22

THE SOUND OF gunfire intensified behind them as Amar and Lena made their way up the stairs with Palepoi and Nishimura.

Amar paused. "What's going on down there, Mak?" he asked.

"Chief," his earpiece said. "Mak here. I think we may have gotten the last of them. We're proceeding into the Enigma chamber."

"Don't fall asleep, Mak," he cautioned. "You don't know what's in there."

On the way up, they paused to look in on Akira and his bunch, who seemed almost bored.

Mak came back just as they reached the top level.

"Nothing moving in here, Chief," she said. "I think we got them all." There was pause. "Weird," the Russian said. "These look sort of like coffins."

Amar peered around the corner. He was now looking down the passage that the bridge opened from, where DeLao's squad was supposed to be.

But the corridor was empty. And the hatch to the bridge was closed.

Someone on the radio link started screaming.

"Mak?" Amar said.

"Chief—" the Russian gasped.

Then nothing, as if her radio had been destroyed. But below, the sound of gunfire began again.

What the hell is happening, he wondered, fighting a sudden, almost overwhelming sense of dread.

Coffins. He remembered Vahlen's lab, the alien-human hybrid in cryosleep. . . .

One thing at a time, he told himself sternly. Do the job in front of you. Trust the other squad leaders to do theirs.

"Where is the access corridor?" he asked Lena.

"Down past the bridge," she said.

"Okay," he said. "The two of us are going down there. Nishimura, Palepoi —cover us."

As they crept down the passage, Amar roved his gaze everywhere, but he paid special attention to the bridge hatch, afraid that it was going to suddenly spring open.

But they passed it uneventfully and reached the stairs.

Then the bridge door opened, and DeLao stepped out. He aimed his rifle at Amar and pulled the trigger.

Amar was already moving, pushing Lena into the stairwell. Two bullets smacked into his armor on his left side and nearly spun him around. He managed to stagger through the hatch before DeLao could shoot him again.

"Amar—" Lena began.

"Just go," he said. "Do it."

His ribs felt like a cinderblock had been slammed into them, and he was sure some of them were broken, but there wasn't any blood.

He leaned out for a look. DeLao was waiting, and now Amar noticed what he hadn't before, at least not on a conscious level.

DeLao's eyes. Empty, glowing, like Nishimura's back in New Kochi.

Bullets thudded into the bulkhead as he drew back again, but not before seeing something else coming out of the hatch, something not human at all.

"Chief?" Nishimura said.

"Try not to kill DeLao if you can help it," he said. "But don't let anything get to the stairs."

Then he started up after Lena as the fireworks began in the corridor.

The narrow stairs took him up past the crew quarters and an unassigned room above them. Beyond that they continued until they reached a long horizontal shaft lit by cool blue light.

Lena was waiting for him. She shot him in the stomach as soon as he stepped into the corridor.

He gasped and staggered back. His legs suddenly felt like rubber, but oddly there was no pain, just the sense of impact. Behind her, he saw a mis-shapen shadow and huge phosphorescent eyes.

"Lena," he pleaded. "Don't. Fight it. I love you."

She took a step forward and aimed at his face. He saw her hand was trembling. Her trigger finger twitched, once, twice.

Amar rolled over so he had a clear shot at the thing and then sprayed it with bullets. It staggered back a meter and then started forward again, screeching. Amar took aim at its huge, onion-shaped head and blew it into fragments.

Lena shrieked and dropped the gun. Amar staggered up and took her in his arms.

"I know," he said, brushing her hair with his palm. "I know."

"I shot you!" she cried. "Oh my god, Amar—I shot you."

"Lena," he said. "Listen. I'll be okay. You have to focus. The kill switches. I have to watch the stairwell. It's okay."

It wasn't, of course. His gut was burning now, and his body felt unreal. He knew he was on the verge of blacking out.

"You can do it," he said. "You have to do it."

She pulled back from him. Her face was streaked with tears, but he recognized the look of determination on it.

"Okay," she said. She started down the corridor.

"I'll watch your back," he said.

"Probably better if you watch the stairs," she said. It took him a few beats to realize she was trying to make a joke.

She went a few meters and then crouched down. "Crap," she said.

"What?" he grunted.

"It's Sam," she called back. "He's dead."

Of course he was. Amar was trying to picture what had happened. The

Sectoids had unobtrusively moved up from below, taken control of DeLao and Sam, and probably some of the others. They had quietly killed everyone else, dragged them into the control room. . . .

He heard something coming up the stairs; he drew a bead on the next landing and waited.

"The kill switches," Lena said. "They've been disabled."

Of course they had.

It came quicker than he thought it would. All limbs and horror, the Chryssalid almost seemed to fly up the stairs. He started firing as soon as he saw it, but it nearly made it all the way to him before finally succumbing. He watched it thrash back down toward the bottom.

"Chief," Nishimura said. "They're coming from everywhere. Swarming. Palepoi is down."

"Fall back," he said. "Defend engineering."

"But Chief—"

"Go," he said. "There's nothing you can do for us alone. I'm in a defensible position."

A streak of green plasma seared past his head, and down on the landing he saw another Sectoid scrambling toward him. It was smaller than the one he'd just killed and much smaller than the one in New Kochi.

It died more easily, too, but there were plenty more behind it.

He ducked back behind the wall to reload. Lena was right there.

"Give me your pistol," she said. "So I can help."

"I've got this," he said. "You need to figure out how to re-enable the kill switches."

"I can't do that," she said. "But there's another option, if you have a grenade left."

"You mean we can just blow it up?" he asked, then fired at the next monster as it started up toward them, forcing it back down.

"Sure," she said. "This is where the AI gets its power. The kill switches were designed to do that without, you know, destroying the whole area. But we don't have the luxury of being neat anymore."

"So we just toss the grenade down there?"

"I'd better place it," she said. "Can it be set for a delay?"

"Up to twenty seconds," he said.

"Okay," she said. "Stand up."

"I'm not sure I can," he said.

"You have to," she said. "Once I set the grenade, we're going to have to run like hell. We don't want to be up here when the power conduits rupture."

"That puts us running down into them," he said, taking another shot.

"Yep," she said. "So stand up and give me your pistol."

He wasn't sure where he found the strength, but using the wall as support, he managed to get back on his feet. She took his handgun and grenade and went back down the corridor.

And that was when the spider tried to get back into his skull.

He tried to focus on the pain, to beat it back. He staggered down a step, to find it, kill it before it could take control of him.

His legs betrayed him, and he stumbled and went crashing down the stairs. He hit the landing, agony digging in his every nerve as he fired blindly, and the spider walked out, but it wasn't dead—he could feel it, waiting. His vision was blurring; he made out vague shapes scrambling up toward him.

Lena was suddenly at his side. She pulled out his sidearm and fired across him, down the stairwell. Another one of the things gibbered in pain.

"Come on," she said. "We've got to go down there."

"We can't," he said.

"We have about six seconds," she said. She put her arm under him and heaved, and once more he gathered his feet under him.

Another one of the little monsters stuck its head around the next landing, and Lena put a hole in it. They managed to stumble down another flight.

Then everything went white, and something slapped him in the back, *hard*.

The next thing he saw was Lena in front of him, legs braced, firing his pistol at something he couldn't see. He started to rise up and saw three plasma bursts sleet through her unarmored body. She took a step forward, and they shot her again.

She fell back next to him. She looked at him and tried to say something, but his ears were ringing, and he couldn't make out the words.

He rolled off of his rifle and shot at the first thing he saw move, but everything was blurring now, and he couldn't find a target. Or move his hand or, finally, see at all.

But he could still hear, and what he heard sounded like gunfire, far off in the distance.

CHAPTER 23

IT SEEMED TO Amar that it had been dark for a long time, dark and deeply silent. If it was night, it was starless and long, as if the world had stopped turning.

Maybe, he thought, morning would never come again.

Part of him hoped it wouldn't.

But then, very faintly, the line of the horizon appeared, dividing first gray and black, then coral and indigo, saffron and azure, until finally—like the eye of a god opening—the edge of the sun appeared.

Again he wondered at how quickly it rose, how beautiful it was. He watched in awe as the golden path appeared on the waters and stretched out to his feet.

He wondered if he walked that path, where it would go, what things he would see. But before he set foot on it, he saw something coming toward him—small with distance, but growing larger by the moment.

A breeze lifted, and very faintly he heard something—not quite music, but a cadence.

And words.

Tyger, Tyger, burning bright,
In the forests of the night;
What immortal hand or eye
Could frame thy fearful symmetry?

The words continued, and the tiger stopped in front of him. For a very long moment, it held his gaze. He saw the faint reflection of himself in the golden spheres of its eyes. He felt its hot breath on his face.

Then it went around him and continued on across the water.

Amar awoke on his back, staring at the ceiling. When he turned, he saw that he was in the infirmary of the Avenger. He had an IV drip in his arm.

Chitto was sitting in a chair next to him. She was just closing a book.

"Hey, Chief," she said. "Glad you're back."

"Yeah," he said.

He remembered. At the end it was messy, but he remembered. Yet he still had to ask.

Chitto told him what he needed to hear, and he nodded.

"Any other questions, Chief?"

"No," he said. "Not right now."

"That's okay, then," she said. "I was just going anyway."

He nodded at her book. "What's that you're reading?" he asked.

"Oh, this?" she said. "It's just some poems by a guy named Blake."

"Where did you get a book all the way out here?"

She shrugged. "I've had it all along," she said. "Brought it with me from home."

Then she left.

***

Lily Shen came to see him later, but how much later he wasn't sure.

"I heard you were awake," she said.

"For what it's worth," Amar replied.

"It's worth a lot," Lily said. "To all of us. If it hadn't been for you—"

"That's . . . I don't want to hear that," Amar said. "Tell me what happened. Obviously we're still alive."

"The aliens were in cryosleep," Lily said. "The AI woke them up. They seem to have deployed the robots first, as a ruse, while the Sectoids infiltrated the bridge area. They took control of DeLao and one of his men, and they killed the other two. We found them on the bridge, along with my father."

"Your father . . ." he began.

"They didn't kill him," she said. "But they interrogated him." Her voice dropped. "It was too much for him," she said. "I don't think he will recover."

"I'm sorry to hear that," Amar said.

"We've all lost loved ones," she said. But he could see on her face and hear in her voice that she wasn't ready to lose him.

He closed his eyes. "So the grenade worked, I guess."

"Yes," Lily said. "The damage was pretty terrific; it will set us back a bit. But we survived. The mission survives. As does hope. Thanks to you and Lena, the AI is completely defanged."

"I've heard that before," Amar said.

She shook her head in the negative. "We got it right this time."

He hoped that was true. He had no interest in a do-over.

"And then Chitto," she said. "More than half of the soldiers were dead, but she somehow pulled together what was left and brought them up to support you. Killed the last of the aliens, rescued you and my father."

He felt an unexpected pulse of pride.

"Chitto?" he said. "She did that?"

"Yes, she did," Lily said.

"Did Nishimura survive?"

"Yes, she made it," Lily said. "She's off on a recruiting mission at the moment."

"How long have I been out of it?"

"Two weeks," she said. "They had to do some pretty complicated surgery on you, and they still weren't sure you were coming out of it—until you did." She smiled her distracted little smile, and he could tell her attention was no longer on him. She had things to do. He was surprised she had spent this long with him. She stood up. "Do you need anything?" she asked.

"No," he said.

Lily took a few steps and then turned back.

"She's a hero, KB," she said. "She saved us all. Even with the aliens dead, we would still have suffocated."

"I know," Amar said.

***

He was in bed for another week before he could slowly, painfully, move around. Lily told him he should take some time off, but he knew that wouldn't do him any good—that he would just think about Lena, about all the time he had wasted before finally bending to his heart.

So he went back to work. There was plenty to do—recruits were flowing in from everywhere. They needed training, and assignments, and a little perspective.

By the time Nishimura returned, he was strong enough to have a beer with her. She was the last living member of his original squad. They toasted their fallen and told a few funny stories about each. It didn't feel good, exactly, but it did feel right.

"I brought up the new guy," she told him.

"Who is that?" He wanted to know.

"The new head of research, Tygan. Pretty sharp guy. He used to work in the gene therapy labs with ADVENT, but he got religion and defected to us."

"He must have been pretty convincing," Amar said. "The security risk involved in bringing somebody like that in . . ."

"We checked him out pretty good," she said. "Anyway, you know as well as I do that there are good people in the cities. They only need to know the truth. Some find it for themselves, and some have to be shown it."

He knew she was talking about Lena, but he wasn't ready to talk about her. He might never be.

When Nishimura saw that he wasn't going to bite, she changed tack.

"What do you think our next mission will be?" she asked.

"No telling," he said.

But he was thinking something else—that maybe he didn't have another mission in him. That he had done his part, given all he could. That maybe it was time for him to go home, see if any of his cousins were alive, help them survive.

***

"We've done good work here," Dr. Shen said, a few days later. "I hope you all know that. I hope you take it to heart."

There wasn't much left of Doctor Raymond Shen. He was shockingly thin and dissipated. His arms quivered uncontrollably, and his speech was slurred.

He was sitting up in his bed, but it looked like he might topple over at any moment. Lily and a nurse stood on either side of him, ready to catch him if he did.

"Unfortunately," he said, "it doesn't appear likely that I will be here to see this ship fully operational, much less the end of what is going to be a long and wearying war. So I would like to discuss what comes next.

"My daughter is more than fit to replace me in engineering. We have our new head of research, so we need not worry about that. But for XCOM to move forward, it needs structure. It needs someone in charge."

He was silent for a moment; it looked as if just that much speaking had worn him out.

"There is a possibility," he said. "It is not yet confirmed. But if it is true, I can die knowing that I left all of this in good hands, that the human race has a fighting chance."

"What possibility, sir?" Amar asked.

"There is quite a bit you need to know," Dr. Shen said. "Things I've kept mostly to myself or shared only with Lily. But time's arrow has found me, and I can't be the sole repository of so much that is so critical."

He seemed to be having difficulty breathing, and for several long moments he tried to get more words out, without success.

"Dad—" Lily began, but he waved her off.

He closed his eyes, and when he opened them he was able to continue, in a wheezing, raspy ghost of a voice.

"The . . . setback . . . was unfortunate. I know the word is too mild," he said, looking apologetically at Amar. "We all lost so much. But you must promise me you will carry on."

In that moment, Amar's doubts dropped away. Lena had once told him he liked to make the easier choices when it came to his feelings. Staying with XCOM was going to be hard. He would be reminded of her every day. He would grow close to comrades and then lose them, too.

But he didn't want to forget her, and if his presence brought one more rookie out of the field alive, it would be worth it.

"I promise," he said.

Dr. Shen died three days later. They buried him in the cloud forest with Lena, DeLao, and all of the rest of the Avenger's dead. Like them, his grave wasn't marked, but its position was recorded to the millimeter.

Because one day they would all have markers, and their names would be known, and history would remember how and when humanity turned the corner and began the fight to take back their planet—and their destiny.

In Flanders fields the poppies blow
Between the crosses, row on row,
That mark our place: and in the sky
The larks still bravely singing fly
Scarce heard amid the guns below.

We are the dead: Short days ago,
We lived, felt dawn, saw sunset glow,
Loved and were loved: and now we lie
In Flanders fields!

Take up our quarrel with the foe
To you, from failing hands, we throw
The torch: be yours to hold it high
If ye break faith with us who die,
We shall not sleep, though poppies grow
In Flanders fields

—John McCrae

EPILOGUE

THE BOY LOOKED even younger dead, he thought. What was his name? Ivan?

Ivan. He and the rest had tried to sabotage a gene therapy clinic, as he heard it. Only two of them got out and made it to the settlement, and one was Ivan.

But the kid had taken a round and died a day later. He had learned about it when he went in for supplies.

He found the surviving kid digging Ivan's grave. The boy watched him as he arrived. He didn't look any older than sixteen. He had wide, expressive eyes that he should have been used to woo girls rather than to look through a rifle sight.

"What do you want?" the boy asked.

"Nothing," he said. "I just came to pay my respects."

"Oh," the boy said. "You knew him?"

"Not much," he replied. "But if you want some advice—forget burying him. Get the hell out of here before a patrol finds you."

"He deserves a burial," the boy said.

"I bet he'd rather you stayed alive, if he had any say in the matter."

The boy straightened, and his eyes narrowed.

"You're him, aren't you? The guy Ivan came to see."

He just shrugged.

"Yes, it's you," the boy said. "Ivan kept going on about what a great man you were, how you could turn everything around, that all he had to do was talk to you. And what did you do? Showed him your back. Great man, my ass. So I've no use for you, *pendejo*—or your advice."

He spat and then went back to digging.

"That's fine with me, kid," he said.

He got his supplies and went back to his hidey hole. He turned on the radio and took a seat, setting a bottle of whiskey in front of him on his "table."

He hadn't listened to the radio for a long time—it was too depressing. But in the last few weeks—well, it seemed like something was starting to happen. Somebody was recruiting, and on a pretty decent scale. Battles were being won. Small victories, true, but victories nonetheless. But more than that, there was a sudden surge of what he could only call hope—and what's more, that hope seemed to have a name.

Avenger.

He unscrewed the cap of the whiskey bottle, thinking about Ivan, about the boy digging his grave who probably wouldn't make it to sundown.

Not his problem. Nothing to be done.

He lifted the bottle.

Then, with a heavy sigh, he set it back on the crate and screwed the cap back on. He went into his shack, found his shotgun, and checked to make sure it was loaded.

Something was happening out there, finally. It was time he found out what.

The boy looked up at him when he returned. He saw the shotgun and jumped for his rifle.

"Hang on, son," he said. "Just give me the shovel so we can get this done and get out of here."

The boy stared at him as if he was kidding, but when it sunk in that he wasn't, he handed him the shovel.

"When Ivan came to see me," he said, pushing the shovel into the dense soil, "he had someone he wanted me to see. Would you know who that was?"

"Yeah," he said. "I think so."

"When we're finished here, you'll take me there. Okay?"

"Yes," the boy said. "Yes, sir."

He kept digging.

"It's Bradford, right?" the boy said, after a moment. "Mr. Bradford?"

He leaned on the shovel and looked at the boy.

"What's your name?"

"Arturo."

"Don't call me that, Arturo," he said. "That's not a name that needs to get around. Just call me Central."

They laid Ivan in the ground, went back to his place, and packed up what few possessions they would need. When the patrol found his shack, he and Arturo were long gone.

THE END

ACKNOWLEDGMENTS

I would like to thank Matt Knoles at 2K Games. To the Firaxis team—Peter Murray, Lindsay Riehl, Garth DeAngelis, Scott Wittbeker, Jacob Solomon, Chad Rocco, and Garrett Bittner—thanks for creating such an amazing universe and navigating me through it. At Insight Editions, thanks to Vanessa Lopez, Elaine Ou, Greg Solano, and Chrissy Kwasnik, and special thanks to my editor, Ramin Zahed.

INSIGHT EDITIONS

PO Box 3088
San Rafael, CA 94912
www.insighteditions.com

 Find us on Facebook: www.facebook.com/InsightEditions
Follow us on Twitter: @insighteditions

PUBLISHER: RAOUL GOFF
ACQUISITIONS MANAGER: ROBBIE SCHMIDT
ART DIRECTOR: CHRISSY KWASNIK
EXECUTIVE EDITOR: VANESSA LOPEZ
SENIOR EDITOR: RAMIN ZAHED
ASSOCIATE EDITOR: GREG SOLANO
PRODUCTION EDITOR: ELAINE OU
PRODUCTION MANAGER: ANNA WAN

COVER ART BY DAVID PALUMBO

ROOTS of PEACE   REPLANTED PAPER

Insight Editions, in association with Roots of Peace, will plant two trees for each tree used in the manufacturing of this book. Roots of Peace is an internationally renowned humanitarian organization dedicated to eradicating land mines worldwide and converting war-torn lands into productive farms and wildlife habitats. Roots of Peace will plant two million fruit and nut trees in Afghanistan and provide farmers there with the skills and support necessary for sustainable land use.

Manufactured in the United States by Insight Editions

10 9 8 7 6 5 4 3 2 1